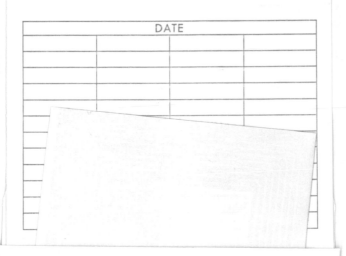

Measuring emotions in infants and children

Volume II

Cambridge Studies in Social and Emotional Development

General Editor: Martin L. Hoffman

Measuring emotions in infants and children

Volume II

Edited by

CARROLL E. IZARD
University of Delaware

and

PETER B. READ
Scarsdale Family Counseling Service

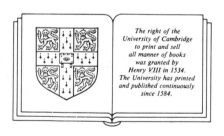

The right of the
University of Cambridge
to print and sell
all manner of books
was granted by
Henry VIII in 1534.
The University has printed
and published continuously
since 1584.

CAMBRIDGE UNIVERSITY PRESS

Cambridge
London   New York   New Rochelle
Melbourne   Sydney

Published by the Press Syndicate of the University of Cambridge
The Pitt Building, Trumpington Street, Cambridge CB2 1RP
32 East 57th Street, New York, NY 10022, USA
10 Stamford Road, Oakleigh, Melbourne 3166, Australia

First published 1986

Printed in the United States of America

Library of Congress Cataloging-in-Publication Data

Measuring emotions in infants and children.
(Cambridge studies in social and emotional
development)
Includes bibliographical references and index.
1. Emotions in children – Testing – Congresses.
2. Facial expression – Congresses.   3. Expression in
children – Congresses.   I. Izard, Carroll E. (Carroll
Ellis), 1923–   .   II. Social Science Research
Council (U.S.).   Committee on Social and Affective
Development During Childhood.   III. Series.
[DNLM: 1. Child development – Congresses.   2. Emotions –
In infancy and childhood – Congresses.
WS 105.5.E5 M484 1978–79]
BF723.E6M43   155.4'12   81-10032

British Library Cataloguing in Publication Data

Measuring emotions in infants and children
– (Cambridge studies in social and
emotional development)
Vol. 2
1. Emotions in children – Testing
I. Izard, Carroll E.   II. Read, Peter B

ISBN 0 521 32367 3

Contents

v

Part V   The conceptualization of emotion

Preface

The first of these two volumes on measuring emotions in infants and children was a product of two conferences sponsored by the Social Science Research Council's Committee on Social and Affective Development during Childhood. We were aware at the conclusion of these conferences that there were some useful methods that had not been presented at the conferences. Various circumstances precluded their inclusion in Volume I. Furthermore, in the years since the last of the two conferences (May 1979) several new methods have proved effective in the rapidly growing field of emotional development.

The present volume consists of invited papers written by individuals who have made significant contributions to research strategy and methodology in the study of emotions in infants and children. Their contributions are clearly distinct from those of Volume I, and the two volumes taken together represent a fairly comprehensive set of research strategies and methods for research on emotions during the early years of life.

As was the case with Volume I, the rapidly growing field of emotional development continues to outpace the publication process. While this volume was in production, new evidence emerged for the usefulness of Everett Water's Q-Sort method of assessing infants and children on a dimension of secure–anxious attachment and for the Kurt Fischer approach to assessing social development. We are disappointed in not having these contributions in the volume but happy that they are in the literature.

Contributors

Marc H. Bornstein
Department of Psychology
New York University

Merry Bullock
Max-Planck Institut für
Psychologische Forschung

Linda A. Camras
Department of Psychology
DePaul University

Richard J. Davidson
Department of Psychology
State University of New York,
Purchase

Nathan A. Fox
Department of Human Development
University of Maryland

Jane M. Gaughran
Department of Psychology
New York University

Karin Grossmann
Institut für Psychologie IV
Universität Regensburg

Klaus E. Grossmann
Institut für Psychologie IV
Universität Regensburg

Jeannette M. Haviland
Department of Psychology
Rutgers University

Peter Homel
Department of Psychology
New York University

Carroll E. Izard
Department of Psychology
University of Delaware

Janet L. Jewett
School of Education
National College of Education

Lynne Sanford Koester
Department of Child Development
and Family Relations
University of North Carolina

Carol Zander Malatesta
The Graduate Faculty
New School for Social Research

Hanuš Papoušek
Max-Planck Institut für Psychiatrie

Mechthild Papoušek
Max-Planck Institut für Psychiatrie

Peter B. Read
Scarsdale Family Counseling Service

James A. Russell
Department of Psychology
University of British Columbia

Nancy L. Stein
Department of Education
University of Chicago

Anna Schwan
Institut für Psychologie IV
Universität Regensburg

Part I

Introduction

1   Introduction

Carroll E. Izard

Volume I of *Measuring Emotions in Infants and Children* grew out of a series of conferences sponsored by the Social Science Research Council (SSRC). Some of the themes discussed in these conferences are now well represented by empirical studies reported in the journals. Indeed, since the initial plans for Volume I were made, there has been a steady increase in research on the development of emotions.

When the first volume of *Measuring Emotions in Infants and Children* was published, it was not possible to include a number of important methods then current, in particular those related to attachment or mother–infant relationships, temperament, emotion comprehension, and emotion–cognition relations. Approaches to measurement in each of these areas are represented in the present volume. In addition, this volume contains some recent developments on measuring facial expressions of emotion and on the psychophysiology of emotions in infants and children. A brief update of the issues raised in the SSRC conferences and discussed in Volume I is presented in the following paragraphs.

Components of emotion

It is still generally accepted that a given emotion involves neurochemical processes, behavioral expression, and subjective experience. Work continues on the problem of defining each of these components and determining their relations and sequence in the emotion process.

The biological level. Although there is steady progress in research on the neural substrates of stress, depression, and anxiety, the neurosciences have still not launched a vigorous research effort focusing on the discrete emotions. Nevertheless, evidence continues to converge on the problem. A summary of this work can be found in Izard & Saxton (in press) and a brief update in Izard & Malatesta (in press). Some interesting new developments in the psychobiology of emo-

3

tional development are presented in Fox & Davidson (1984) and in their contribution to this volume, Chapter 2.

The behavioral–expressive level. The behavioral–expressive level probably continues to be the most active area of research in the field of emotional development, particularly in the infancy period. The value of measuring emotion expression in infants is becoming more widely accepted, but the issue of coherence between expression and subjective experience is still unsettled (Izard & Malatesta, in press; Kagan, 1984; Lewis & Michalson, 1983). Evidence related to the significance of facial and vocal expressions is presented in Chapters 2, 3, 4, 5, and 7. These chapters fall in three different parts of this volume, testifying to the use of expression measurement in a variety of research areas.

The subjective–experiential level. No self-report measures of any sort have ever been widely accepted as useful and valid methods in experimental psychology. They have, however, continued to prove useful to many researchers in emotions, personality, and clinical psychology. For example, self-report measures have been widely used in the study of anxiety (Spielberger, 1972) and depression (Blumberg & Izard, 1985). Chapter 10 of Volume I describes a discrete-emotions approach to measuring the subjective experience of emotion, and Chapter 8, by Bullock and Russell, in the present volume shows the value of both the discrete-emotions approach and the measurement of dimensions of emotion experience such as pleasantness and activation.

Emotion–cognition relations

Perhaps because of the prominent place of cognitive studies in behavioral science for the past two decades and the current renaissance in emotions research, the topic of emotion–cognition relations has generated considerable theoretical debate and empirical research. Two volumes have appeared on the topics since the publication of Volume I of *Measuring Emotions in Infants and Children* (Clark & Fiske, 1982; Izard, Kagan, & Zajonc, 1984). That there are workable methods for studying the relations between emotion and cognition is evident in this volume in Chapter 8 and in Chapter 9 by Stein and Jewett.

Although progress is being made in the study of emotion–cognition relations, important issues remain unresolved. The most significant of these is the matter of construct boundaries or definition. Some theorists (Plutchik, 1980) hold that cognition is an integral part of emotion, whereas others (Izard, 1977) maintain that the subjective experience of emotion is a feeling state and that emotion feeling interacts with cognition to form affective–cognitive structures. In their developmental theory of emotion, Izard & Malatesta (in press) attempted to set boundaries for cognition and emotion that make the study of their interaction plausible. In brief they maintained that cognition begins with learning- or experience-based schemas and always involves representations constructed through experience. In contrast, the conscious component of emotion is a feeling state, the direct derivative of activities in its underlying neurochemical substrates. Thus, emotion feeling can be activated and exist in consciousness as a central motivational state, independent of cognition as defined above.

An alternative to Izard and Malatesta's position is presented by Mandler in Volume I and by Averill (1984). They maintain that emotion experiences, like cognitive schemas, are constructed through social learning. The difference between the two positions is subtle but profound. The constructions (emotion experiences) described in the cognitive theories of Mandler and Averill are similar to the affective–cognitive structures in Izard's differential emotions theory; and in the affective–cognitive structure, the affective component supplies the motivation for subsequent behavior. Cognitive theories are not much concerned with the motivational and social signal aspects of emotions, but these aspects are central to differential emotions theory and the positions of such developmentalists as Campos & Barrett (1984), Cicchetti & Hesse (1982), Emde (1980), Hoffman (1975), and Sroufe (1979). A cognitively oriented approach to children's emotion experiences is aptly represented in this volume by Stein and Jewett, who have been influenced by Mandler and Russell.

Overview of the volume

Fox and Davidson (Chapter 2) argue that a full understanding of emotional development will require studies that use behavioral and physiological measures simultaneously. That such time-locked measures are feasible is demonstrated by the methods they describe and the research they summarize. For example, in their own research they have shown that the right and left frontal lobes of 10-month-old infants respond differentially while the infants are viewing positive and negative emotion expressions. They also detail some recent advances in methods of measuring heart rate variability and vagal tone and techniques for examining the balance between the two branches of the autonomic nervous system. Indices derived from these methods in early infancy are significantly related to objectively measured discrete facial expressions of emotion and predictive of affective response to separation at 1 year of age.

In Chapter 2, Fox and Davidson present a review of research strategies and important findings that have advanced our knowledge of the psychophysiology of emotions. They begin with a cogent analysis of the issues in the measurement of physiological indices of emotion. In later sections they discuss developmental processes that must be taken into account in psychological studies. They indicate, for example, that developmental changes occur in electroencephalographic alpha, noting that alpha activity in infants is much slower than the 8–13 Hz in adults. Documenting the significance of measuring central nervous system indices of emotions constitutes an important thrust of Fox and Davidson's chapter. Studies from their own laboratories have shown differential involvement of the right and left cerebral hemispheres in emotion processes in young infants and suggested that even in the early months of life the left hemisphere is relatively more involved in mediating the positive emotion of interest and the right hemisphere some of the negative emotions.

They recognize the continued importance of assessing autonomic nervous system indices of emotion, but they emphasize some new strategies, particularly for indexing cardiac responses. They review work suggesting that vagal tone and heart rate variability patterns in early infancy predict personality traits and coping styles at later ages.

In Chapter 3, Malatesta and Haviland demonstrate that a microanalytic method and a more global approach can complement one another in the study of emotions in mother–infant interactions. They used a fine-grained facial movement coding system (Maximally Discriminative Facial Movement Coding System, or Max) (Izard, 1979) to measure emotion signaling and a standardized parent questionnaire (Infant Behavior Questionnaire, IBQ; Rothbart, 1981) to assess temperament. They discuss several important practical considerations in the application of the microanalytic facial coding method to lengthy videotaped records. In their longitudinal study of mother–infant interactions, they found a number of significant correlations between emotion expression indices derived from Max and temperament dimensions measured by the IBQ. They suggest that it may be useful to think in terms of emotion expression patterns or styles that are characteristic of individual infants. In the Max coding of mothers' facial behavior, they found evidence that mothers' facial behavior has an impact on their infants' temperament.

In Chapter 4, Camras examines the relative signal value of facial expressions and contextual cues. She considers a number of dimensions of each of these sources of information, particularly the strength, salience, and clarity of the cues. She discusses several ways that display rules may affect children's judgments of facial expressions and presents relevant evidence. She also shows that the form of a subject's response can affect estimates of emotion recognition ability. Finally, she presents an original empirical study illustrating how kindergarten children can utilize both facial and situation cues to decode emotion expressions.

In Chapter 5, Papoušek, Papoušek, and Koester present their microanalytic methods for studying emotions in parent–infant communications. They focus on the early, preverbal period, and they describe techniques for analyzing facial and vocal expressions of mothers and infants. They are especially concerned with relations between the pleasure–displeasure dimension of emotions and the integrative processes of young infants and with the interaction of biological and ecological influences. Building on the Papoušeks' earlier work, the authors evaluate the role of expectancy and contingency in mother–infant interactions. They summarize two new empirical studies on emotion expressions in early mother–infant interactions. Their intensive studies and microanalytic methods yielded a number of new and interesting findings. They found meaningful patterns of facial and vocal expression in parents and infants. For example, both mothers and fathers used melodic contours at a higher than average pitch and a wider range of pitch when addressing 3-month-old infants. They also describe several age-related changes in infants' facial and vocal expressions.

In Chapter 6, Grossman, Grossman, and Schwan present a new method for analyzing infant emotion communications after brief separation. Their research program on mother–infant relationships and communications began with studies using the Ainsworth Strange Situation and Ainsworth's system for classifying infants according to type of attachment. When they found that about two-thirds of German infants were classified as insecurely attached by the original Ainsworth criteria, they began developing a wider view of attachment. This wider view called for a more fine-grained method of observing and analyzing infant emotion communications that would provide more detail on the characteristics of infants classified by Ainsworth's scheme as avoidant (A), secure (B), and ambivalent/resistant (C). Chapter 6 presents this new method and some of the results of its application. Although Grossman, Grossman, and Schwan confirmed a number of Ainsworth's original hypotheses regarding the meaning and usefulness of the Strange Situation, they added new insights on the characteristics of Group A, B, and C babies. They found, for example, that either Group A or Group B babies may be either happy or unhappy. Some Group A babies managed the Strange Situation quite well, showed no signs of distress or impairment in quality of play, and had apparently done well in meeting their mothers' demands for independence. The new methodology has yielded data that challenge the previous characterizations of types of attachment and add new insights on the qualitative differences in mother–infant relationships.

In Chapter 7, Bornstein, Gaughran, and Homel assess the issues in measuring infant temperament. They point out several problems in current infant temperament questionnaires. Their survey of the literature shows that most instruments have poor inter-rater reliability, low internal scale consistency, and little or no evidence of short-term test–retest reliability. They also show that most of the research on validity of temperament measures has been concerned with concurrent validity, which is necessary but insufficient. They argue for the study of the validity of temperament measures in the context of related variables, or what Cronbach and Meehl called the "nomological network." The authors present an empirical study using their own approach to the measurement of infant temperament. They compared data obtained with their infant temperament measure administered to mothers with independent observer ratings. They obtained high mother–observer correlations and short-term stability of both mother and observer ratings, correlations in the mid-80s. They explained their success in obtaining high reliability in terms of the limited number of concrete observable items included in the inventory. The authors describe what appears to be a promising instrument for measuring temperament, discuss its limitations, and suggest ways for establishing its validity. They provide a number of suggestions to other researchers who may be interested in developing or assessing infant temperament measures

In Chapter 8, Bullock and Russell present two methods of measuring children's concepts of emotions. These two approaches – the discrete-emotions, or structural, approach and the dimensional approach – have been considered by some to be conflicting or competing approaches. Bullock and Russell make it clear that the discrete-emotions approach and the dimensional approach to the study of emotions can complement one another. They point out the strengths and weaknesses of each approach and report a number of recent studies showing how each approach yields interesting and useful data. Bullock and Russell show that everyday emotion concepts or categories, like most everyday concepts, lack the necessary and sufficient features to give them precise definition. That is, when we attempt to measure an emotion concept such as anger or fear by methods depending on language, we find that these concepts have fuzzy borders. The fuzzy borders derived by the discrete-emotions approach can also be understood as meaningful semantic overlap between categories. A complete structural approach, therefore, describes the way in which categories overlap and interrelate. Similarly, an analysis of the dimensions in the semantic space of emotion words also has limitations. It is not always clear how many dimensions are required or what precisely the dimensions represent. No set of dimensions ever accounts for all of the variance in the semantic space of emotion symbols. Despite these limitations, Bullock and Russell show that both approaches can enlighten us on the nature of children's concepts of emotion and on the development of these concepts as the child matures. In general their work supports that reported by Stein and Jewett in Chapter 9, affirming that children of ages 3 to 5 are quite successful in dealing with a number of emotion concepts. In addition Bullock and Russell show that preschool children have some understanding of the affective dimensions of pleasantness–unpleasantness and activation as they apply to emotion symbols and emotion expressions.

In Chapter 9 Stein and Jewett present both a conceptual analysis of the meaning of negative emotions and a method of measuring children's conceptions of emotions. Their focus is on the child's understanding of emotions, their causes, and their consequences. They review previous research (Trabasso, Stein, & Johnson, 1981) that showed that 3-year-old children could accurately distinguish positive from negative emotion states and causes from consequences. This study also produced the rather remarkable finding that 3-year-old children understand the causes of anger, sadness, and fear in about the same way that 6-year-old children do. Stein and Jewett present an original empirical study of 6-year-old children's conceptions of anger, fear, and sadness. They extend Mandler's (1975) concept of the cognitive or evaluative component of emotion by describing dimensions that can be used to distinguish positive from negative emotions and to differentiate among negative emotions. Their approach to the meaning analysis of emotion states, influenced by Roseman (1979), is based on the persons' desires, attainments, and expectations. The last dimension consists of a person's appraisal of the certainty of a future event. The latter dimension distinguishes fear from anger and sadness, and anger and sadness are distinguished in part by the person's focus of attention. Attention to the cause of a loss may create anger, whereas attention to the consequences of the loss may elicit sadness. Stein and Jewett's empirical study of children's knowledge of negative emotion states includes a paradigm for the study of emotion–cognition relations in children. Their results led them to challenge previous research in terms of the constraints it has placed on 6-year-old children's understanding of the causes and consequences of the negative emotions of sadness, anger, and fear. They concluded that 6-year-old children are capable of feeling both positive and negative emotions toward the same person and that they are actually quite sensitive to simultaneously existing emotion states.

These chapters, when combined with those of Volume I, represent the wide range of methods currently employed to study emotions in infants and children. Yet as this summary indicates, methodology is intimately linked to critical theoretical issues. And these volumes are more than a description of methods and research strategies. They reveal the conceptual tools required to study emotions in relation to other processes in the stream of early development.

References

Averill, J. R. (1984). The acquisition of emotions during adulthood. In C. Z. Malatesta & C. E. Izard (Eds.), *Emotion in adult development* (pp. 23–43). Beverly Hills, CA: Sage.

Blumberg, S., & Izard, C. E. (1985). Affective and cognitive characteristics of nondepressed and depressed 10-year-old children. *Journal of Personality and Social Psychology, 49*(1), 194–202.

Campos, J. J., & Barrett, K. C. (1984). Toward a new understanding of emotions and their development. In C. E. Izard, J. Kagan, & R. B. Zajonc (Eds.), *Emotions, cognition, and behavior* (pp. 229–63). Cambridge University Press.

Cicchetti, D., & Hesse, P. (1982). Perspectives on an integrated theory of emotional development. In D. Cicchetti & P. Hesse (Eds.), *Emotional development* (pp. 3–48). San Francisco: Jossey-Bass.

Clark, M. S., & Fiske, S. T. (1982). *Affect and cognition*. Hillsdale, NJ: Erlbaum.

Emde, R. N. (1980). Toward a psychoanalytic theory of affect. I. The organizational model and its propositions. In S. Greenspan & G. Pollock (Eds.), *The course of life: Psychoanalytic contributions toward understanding personality development* (pp. 63–83). Washington, DC: U. S. Government Printing Office.

Fox, N. A., & Davidson, R. J. (1984). Hemispheric substrates of affect: A developmental model. In N. A. Fox & R. J. Davidson (Eds.), *The psychobiology of affective development* (pp. 353–81). Hillsdale, NJ: Erlbaum.

Hoffman, M. L. (1975). Developmental synthesis of affect and cognition and its implications for altruistic motivation. *Developmental Psychology, 11,* 607–22.

Izard, C. E. (1977). *Human emotions*. New York: Plenum.

Izard, C. E. (1979). *The Maximally Discriminative Facial Movement Coding System (Max)*. Newark: University of Delaware, Instructional Resources Center.

Izard, C. E., & Saxton, P. M. (in press). Emotions. In R. C. Atkinson, R. J. Hernstein, G. Lindzey, D. Luce, & R. Thompson (Eds.), *Steven's handbook of experimental psychology*. New York: Wiley-Interscience.

Izard, C. E., Kagan, J., & Zajonc, R. B. (1984). Introduction. In C. E. Izard, J. Kagan, & R. B. Zajonc (Eds.), *Emotions, cognition, and behavior* (pp. 1–14). Cambridge University Press.

Izard, C. E., & Malatesta, C. (in press). A developmental theory of the emotions. In J. D. Osofsky (Ed.), *Handbook of infant development*. Revised. New York: Wiley Interscience.

Kagan, J. (1984). The idea of emotion in human development. In C. E. Izard, J. Kagan, & R. Zajonc (Eds.), *Emotions, cognition, and behavior* (pp. 38–72). Cambridge University Press.

Lewis, M., & Michalson, L. (1983). *Children's emotions and moods: Developmental theory and measurement*. New York: Plenum.

Mandler, G. (1975). *Mind and emotions*. New York: Wiley.

Plutchik, R. (1980). *Emotion: A psychoevolutionary synthesis*. New York: Harper & Row.

Roseman, I. (August 1979). *Cognitive aspects of emotion and emotional behavior*. Paper presented at the annual meeting of the American Psychological Association, New York.

Rothbart, M. K. (1981). Measurement of temperament in infancy. *Child Development, 52,* 569–78.

Spielberger, C. D. (1972). *Anxiety: Current trends in theory and research* (Vols. 1 and 2). New York: Academic Press.

Sroufe, A. L. (1979). Socioemotional development. In J. D. Osofsky (Ed.), *Handbook of infant development* (pp. 462–516). New York: Wiley Interscience.

Trabasso, T., Stein, N. L., & Johnson, L. R. (1981). Children's knowledge of events: A casual analysis of story structure. In G. H. Bower (Ed.), *The psychology of learning and motivation* (Vol. 15). New York: Academic Press.

Part II

Psychophysiological approaches

2 Psychophysiological measures of emotion: new directions in developmental research

Nathan A. Fox and Richard J. Davidson

The use of psychophysiological measures of emotion in infants has recently undergone a significant change parallel to the changes taking place in the study of emotional development itself. During the past decade, there have been two major advances in the measurement of phenomena that reflect emotion. The first of these involves detailed coding systems for quantifying facial signs of emotion from videotaped records. These systems allow the precise specification of moment-by-moment changes in facial expression. In light of the evidence linking specific facial expressions to particular emotions across cultures, the use of facial behavior as a finely differentiated index of affective state assumes particular importance. The second advance involves the delineation of major biological processes subserving the experience or expression of affect and the use of non-invasive methods to measure these events. The new direction in research involves combining the assessment of facial expression changes with the measurement of underlying patterns of physiological activity.

The purpose of this chapter is to present research on the use of physiological measures of emotion in infants and young children. The first section reviews general issues in the measurement of physiological manifestations of emotion. The second section presents relevant methodological approaches to the study of central nervous system (CNS) manifestations of emotion, including work with animals, as well as brain-damaged and normal adult populations. The third section outlines directions for future research on the CNS substrates of emotion and presents examples of data on the relation between EEG asymmetry and emotion in both adults and infants. The fourth section discusses methodological approaches to the measurement of autonomic nervous system (ANS) manifestations of emotion with emphasis on heart rate. Infant emotion research that has utilized heart rate is briefly reviewed. The fifth section presents directions for future research on ANS substrates of emotion with emphasis on measurement of para-

Preparation of this chapter was supported by a grant from the National Science Foundation (BNS-83/7229) to Nathan A. Fox and Richard J. Davidson.

13

sympathetic activity and its relation to emotion in infants. Examples of research that combines precise recording of emotion expression and physiological patterning are reviewed.

General issues in the measurement of physiological manifestations of emotion

Several important general considerations in the study of physiological concomitants of emotion are worth noting at the outset. These issues apply to the use of any physiological measure that is purported to reflect emotion. The first and probably the most important is the problem of the temporal resolution of the measure. Depending on how one defines emotion, its time course may vary. However, according to most accepted definitions, emotion can be, and often is, fleeting. Instances of relatively "pure" emotion rarely last more than several seconds. Although tonic individual differences may exist in temperament or mood, these differences can be best conceptualized as differences in the probability that particular emotions will occur (for a discussion of distinctions among emotion, mood, emotional trait, and emotional disorder see Ekman, 1984; Izard, 1971). It is imperative that the investigator of the psychophysiology of emotion specify which aspect of affective functioning he or she believes is being measured. It is also critical, if emotion is the target class of behavior to be studied, that the temporal resolution of the physiological measures selected for study conform to the temporal characteristics of the phenomenon itself. The temporal resolution of particular physiological measures is often constrained, not just by the actual physiological substrates and properties of the response system under study, but also by the analytic procedures used to quantify the measure.

Many studies on the psychophysiology of emotion have used measures that have a much longer time constant than the emotional behavior of interest. This results in a decrement in precision, with differences among emotion conditions often attenuated. One of the reasons that the notion of physiological differentiation among emotions has taken so long to become established is this methodological shortcoming in some previous research.

A second general issue concerns how epochs associated with emotion are extracted for analysis. In the literature on adult emotion, the independent variable is typically some particular affect elicitor such as a slide or a short film. Responses evoked by the stimulus are then averaged for the period of time the stimulus is present. Investigators often assume that the independent variable will have fairly consistent effects across people and therefore consider it appropriate to average the data in this fashion. This belief is often based on the fact that many of the stimulus materials used in contemporary emotion research have been extensively tested in large groups of subjects and produce fairly consistent self-reports of emotion. The major problem with this strategy, particularly with stimuli longer than a few seconds, is that an individual's affective response changes over time. Therefore, even if self-reports are relatively consistent across individuals, these ratings represent averages over a particular epoch and do not preserve the variability over time in the experience of emotion.

Most affect elicitors produce blends of emotion. Only rarely does an elicitor produce "pure" emotion. Here the term "pure emotion" refers to the presence of prototypical facial muscle configurations that reflect discrete, primary emotions (Izard, 1971). A pure emotion would be present if one of the patterns of facial musculature indicative of that emotion were expressed. Variations in the "purity" of the emotion might involve blends of different "pure" emotions. This fact is extremely important for physiological research on emotion. If a principal goal of research is to establish the nature of physiological differentiation among emotions, it is critical to compare instances of relatively "pure" emotion. If epochs are not selected for comparison on the basis of that "purity," the investigator may inadvertently compare two epochs of relatively impure emotion that contain significant overlap. This methodological weakness would also contribute to an underestimation of the differentiation among emotions (Ekman, 1983). Correcting this deficiency requires that epochs be selected for analysis on the basis of some independent criteria for the presence of a particular emotion. When these criteria are satisfied for the presence of a discrete emotion, then and only then can the investigator have confidence that the analysis is being performed on segments during which specific emotions are occurring. It is insufficient to rely solely on the nature of the independent variable.

The necessity of extracting epochs based on criteria independent of the physiology raises the technical and methodological problem of synchronizing the physiological measures to other, typically behavioral signs of emotion. Most of the studies that have used this strategy in both the adult and infant literature have used facial behavior as the "marker" of epochs containing emotion. In a sense, these studies have used the face as the final arbiter of whether an emotion was present and what it was. This research strategy requires videotaping the subjects along with recording their physiological reaction. In studies of adults, it is imperative that the video camera be unobtrusive, since display rules dramatically modify facial behavior in situations in which the subject is aware of being videotaped.

In order to synchronize the videotaped record of the facial behavior with the physiology it is imperative to have, at the very least, a signal marker to indicate the onset and offset of each event placed simultaneously on both the videotape and on whatever medium is being used to store the physiological data. In this way, it is possible to establish the location of epochs of physiology that are coincident with the display of particular facial signs of emotion with an adequate degree of precision. The use of digital time code generators and readers provides an even more accurate means of synchronization. With these devices, a unique digital code is placed on each frame of the video and also on either an FM tape (an analog storage medium) or a computer. An investigator can then locate the physiological activity corresponding to a particular video frame with absolute precision. As more subtle relations between aspects of physiological and facial behavior are examined, it will be increasingly necessary to utilize precise and sophisticated methods for behavior–physiology synchronization.

The set of general issues described above regarding the measurement of the physiological manifestations of emotion raises another set of important methodological problems. The most serious problem, particularly with the measurement of electroencephalographic (EEG) events related to emotion, is that of movement-related artifact. When epochs of physiology are selected for analysis based on the presence of discrete facial signs of emotion, the segments thus extracted are often those most confounded by muscle artifact. This is not particularly surprising in light of the association of movement with expressive signs of emotion. It does, however, pose very serious methodological problems for the investigator wishing to examine those periods during which the most intense emotion has occurred. If the traditional method of handling this problem is adopted, only segments during which no artifact is present will be retained for analyses. This might sometimes be acceptable, depending on the severity of the artifact problem. However, the data loss will often be excessive. Moreover, the segments that are discarded are often those containing the most intense periods of emotion. For these reasons, it is advantageous to develop procedures allowing the retention of EEG data that are coincident with the presence of movement artifact. Davidson (in press) has reported on the development of one procedure for statistically partialing out the variance in the EEG that is accounted for by muscle activity.

Central nervous system manifestations of emotion

Relatively little empirical work has directly examined CNS activity associated with emotion. Most of the physiological measures that have been recorded in studies of emotion are autonomic. This bias goes back to the early days of research on emotion, when Cannon (1927) and others (Malmo, 1959) observed profound changes in components of the ANS during fight or flight responses in animals. The relative preponderance of studies on the ANS manifestations of emotion also derives from introspective psychological report. When adult subjects describe sensations associated with emotion, these reports often include references to ANS changes. For example, the phrases ''white with fear'' and "red with anger" presumably refer to changes in blood flow in the face that are different in these two emotions. Symptoms such as heart pounding and excessive sweating also refer to autonomic changes. Obviously, ANS changes are significant in emotion and may indeed play an essential role in affecting the subjective experience of emotion. However, these ANS changes are themselves generated by changes in certain regions of the CNS. What is unclear is whether these ANS changes are necessary conditions for the experience/expression of particular emotions or should be regarded as correlates of these states. According to the latter view, the ANS changes typically occur in subjects with no history of neurological or psychiatric disorder and in ordinary contexts in which the masking of particular signs of emotion would not be thought to occur. However, this position would hold that not all of these changes are necessary for the experience of a particular emotion. The requisite studies have not been performed to answer this question unambiguously. It is likely that some of the ANS changes will be found to be necessary, whereas others might be more appropriately regarded as correlates of the state. In any case, the direct measurement of the CNS manifestations of emotion might potentially put us closer to the "source" of the physiological changes that distinguish among emotions. A growing literature has developed over the past decade on the CNS substrates of emotion. Comparatively little has been done in this area in infants.

The increased attention to the central substrates of emotion in adults was catalyzed by observations of the affective consequences of localized brain damage. Many investigators began to note reliable changes in the affective state of patients with particular lesions to the CNS. These affective changes came to be viewed as representing primary consequences of the brain damage and not changes secondary to the loss of particular cognitive or motor functions.

A second catalyst for research in this area has been the extensive studies performed during the past two decades on the effects of experimentally produced lesions in animals on affective behavior (see review by Panskepp, 1982). These studies have underscored the suggestion that different brain systems subserve different emotions and have highlighted the specific role that different neurotransmitters play in the production and modulation of a range of emotional behavior.

The following section provides an overview of the methods used to make inferences about both the CNS and ANS substrates of emotional behavior. Methodological advantages and disadvantages of each of these approaches are described. Data on one of the most well studied features of CNS involvement in emotion – lateralization – are reviewed. The last part of the section reviews our own work on asymmetries in brain electrical activity associated with emotion in infants during the first year of life.

Methodological approaches

Experimentally produced brain manipulations in animals. A variety of studies have established that stimulation of different regions of the hypothalamus produce different patterns of affective behavior in animals. For example, stimulation of the lateral hypothalamus elicits exploratory behavior, whereas stimulation of the ventral–medial region elicits rage (growling, hissing, and biting) (Panskepp, 1982). Moreover, different neurotransmitters have been found to predominate in each of these regions, the lateral hypothalamus containing a preponderance of dopaminergic neurons and the ventral–medial hypothalamus containing primarily cholinergic neurons. Data based on these approaches have been extensively reviewed elsewhere (Kelley & Stinus, 1984; Panskepp, 1982) and are not considered further here. Our point in introducing these data is simply to underscore the fact that powerful alterations in affective behavior are observed with direct manipulations to certain regions of the CNS in animals.

Brain damage in humans. The affective consequences of localized damage to the human brain have been studied in brain-damaged patients. The basic strategy in these studies has been to compare two groups of patients, each with relatively circumscribed lesions in different brain regions. The patients are typically matched on basic descriptive characteristics. Many studies have simply utilized relatively crude clinical ratings to assess the affective state of the patients. Comparatively fewer have used more standardized testing situations. Alterations in both the perception of emotion and its expressive features have been reported to occur with different patterns of brain damage. The lack of better measures of emotional responsiveness has been one of the most significant problems in this literature.

One of the earliest observations on the emotional consequences of localized brain damage was Babinski's (1914) observation that patients with right-hemisphere lesions often seemed indifferent or euphoric. Goldstein (1948) noted that patients with left-hemisphere damage often were profoundly depressed, a syndrome he termed the "catastrophic reaction." Together, these observations were among the first to suggest that the two hemispheres of the brain may be differentially lateralized for certain positive and negative emotions.

The results of recent studies argue against an early suggestion that these affective changes are secondary to the cognitive dysfunctions that unilateral hemispheric lesions produce. Some studies matched left- versus right-hemisphere-damaged patients on the severity of cognitive and motor dysfunctions and still revealed profound differences in the nature of affective responding. For example, Gasparini, Satz, Heilman, and Coolidge (1978) matched a group of left- and right-damaged patients on IQ and motor skills. They then administered the Minnesota Multiphasic Personality Inventory (MMPI) to these patients and found that the left-damaged group showed a marked elevation on the depression scale, whereas the right-damaged patient did not. Since these subjects had been carefully matched on cognitive and motor dysfunctions and in light of the fact that completion of this personality inventory does not require the perception or expression of emotional information, these findings suggest that localized brain damage was primary in producing these different emotional reactions.

The literature on the emotional consequences of localized brain damage has been extensively reviewed, and the reader is referred to these sources for additional information (Davidson, 1984a,b; Heilman, Watson, & Bowers, 1983). Additional data on the effects of right- versus left-sided lesions are briefly considered in a later section on hemispheric asymmetry and emotion.

Behavioral studies of intact subjects. Virtually all of the behavioral studies in humans on the neuropsychology of affect have centered around the issue of lateralization. The available behavioral methodology lends itself to the exploration of this issue since techniques have been developed for the presentation of lateralized stimuli that project initially, predominantly, or exclusively to one hemisphere. Using these procedures, an investigator can study differences in the response to identical information by one versus the other hemisphere. This technique has been used with both visual and auditory information. In the auditory modality, most studies have adopted the dichotic presentation technique. Very few studies using dichotic techniques have examined responses to emotional information (see, e.g., Safer & Leventhal, 1977). With visual hemifield presentation, information presented to the left side of space projects initially to the right hemisphere, and vice versa for information presented to the right side of space. The pathways in the visual system are almost completely decussated, resulting in mostly contralateral projections. It should be noted, however, that once information reaches the cortex, it is routinely transferred to the opposite hemisphere via the commissural pathways. Any differences in the response to information presented to the two visual fields therefore arise as a function of the hemisphere to which information is initially presented.

A variety of responses have been utilized in hemifield presentation paradigms. Often, reaction time to a motor response is used in studies of facial expression recognition (e.g., Strauss & Moscovitch, 1981). Other experiments have used accuracy of judgment. Comparatively fewer studies have examined the impact of lateralizing stimulus presentations on emotional responsiveness. Most experiments have focused on the perceptual side. In studies that have assessed the differential effects of left versus right stimulus presentations on emotional responses, subjects have been asked to rate the degree to which emotions were experienced in response to the identical stimuli presented to the right versus left visual field. Several studies have revealed small but reliable differences in the self-reports of subjects in response to affective information presented in this fashion initially to the left and right hemisphere (e.g., Davidson, Schaffer, & Saron, 1985; Davidson et al., in press. Dimond, Farrington, & Johnson, 1976).

In most experiments using this method, stimuli are presented for less than a saccade (approximately 175 msec). The reason for this is that fixation is typically not monitored, other than to ensure that subjects are fixating on the central fixation point before stimulus presentation. By presenting the stimuli for a duration less than a saccade, the investigator ensures that even if the subject moves his or her eyes away from the central point, insufficient time will be available to foveate the stimulus. In other words, stimulus offset would have occurred by the time the subject was able to fixate on the location where the stimulus was presented. Using careful electrooculographic or video monitoring of fixation, it is possible to present stimuli for considerably longer than a saccade (e.g., Davidson, et al., 1985; Reuter-Lorenz & Davidson, 1981). This is useful when short tachistoscopic durations are too brief to perform more complex tasks. Because visual acuity drops off steeply as stimuli are presented laterally to the fovea, longer stimulus exposure is often necessary for certain discrimination tasks that have been used in adults.

An interesting property of the infant brain is that the commissural pathways are less developed than those of an adult, presumably resulting in less interhemispheric transfer (see reviews by Denenberg, Hofmann, Rosen, & Yutzey, 1984; Fox & Davidson, 1984b). This should accentuate the magnitude of visual field asymmetries. Unfortunately, it is difficult to present visual stimuli in this fashion to infants because it is necessary to have the subjects fixating a central target for stimuli to fall on the appropriate retinal location. Despite these apparent difficulties, this paradigm has been successfully utilized with infants (G. Turkewitz, personal communication, 1984). It offers the possibility of observing different affective responses to the identical stimuli presented initially to the right versus left hemisphere. In infants, either physiological or behavioral responses to lateralized stimulus presentation can be measured. One elegant feature of this type of design is that the physical stimulus remains identical. The difference between conditions is solely a function of whether the stimulus is presented initially to the left or right hemisphere. In this way, the unique contribution of each hemisphere to the affective response can be discerned.

Electrophysiological studies. Most of the studies that have examined electrophysiological manifestations of emotion have assessed EEG asymmetry in response to certain affect elicitors. The advantage of using EEG is that recordings can be made during the performance of "real-life" behavior. In adults, a variety of affect elicitors have been used, such as films, slides, and self-generated emotion. Typically, the EEG is monitored during the presentation of the affective stimulus and averaged for the duration of time during which the stimulus was present. The activity during this epoch is then compared with activity during either a period of no emotion or during the presentation of another affect elicitor designed to produce a different type of emotion (for reviews of such studies in adults, see Davidson, 1983).

The manner in which the EEG is analyzed is typically to examine power in one or more frequency bands. In the adult literature, the most common measure is power in the alpha band. Greater alpha power is taken to be indicative of decreased activation (see Lindsley & Wicke, 1974; Shagass, 1972). Thus, an inverse relation is assumed between activation and alpha. By comparing the relative amounts of alpha on the two sides of the head, differences in degree and direction of asymmetrical activation can be inferred. It is known that over the course of development there are important changes in the frequency of the alpha rhythm. At least from birth to young adulthood, the frequency of the alpha rhythm increases. Therefore, the frequency band in infants that corresponds to adult alpha is considerably slower than 8–13 Hz (the frequency of alpha in adults). Examples of the use of EEG to infer asymmetries in hemispheric activation in infants are presented below.

The nature of the independent variable (i.e., which emotion is indeed elicited by the stimulus) is usually inferred from the self-reports of the subjects or from some type of a priori classification procedure. Using these procedures, several studies have provided evidence for right-hemisphere activation in the frontal region during the experience of certain negative emotions and left-sided activation during the experience of certain positive emotions (e.g., Davidson, Schwartz, Saron, Bennett, & Goleman, 1979; Tucker, Stenslie, Roth, & Shearer, 1981). Individuals who characteristically display a negative affective set (i.e., depressed individuals) have been found to show greater right-sided frontal activation during rest than nondepressed control subjects (Schaffer, Davidson, & Saron, 1983). Parietal EEG asymmetry did not discriminate between the positive versus negative conditions or between depressed and nondepressed subjects in any of these studies. These EEG findings are consistent with other studies using different methodological approaches.

We have applied these techniques to the assessment of asymmetries in activation during the presentation of affect elicitors in infants (Davidson & Fox, 1982; Fox & Davidson, 1984a, in press). In general, the data are consistent in direction with the adult findings and suggest that asymmetries for positive versus negative emotion are present early in the first year of life. These findings are reviewed in detail in a later section.

The general strategy of averaging the EEG over the epoch during which the affect elicitor was presented can obscure potentially important information. In order to extract epochs of EEG during which relatively "pure" emotion was being expressed requires that certain specific criteria be specified for the presence of an affective state. The presence of the state cannot be inferred from the simple fact that the stimulus was presented. This methodological approach recognizes that individual differences exist in the degree to which particular stimuli exert emotional effects. By using objective, behavioral measures of affect expression, one can extract segments of physiology that are associated with the same facial signs of emotion. This may be an effective method for reducing variability extraneous to the central questions under study. This strategy requires that relatively short epochs of EEG be extracted for analysis. This requirement imposes other, quite formidable constraints on the data analytic effort. For example, a method must be available for extracting EEG at a specific location in time for durations that vary as a function of the duration of the affect expression. In order to achieve effective time resolution, data must be extracted for overlapping windows since 2 sec of EEG is about the minimum-duration epoch for an FFT (fast Fourier transform) with sufficiently accurate frequency resolution for the purposes described. The FFT is a mathematical transform that is used to decompose the complex EEG signal into its underlying frequency components. On the basis of an FFT, a power spectrum can be computed that reflects the amount of power at each frequency. To get time resolution better than 2 sec, FFTs must be computed on overlapping 2-sec chunks. This is accomplished by moving the 2-sec window in half-second increments and computing separate FFTs for each of these overlapping windows. Since the FFT reveals the power at each frequency in the EEG at the midpoint of the window, the overlapping chunk approach increases the temporal resolution of the method. Special care must be taken either to restrict the data set to those epochs unconfounded by movement-related artifact or to use a regression-based correction procedure for removing the movement-related component in the EEG.

An additional issue in the recording of EEG involves the choice of a reference electrode site. Most studies of EEG asymmetry in adults, and our own work with infants, have used the common vertex as a reference. However, potential problems are associated with this choice. Specifically, if electrical activity at Cz varied among conditions as a function of changes in arousal, this would confound the interpretation of the activity recorded from the lateral scalp regions. In this case, use of a Cz reference would be potentially misleading. Alternative montages include the use of linked ears or other noncephalic sites. There are, however, a number of points worth noting with regard to the choice of a linked-ears reference. (a) Some evidence suggests that this reference artifactually attenuates the magnitude of asymmetries in brain electrical activity (see Nunez, 1981). Nunez (1981) suggests that this occurs as a function of placing a low-resistance shunt across the head. Thus, although a linked-ears reference eliminates some of the problems associated with Cz, it may introduce others. (b) Some data indicate that measures of alpha asymmetry in adults from a linked-ears and a vertex montage are significantly correlated (Davidson, Taylor, Saron, & Stenger, 1980).

Directions for future research: asymmetry and emotion

Work with adults

By means of the methods described above, several important observations have been made regarding hemispheric differences in the experience/expression of emotion. These findings call into question the early hypothesis (e.g., Schwartz, Davidson, & Maer, 1975) that the right hemisphere is involved in all emotion. They are more consistent with the notion of differential lateralization for at least certain positive and negative affects. More formally stated, this hypothesis holds that certain regions of the left hemisphere are specialized for the processing of certain forms of positive affect and that certain regions of the right hemisphere are specialized for the processing of certain forms of negative affect.

Two major qualifications in the statement of this hypothesis should be noted: (a) The specific regions within a hemisphere associated with affective asymmetry are unstated, and (b) the precise emotions for which this asymmetry exists are not indicated. More detailed information on these two points is lacking because of insufficient data. A brief and selective review of these findings is presented below. For more complete reviews see Davidson (1984a,b).

The differential role of the two cerebral hemispheres in emotion was first apparent in early observations of brain-damaged patients. Several investigators noted that, after unilateral left-hemisphere damage, patients displayed a high incidence of negative affect and "catastrophic reactions" (Alford, 1933; Goldstein, 1939). This reaction is characterized by excessive negative affect, tears, and pessimism about the future. After right-hemisphere damage, a very different affective reaction was noted. Patients with this pattern of damage displayed either indifference or euphoria (e.g., Denny-Brown, Meyer, & Horenstein, 1952). A number of more recent studies have evaluated the effects of the caudality of lesion (i.e., where in the anterior–posterior plane the lesion occurs) on affective response. Depressive reactions associated with left-hemisphere damage are particularly apparent with damage to the left frontal region (e.g., Robinson & Szetela, 1981).

These findings suggest that the two cerebral hemispheres may play different roles in positive and negative affect. However, none of the studies systematically evaluated the affective state of the patient. The dominant emotional characteristic of the patient was typically inferred from clinical judgments. This resulted in an inability to characterize the affective state of the patient with any precision. However, the data do suggest that the anterior regions of the two cerebral hemispheres may play a differential role in at least certain positive and negative emotions.

Another way to explore the question of hemispheric differences in the control of positive and negative emotions is to examine activation asymmetries in depressed subjects. These individuals can be assumed to be tonically in a negative affective state. Various reports have indicated that depressed patients have greater right-hemisphere activation in temporal, central, or frontal leads (e.g., Flor-Henry, Koles, Howarth, & Burton, 1979; Schaffer et al., 1983). However, some findings suggest that activation asymmetry varies as a function of the nature of depressive symptoms (Perris & Monakhov, 1979). Schaffer et al. (1983) found the subclinically depressed subjects classified on the basis of Beck Depression Inventory (BDI) scores were reliably distinguished from matched controls on the basis of a 1-min sample of resting eyes closed EEG. The depressed subjects exhibited significantly greater relative right frontal activation than control subjects. No group differences were found on parietal activation asymmetry for the same epochs.

Research performed on normal populations supports and extends the clinical evidence described above. Most of the behavioral studies on normal individuals have focused on the perception of emotion. This fact is as much a function of methodological constraints as anything else. Brief, single exposures of affective stimuli rarely evoke much emotion. These techniques, however, are well suited to the study of the perception of emotion. These studies have been performed in both the visual and auditory modalities. Typically, affective stimuli are presented to either the right or left visual fields or to the right or left ears, and accuracy and/or reaction time of recognition are assessed (see Bryden & Ley, 1983, for a review). In general, these studies have shown that affective stimuli are processed more accurately and/or efficiently when they are initially presented to the right hemisphere irrespective of the affective valence of the stimulus. However, in certain behavioral paradigms that minimize the degree of cognitive processing required to perform the task, evidence in support of differential lateralization for positive and negative emotions has been obtained (Reuter-Lorenz & Davidson, 1981; Reuter-Lorenz, Givis, & Moscovitch, 1983).

One interpretation of the finding of right-hemisphere superiority in the perception of emotion invokes the cognitive specialization of the right hemisphere. According to this view, the right hemisphere holds an advantage in the perception of emotion as a function of its superiority in holistic, parallel processing. A corollary of this position is that performance on tasks of emotional face recognition should be correlated with performance on tasks of basic visuospatial processing. Recent evidence in both normal subjects (e.g., Ley & Bryden, 1979) and brain-damaged patients (e.g., Bowers, Bauer, Coslett, & Heilman, 1985) does not support this position. Rather, the brain damage evidence indicates that the deficit displayed by right-brain-damaged patients on emotional face recognition tasks remains after performance on a task requiring judgments of facial identity has been partialled out (Bowers et al., 1985). Similarly, in normal subjects performance on tasks requiring emotion recognition is independent of performance on tasks requiring recognition of facial identity (Ley & Bryden, 1979). These findings have been interpreted by some (e.g., Etcoff, in press) to indicate that the recognition of emotion is subserved by an independent processing module in the right posterior region. Both views of the role of the right hemisphere in the perception of emotional information would hold that during tasks requiring the perception and recognition of emotional material, irrespective of their valence, the right parietal region should be relatively more activated than the homologous region on the left side. Indeed, in many studies of EEG asymmetries associated with emotion, right parietal activation has been consistently found during both positive and negative emotion. This finding has been obtained in adults as well as in infants (see Davidson, 1984a,b, for reviews).

Electrophysiological studies of activation asymmetries associated with emotion in adults have helped to localize more precisely the regions showing differential lateralization for positive and negative emotion. Davidson and colleagues (1979) reported that frontal activation asymmetry discriminated between epochs self-rated as associated with positive and negative emotion. In this study, subjects were exposed to video segments designed to elicit a range of emotions. Subjects were instructed to press up or down on a pressure-sensitive gauge according to the degree to which they liked or disliked what they were viewing. Epochs that subjects rated most positive were then selected and compared with epochs judged to be most negative. The data revealed that the positive epochs were associated with significantly greater left frontal activation than were the negative epochs. Parietal asymmetry from the same points in time did not discriminate between segments. The parietal leads showed right-hemisphere activation throughout both the positive and negative periods. Data from other laboratories have replicated this basic pattern of findings with other affect elicitors (e.g., Tucker et al., 1981).

Collectively, the data on asymmetry and emotion in adults suggest that the two cerebral hemispheres play different roles in emotional behavior. Both the brain damage and electrophysiological data reveal that the anterior cortical regions show differential lateralization for positive and negative emotion. These findings suggest that the left anterior region is more involved in positive emotion, whereas the right anterior region is more involved in negative emotion. Other evidence suggests that the posterior right-hemisphere region may play a special role in the perception of affective information irrespective of the valence of the stimulus. Many questions remain unanswered. Precious little evidence is available on the specific positive and negative emotions that show these asymmetrical effects. Further progress in this area will require more sophisticated measures of affect such as discrete coding of changes in facial musculature. The specific subcomponents of emotion that are lateralized also remain to be characterized. For example, is it hedonic tone that is differentially represented in the two hemispheres? Do the two hemispheres differ in the degree to which they are involved in the control of emotion? Finally, questions about the development of asymmetries for emotion have not yet been considered. In the next section, we present an overview of our collaborative program of research in this area and illustrate how some of the basic outstanding questions concerning emotion and asymmetry can be approached in developmental research.

Work with infants

In two studies, Davidson and Fox (1982) attempted to extend to infants the findings on differences in adult frontal EEG asymmetry between positive and negative affective stimuli. A total of thirty-eight 10-month-old female infants were seen. Ten-month-old infants were chosen for this study because previous developmental research (Sroufe, 1979) had demonstrated that 10-month-olds are capable of expressing a wide range of emotions, including joy and sadness. Only infants born to right-handed parents were tested. The infant sat in her mother's lap facing a 21-in. (diagonal) video monitor. The EEG was recorded from the left and right frontal and parietal regions (F3, F4, P3, P4) referred to a common vertex (Cz) and stored on separate channels of FM tape.

Positive and negative affective facial stimuli were embedded in a video recording of "Sesame Street." The stimulus tape was sequenced in the following manner: 10 sec of a "Sesame Street" segment followed by 90 sec of an affective face segment that was either happy or sad (counterbalanced across subjects). After the first affective segment, the infant viewed 90 sec of "Sesame Street," after which the second 90-sec affective segment was presented. In each affective segment, a female actress maintained a neutral face for 15 sec and then spontaneously broke into either smiling and laughter (happy segment) or frowning and crying (sad segment). The face was relatively static for the entire epoch. The audio portion was edited out so as to match the happy and sad segments.

The EEG in response to each segment from each of the four leads was reviewed and edited for gross eye movement and muscle and movement artifact. From the original 38 subjects in the two studies, we obtained artifact-free data on 24 infants. Artifact-free epochs were filtered for 1- to 12-Hz activity using Rockland variable bandpass filters with 48-dB octave cutoffs. The filtered output was digitized using Coulbourn digital logic, and activity (in microvolt seconds) in the 1- to 12-Hz band was computed for each of the four leads separately for each of the affective epochs.

Table 2.1. *Means and standard deviations of the frontal laterality ratio scores by condition*

Study 1 ($N = 10$)		Study 2 ($N = 14$)	
Happy	Sad	Happy	Sad
0.021	−0.001	0.073	0.032
(0.051)	(0.032)	(0.10)	(0.115)

Note: Higher numbers indicate greater relative left-sided activation.
Numbers in parentheses are standard deviations.
Source: Davidson and Fox (1982).

Studies 1 and 2 were identical except that in the second study an observer blind to the affective condition coded the infant's visual fixation and EEG was examined only for artifact-free epochs during which the infant was fixating on the monitor.

The results indicated that, in both studies, infants displayed greater relative left frontal activation in response to happy versus sad epochs. Across both studies, 20 of the total of 24 infants showed equal or greater relative left frontal activation during happy versus sad epochs. Parietal asymmetry failed to discriminate between these conditions (Table 2.1).

We performed a third study designed to explore the origins of this asymmetry for affect by eliciting positive and negative affective responses in newborn infants while simultaneously recording EEG (Fox & Davidson, in press). Twenty-six infants 2 to 3 days of age (9 males and 17 females) were recruited from the newborn nursery at a large metropolitan hospital. All infants had 5-min Apgar scores of 9 or 10 and evidenced no congenital or neurological abnormalities. Parental handedness was recorded by having the mother fill out the Edinborough Inventory for both herself and her spouse. Twenty-five of the 26 parents were right-handed. The data from the infant born to a left-handed parent were not included.

All infants were seen midway between feedings while they were in a quiet, alert state. The infant was tested in his or her bassinet in a laboratory adjacent to the nursery. Foam rubber and towels were positioned at the top of the bassinet around the infant's head to keep the head in midline and to prevent, as much as possible, the head from turning during the stimulus presentations. The EEG was recorded with a specially designed Lycra stretchable cap constructed to accommodate a normal range of head circumferences among newborns. The EEG was recorded from left and right frontal and parietal scalp regions (F3, F4, P3, P4), all referred to a common vertex (Cz) reference. The EEG was amplified on a

Table 2.2. *Means and standard deviations (in sec) for the duration of facial signs of interest and disgust for each of the three taste conditions*

Facial expression	Water	Sugar	Citric
Interest			
Mean	2.41	2.65	2.65
SD	2.52	3.48	3.14
Disgust			
Mean	1.43	0.48	1.55
SD	2.22	1.25	1.81

Note: Interest and disgust were the two facial expressions that occurred with the most frequency.

Grass model 7 polygraph and stored in analog form on FM tape. The infant's face was videotaped during the stimulus presentations, and the videotape was synchronized to the physiological recordings.

Four different stimuli were presented to the infant: (a) distilled water, (b) sucrose solution (25%, 0.73 M), (c) citric acid solution (2.5%, 0.12 M), and (d) quinine sulfate solution (0.25%, 0.0003 M). Solutions were presented at room temperature with separate sterile glass graduated pipettes. Four milliliters of liquid of each solution were presented to each infant. Distilled water and sucrose solution were always presented first, followed by either quinine or citric acid. (The latter two were randomized across subjects.) The quinine solution did not elicit reliably coded changes in infant facial expression, and data from this condition were dropped from further analysis.

Facial behavior in response to the stimulus conditions was analyzed for 30 seconds following taste presentation using Izard's Max coding system. Table 2.2 presents the means and standard deviations of the duration of each emotion that was observed for the water, sucrose, and citric acid taste stimulus conditions. As can be seen, the duration of interest is comparable among the three taste conditions. The duration of disgust is shorter during the sucrose stimulus condition than during the water and citric acid stimulus conditions, both of which elicited comparable durations of facial signs of disgust. These facial data seem to suggest that the first introduction of the pipette into the infant's mouth (i.e. the water condition) might be an event associated with the elicitation of facial signs of negative affect.

Power was computed in three different frequency bands for the EEG data: 1–3 Hz, 3–6 Hz, and 6–12 Hz. These data were log-transformed and subjected to a multivariate analysis of variance with Condition (water, sugar, citric acid),

Table 2.3. *Means and standard deviations for log power in the*
3- to 6-Hz band separately for the left and right frontal and
parietal regions, by condition

Conditon	Frontal		Parietal	
	Left	Right	Left	Right
Water				
Mean	0.352	−0.141	1.418	1.226
SD	1.418	1.545	0.956	1.009
Sugar				
Mean	0.442	0.697	1.064	1.379
SD	1.118	1.001	0.928	0.816
Citric				
Mean	0.334	0.340	1.423	1.385
SD	1.592	1.465	0.995	0.776

Region (frontal, parietal), and Hemisphere (left, right) as repeated measures. The data revealed a significant main effect for Region [$F(1,10) = 17.54$, $p = .002$]. This effect was a function of more power in the parietal than in the frontal region. There was also a significant Condition × Hemisphere interaction [$F(2,20) = 5.56$, $p = .03$]. This multivariate interaction was decomposed by computing separate univariate ANOVAs on log power in each of the three bands.

The two bands that revealed significant condition effects were the 3- to 6-Hz and 6- to 12-Hz bands. A significant Condition × Hemisphere interaction for the 3- to 6-Hz band [$F(2,18) = 4.90$, $p = .04$] (see Table 2.3) revealed that in response to the water stimulus less power is present in the right hemisphere (i.e., more right hemisphere activation) than the left in both regions. In response to the sugar stimulus the opposite pattern was observed (i.e., less power in the left hemisphere in both regions). Little hemispheric difference was observed in response to the citric acid condition in either region.

The significant Condition × Hemisphere interaction for the 6- to 12-Hz band [$F(2,26) = 4.69$, $p = .04$; see Table 2.4] revealed that there was less power (i.e., more activation) in both the right frontal and parietal regions than in the left during the water condition, whereas the sugar stimulus condition elicited the opposite EEG pattern, that is, less power in the left than in the right frontal and parietal regions.

The results of this study indicate that newborn infants show differences in asymmetry of brain electrical activity in response to different taste conditions. The surprising finding in these data was the pattern of EEG asymmetry that

Table 2.4. *Means and standard deviations for log 6- to 12-Hz power separately for the left and right frontal and parietal regions, by condition*

	Frontal		Parietal	
Condition	Left	Right	Left	Right
Water				
Mean	−1.219	−1.562	−0.601	−0.751
SD	1.373	1.282	0.819	0.741
Sugar				
Mean	−1.293	−0.925	−0.701	−0.314
SD	1.747	1.343	0.923	0.813
Citric				
Mean	−1.603	−1.360	−0.281	−0.601
SD	1.669	1.267	0.775	0.697

accompanied the water condition. In both the frontal and parietal regions, less power was observed in the right than in the left hemisphere. The presence of facial signs of disgust during the water condition suggests that this condition elicited an aversive response in the newborn infants, with the concurrent changes in brain electrical activity.

It is of interest that contrary to our previous data on 10-month-old infants (Davidson & Fox, 1982) no reliable differences were observed between activation asymmetries in the frontal and parietal scalp regions. These data raise the possibility that the brain of the newborn has not yet developed the functional specificity found in older subjects. Studies on higher nonhuman primates indicate that the frontal region does not participate in complex cognitive and affective processes until relatively late in ontogeny (Goldman, 1976). The EEG that we recorded from this scalp region in newborn infants may be generated from sources in other cortical and/or subcortical locations. Future studies with this age group might profitably examine the coherence between the EEG recorded from anterior and posterior regions in response to specific stimuli in order to make more valid inferences about common source generators.

The data from these infant studies indicate that the expression of certain positive and negative emotions seems to be lateralized in infants during the first year of life. The elicitation of strong approach and withdrawal responses in the neonatal taste study and the associated changes in brain electrical activity support the suggestion that the essential distinction between the hemispheres in the affective domain, at birth, is based on approach and withdrawal (see Davidson, 1984; Fox & Davidson, 1984b; Fox, 1985).

Autonomic nervous system manifestations of emotion

There is a long history of using heart rate as a measure of emotional response. William James in 1890 stressed both bodily (autonomic) changes and the conscious feeling of these bodily changes as integral parts of the experience of emotion. James relied on the subject's introspection of his or her feelings plus the occurrence of somatic changes to define an emotion. Although this model met with important criticism by Cannon in the 1920s (Cannon, 1927), research on emotion continued to focus on physiological changes caused by emotion-inducing stimuli. Two major positions in the research literature can be highlighted. The first argued for measurement of physiological changes during emotional situations as an indication of the arousal level of the organism. Major theorists like Duffy (1962), Malmo (1959), and Lindsley (1951) presented models relating general physiological arousal to the experience of emotion. The second position examined the possibility that different affective states might be associated with different patterns of physiological response. Ax (1953), for example, attempted to differentiate between certain negative emotions (e.g., anger and fear) with a number of ANS measures. Investigators adopting the latter perspective argued for the existence of unique psychophysiological profiles for the discrete emotions. Included in this differentiated response patterning is facial behavior.

Facial expressions of emotion are held to be universal (i.e., they have similar meaning across different human cultures) and are important communicators of information (Ekman & Friesen, 1975; Ekman, Friesen, & Ellsworth, 1982). Performance of these responses (e.g., facial expressions) may be related to discrete patterns of both CNS and ANS response. This model of emotion and its physiological substrates has been challenged by a number of theorists (Mandler, 1962; Schacter & Singer, 1962) who argue that the experience of emotion requires only a general arousal state in combination with the subject's appraisal of that state via situational cues. Thus, they suggest, there may be no set of specific ANS or CNS responses corresponding to a set of felt emotions.

Implicit in the models postulated by the arousal theorists and later by those espousing a cognitive view of emotion (e.g., Schacter & Singer, 1962) was the assumption that autonomic responses were nondifferentiated and merely reflected nonspecific arousal. This view of nondifferentiated autonomic activity was challenged in the late 1950s (Lacey & Lacey, 1958). Research revealed fractionation of ANS responses as a function of the organism's response to stimuli in the environment. In addition, Lacey and Lacey (1958) proposed that changes in the direction of heart rate may physiologically mediate certain cognitive and emotional responses. Subsequently, Graham and Clifton (1966) adapted these notions and those of Sokolov (1963) and proposed a response dichotomy based on deceleration or acceleration interpreted as orienting intake and defensive rejection. In light of the strong support for physiological differentiation, the notion of undifferentiated arousal that is central to cognitive views of emotion has been convincingly refuted (for a review, see Leventhal and Tomarkin, 1986).

Methodological approaches

The OR–DR dichotomy. The orienting response (OR)–defensive response (DR) interpretation of phasic heart rate responses also served as a model for investigators of infant emotional response. Phasic heart rate changes were linked to the infant's positive or negative emotional response. Heart rate deceleration was viewed as accompanying positive emotions, whereas acceleration accompanied negative emotions (Campos, Emde, Gaensbauer, & Henderson, 1975). This extension of the OR–DR dichotomy to emotion research suffers, however, from a number of important conceptual and methodological problems. For example, research with adults (and in some cases infants; see Sroufe & Wunsch, 1972) has demonstrated that an accelerative response may accompany a positive emotion expression, whereas a decelerative response may accompany a negative emotion (Ekman, Levenson, & Friesen, 1983). And the dichotomy of positive–negative emotions related to the OR–DR fails to differentiate among different positive or negative emotions. All negative emotions may not elicit heart rate acceleration or, conversely, all positive emotions may not elicit heart rate deceleration. Most researchers, however, have demonstrated only directional changes in heart rate between positive versus negative emotions (e.g., Provost & Gouin-Decaire, 1979).

There are a number of conceptual and methodological problems in the interpretation of a phasic heart rate response. For example, there have been few attempts to explain differences between emotions along the continuum of intake–rejection (but see, Plutchick, 1984). Although this dichotomy may describe the correlates of certain global emotional responses, it does not explain the physiological substrates of a particular emotion. Noting the presence of an acceleration or deceleration does not clarify the physiological basis for that response. Such phasic changes may, in some instances, reflect somatic changes that accompany a positive or negative emotional response (Obrist, Webb, Sutterer, & Howard, 1970). Finally, there are important methodological issues in defining individual differences in phasic heart rate changes.

Most research has utilized a difference score between a mean baseline heart rate base (ranging from 1 to 15 sec of baseline heart rate) and heart rate during a stimulus event. However, a mean baseline value may obscure a pattern of acceleration and deceleration in the resting heart rate, which may influence response to a stimulus. Porges (1972, 1973; Porges & Humphrey, 1977), for example, demonstrated that individual differences in baseline heart rate variability influence the subsequent direction of the stimulus-related heart rate response.

Although examination of the relation between discrete emotions and phasic heart rate may be problematic, a number of studies have used heart rate change as a response to emotion-eliciting stimuli. Three different emotion-eliciting situations have been examined: the visual cliff, stranger approach, and the Ainsworth and Wittig Strange Situation. In a series of studies using the visual cliff apparatus, Campos (Campos, Hiatt, Ramsay, Henderson, & Svejda, 1978; Campos & Langer, 1971; Campos, Langer, & Krowitz, 1970; Schwartz, Campos, & Baisel, 1973) recorded heart rate and facial and vocal behavior from infants ranging in age from 2 to 9 months during placement on either the deep or the shallow sides of the cliff. In general, Campos found that before 7 to 9 months of age infants show heart rate deceleration to the deep side of the visual cliff. Nine-month-old infants or infants with locomotor experience exhibited heart rate acceleration to the deep side along with behavioral signs of fear. Campos interprets the developmental data as reflecting a biobehavioral shift in emotional response reflected in the change in direction of the heart rate response. Deceleration reflects attention, whereas heart rate acceleration during placement on the deep side reflects a defensive or fear response. Although the 9-month-old infant's refusal to cross the deep side of the visual cliff is a well-established phenomenon in both human and other animal species, the precise emotion associated with this response is unspecified. Specific coding of facial patterning was completed in only one study (Hiatt, Campos, & Emde, 1979), which did not record heart rate so that the temporal relation between facial signs of fear to the cliff and heart rate acceleration is unknown. In addition, the muscle tension increase in infants that accompanies being lowered onto the deep side of the cliff (in the direct placement procedure) may contribute to the direction of the heart rate response (Obrist et al., 1970).

A number of studies have recorded infant heart rate during the approach of an unfamiliar person (Campos et al., 1975; Emde, Gaensbauer, & Harmon, 1976; Lewis, Brooks, & Haviland, 1978; Sroufe, Waters, & Matas, 1974; Waters, Matas, & Sroufe, 1975) or during the Ainsworth and Wittig (1969) Strange Situation (Donavan & Leavitt, 1982). In general, these studies have shown a relation between behavioral wariness to the stranger and heart rate acceleration (see, however, Lewis et al., 1978). The most common interpretation of the acceleration is that it is indicative of negative affect (see Vaughn & Sroufe, 1979) and that such a relation may be seen in the absence of overt distress (e.g., crying; see Waters et al., 1975). Three points should be emphasized with regard to these studies. First, the data do not rule out a cardiosomatic coupling explanation, even when the study examined only infants who did not cry. Data from adults have demonstrated the presence of muscle tension, which can be recorded via electromyographic (EMG) electrodes in the absence of overt muscle movement (Schwartz, Fair, Salt, Mandel, & Kleiman, 1976). Such evidence suggests that heart rate acceleration that occurs in the absence of overt muscle movements may be associated with covert muscle tension, which is reflected in EMG activity. Second, certain situations that evoke laughter, smiling, or positive emotion elicit heart rate acceleration (Sroufe & Wunsch, 1972). Therefore, a strict acceleration–defensive response–negative affect model may be too limiting. Third, there has been little attempt to disentangle the underlying physiological bases of the heart rate acceleration and its relation to the expression of negative affect. Specifically, it is unclear whether the accelerative response is a result of sympathetic arousal, parasympathetic inhibition, or some combination of both. Research dedicated to clarifying the heart rate response associated with emotion is crucial for furthering our understanding of its biobehavioral substrates.

Heart rate, arousal, tension, and development of emotions. Measurement of infant heart rate has played an important role in a number of tension-modulation models of emotion development (Sroufe, 1979). These models usually involve the concepts of tension, arousal, and the modulation of tension via affective display. In brief, the development of emotion is viewed as a by-product of the infant's increasing ability to modulate his or her response to the environment and effectively deal with the buildup of tension. Tension, in this model, is not the result of stimulation per se but the product of the infant's ability or inability to engage a stimulus. Sroufe's (1979) description of the onset and meaning of smiling and the emotion of joy will illustrate this model. Infant smiles are "content-mediated" and are the result of successful assimilation of an event. The emotion of joy is the result of a cognitive process – a connection between infant and environment or the smile of assimilation (see Kagan, 1971).

There is a temporal dimension to this process of tension, appraisal, and emotion outcome. With the presentation of a salient event, orienting and appraisal occur and tension is generated. The outcome of tension may be a positive or negative emotion, depending on the context or nature of the stimulus. Thus, a major determinant of an emotion response is the infant's ability to assimilate the stimulus event.

A number of studies have recorded infant heart rate while testing this model of tension–arousal–modulation (Field, 1981; Fogel, Diamond, Langhorst, & Demos, 1981; Stoller & Field, 1982; Waters et al., 1975). Heart rate has been used as a measure of arousal as well as assimilation. According to this view, heart rate acceleration indicates increases in arousal or tension, motor discharge, and possibly unsuccessful assimilation, whereas heart rate deceleration indicates resolution of tension and assimilation. Two issues emerge in the use of heart rate in this model. First, phasic heart rate responses are not emotion specific. Tension and heart rate acceleration could precede positive emotion expression as well as negative emotion displays. Thus, there is no differentiation among different positive or negative emotions in relation to a specific ANS response. Second, as with the work relating acceleration or deceleration to orienting or defensiveness and positive versus negative affect, there has been little attempt to interpret the physiological substrates of the acceleration or investigate the physiological basis for the fluctuations in heart rate pattern. Rather, phasic heart rate changes seem to be correlates of some general central state that changes as a result of the infant's transaction with the environment.

The most common paradigm examining the tension–arousal model records infant heart rate during a face-to-face interaction session. For example, Field (1981) recorded infant gaze behavior and heart rate while she varied maternal activity in a face-to-face session so that 4-month-old infants received low, moderate, or high levels of stimulation. She reported that infant gaze aversion and heart rate were higher during the low- or high-activity condition than during the moderate-activity condition. Field interpreted the increase in infant heart rate during the high- and low-maternal-activity conditions as reflecting an increase in emotional tension. She also examined periods of gaze aversion and heart rate during the moderate-activity condition and found that heart rate accelerated before the onset of gaze aversion and decelerated during the periods of gaze aversion. A similar finding was reported by Sroufe (Waters et al., 1975), who investigated heart rate changes in infants who averted their gaze during a stranger approach episode. Sroufe reported that heart rate accelerated before gaze aversion and decelerated during the gaze aversion period. Both Field (1981) and Sroufe (1979) argue that gaze aversion represents the infant's "time-out" period, during which the infant may process environmental information or reduce tension via assimilation. Thus, heart rate acceleration before gaze aversion represents an increase in tension. The gaze aversion itself is a behavioral attempt by the infant to modulate this tension or "cut off" and cope with the increase in tension. And if assimilation is successful and leads to a positive emotional response, it would be accompanied by a decrease in heart rate.

In each of these studies phasic heart rate response was utilized as a correlate of behavioral or somatic changes (e.g., gaze aversion) or as an indicator of general arousal. To date, however, there has been little investigation of the relations between the described emotion changes and their physiological substrates.

Directions for future research: vagal tone and emotion expressivity

Three general problems are raised by the research on ANS activity and emotion reviewed above. First, most investigators using heart rate to measure emotion response in infants have not specified the precise emotion under study but have instead examined emotional response along a positive–negative continuum or with non-emotion-specific behaviors such as gaze. A potential improvement in methodology may be to define emotion expressions precisely via discrete facial action coding systems (e.g., Max, Izard, 1979; or FACS, Ekman & Friesen, 1978). A second problem is the time locking of heart rate to emotion. It is important not only to specify the precise emotion or blend that is elicited but also to synchronize physiological recording to the changes in emotion expression. Although time locking of heart rate and gaze aversion has been utilized, there are fewer instances of synchronization of heart rate to changes in discrete facial affect (see, however, Lewis et al., 1978). Third, an attempt must be made to examine in the ANS the physiological substrates of emotion and emotion development. It is no longer satisfactory to speak of accelerations or decelerations in the absence of an interpretation of the physiological meaning of these changes.

A number of strategies may be adopted to investigate the physiological substrates of emotion and the meaning of phasic heart rate changes. One promising statistical technique, forecasting, can be used to examine phasic heart rate responses. Essentially, a mathematical model of the resting baseline heart rate is built and the heart rate response poststimulus onset is compared with the baseline model. Thus, one can examine the individual's heart rate response (acceleration or deceleration) based on the prestimulus heart rate pattern rather than the mean of a prestimulus period, which may obscure variations in individual heart rate.

A second strategy for investigating the physiological basis of heart rate responses involves the use of recently developed measures of sympathetic and parasympathetic influences on the heart. For example, a number of cardiovascular measures of sympathetic activity have been used in studies of adult response to stress (Light, 1981; Obrist et al., 1978). Obrist and colleagues have used, for example, pulse transit time as a measure of sympathetic activity during a stressful task. This measure can be easily used with infant subjects and would significantly add to an interpretation of heart rate changes during an emotion-eliciting situation. Similarly, Porges (1983) has described a statistical technique for partitioning the variance in the oscillations of heart rate in order to isolate that component of the heart rate pattern that is influenced solely by cholinergic (vagal) activity.

Vagal tone as a measure of parasympathetic activity

The pattern of resting heart rate or heart rate variability has been used as an estimate of neural control over the heart and, thus, indirectly as a measure of CNS integrity (Katona & Jih, 1975; Lowensohn, Weiss, & Hon, 1977; Nelson, 1976). For example, Kero, Antila, Ylitalo, and Valimaki (1978) described the relation between heart rate, in the absence of beat-to-beat variability, and brain death. Heart rate variability has also been related to subsequent perceptual–cognitive performance. In a series of studies, Porges (1972, 1973; Porges & Humphrey, 1977) found that subjects with greater baseline heart rate variability had faster reaction times and were better able to focus attention in a perceptual task than subjects with low baseline heart rate variability.

More recently, Porges, McCabe, and Yongue (1982) have demonstrated the possibility of statistically filtering from the heart rate pattern the variance contributed by extraneural factors, thus identifying the rhythmic heart pattern associated exclusively with respiration (i.e., respiratory sinus arrhythmia [RSA]).

In a series of studies with animal preparations, Porges and associates demonstrated that the amplitude of RSA is primarily the result of parasympathetic or vagal influence to the heart. Stimulation of the aortic depressor nerve in the rabbit reflexively increased vagal tone and increased the amplitude of RSA (McCabe, Yongue, Porges, & Ackles, 1984). The administration of pharmacological agents that are known to increase (phenylephrine) and decrease (atrophine) vagal tone resulted in parallel effects on RSA in unanesthetized moving rats (Yongue et al., 1982). A review of the physiological basis of the amplitude of RSA as an estimate of vagal tone was presented by Porges, McCabe, and Yongue (1982). Porges labeled the amplitude of RSA derived through his procedures $\hat{V}$ to emphasize that the amplitude of RSA is a robust estimate of vagal tone. Thus, $\hat{V}$ reflects neural control of the heart and may be more sensitive to the general status of the CNS than other measures of heart rate. Fox and Porges (1985) demonstrated a relationship between $\hat{V}$ and developmental outcome in a population of high-risk infants.

In addition, the use of $\hat{V}$ may make it possible to examine the balance between the two branches of the ANS. In the study of individual differences in psychopathology, investigators have attempted for a long time to quantify the dynamic balance between the branches of the ANS (Eppinger & Hess, 1915; Gelhorn, 1957; Wenger, 1941). If the vagal tone measure reflects the parasympathetic contribution to heart rate variability, one can examine individual differences in this measure as a reflection of one part of autonomic balance. Porges (1976) has, in fact, suggested that extreme differences in vagal tone (and hence autonomic balance) may be linked to certain forms of psychopathologies.

Heart rate variability and emotion expressivity in infants

The model suggested by Porges (1976) predicted differences in attentional and motor behavior based on the relative balance of sympathetic and parasympathetic influences on the heart. Differences in vagal tone may be associated with differences in reactivity and the ability to modulate motor activity. Using this model,

Table 2.5. *Intercorrelation matrix for resting EKG measures and infant facial behavior and maternal behavior during a face-to-face interaction* (N = 11)

	Infant behavior		
EKG measure	Duration interest	Duration joy	Duration surprise
Heart period	−.01	−.35	−.30
Long-term variability	.32	−.03	−.11
Short-term variability	.64*	.01	.25
	Maternal behavior				
	Presents toy	Turns away	Turns toward	Touches	Kisses
Heart period	.01	−.04	−.25	−.02	−.21
Long-term variability	.32	.73**	.48	.04	.38
Short-term variability	−.01	.44	.57*	.18	.60

*p < .05.   **p < .01.

Fox and Gelles (1984) investigated whether variations in heart rate were related to individual differences in facial expression. Twelve 3-month-old infants were videotaped for 2 min in a spontaneous face-to-face interaction session with their mothers. Before the interaction session, 3 min of electrocardiogram (EKG) were recorded from each infant as he or she sat quietly in an infant seat. Measures of heart period as well as long- (range) and short-term (mean successive differences score) variability were derived from the EKG data. The latter variable (short-term variability) approximates parasympathetic influence on the heart (Katonah & Jih, 1975) and is highly correlated with $\hat{V}$, a measure of vagal tone (Porges, 1983), whereas long-term variability may reflect the phasic alternations in the two branches of the ANS. The videotaped facial expressions of the infants were coded by a trained observer using the Maximally Discriminative Facial Movement Coding System (Max, Izard, 1979), producing a set of emotion expression variables. The data revealed (Table 2.5) a significant association between short-term variability and duration of interest expression. Infants with greater short-term variability displayed longer duration of interest facial expressions. The mother's behavior during the session was also coded, and correlations between these behaviors and baseline infant heart rate were computed. As can be seen in Table 2.5 there was a significant association between maternal positive affect and infant short-term heart rate variability as well as between infant short-term variability and mother turning toward her infant. In addition, infants exhibiting high long-term variability had mothers who more frequently turned away during the interaction. These data demonstrate an association between greater short-term variability and more attentive facial behavior during the face-to-face inter-action. A similar relationship between facial expression and resting heart rate has been reported by Field (1983). Infants with high baseline heart rate and low heart rate variability were rated less facially expressive in an imitation task than infants with high baseline heart rate variability. In addition, infants who displayed fewer facial expressions displayed higher heart rate during the interaction.

In a follow-up study, Stifter (1986) recorded 3 min of EKG from 5- and 10-month-old infants during a quiet resting state before an experimental session. During the session the infant's facial expressions were videotaped as he or she was approached by an unfamiliar person or by the infant's mother. Infant facial behavior was coded using Izard's Affex system (Izard, 1979). The EKG data were digitized and edited, and measures of heart rate variability including the vagal tone measure (Porges, 1983) were derived. The data from this study again revealed a significant association between infant expressivity and heart rate var-iability. Specifically, 5-month-old infants with high vagal tone displayed greater emotion expressivity to both mother and stranger than infants with low vagal tone.

In addition to the association with emotion expressivity, differences in heart rate variability may also reflect a more general temperamental dimension re-flected in behavioral reactivity to mild stress and motor inhibition (Fox, 1984; Porges, 1976). Children varying in their ability to explore an environment ac-tively or cope with uncertainty may also differ in tonic heart rate variability. A number of research programs have reported data that seem to support such a relation (Garcia-Coll, Kagan, & Resnick, 1984).

Fox (1984), for example, examined the relation between neonatal heart rate variability and attachment behaviors at 12 months. Resting EKG data were re-corded on 60 infants at the neonatal period, and measures of heart rate variability were derived. The infants were again seen at 12 months in a brief separation–reunion episode. Four behaviors were coded during separation: latency to cry, degree of distress, search behavior, and duration of play. At reunion, latency to begin playing once the mother had returned was coded. The data from this study revealed that infants with greater short-term variability were more distressed at separation than infants with low short-term variability. In addition, infants who exhibited less heart rate variability had exhibited a longer latency to begin play-ing after reunion. Thus, individual differences at the neonatal period displayed a significant association with socioemotional behavior when infants were 12 months of age.

In a second study, Fox, Porges, and Stifter (1984) observed 60 infants at 24 months of age in a free-play and toy-pick-up session. Before the sessions, 3 min of resting EKG were recorded and the vagal tone measure was derived. The 60 infants were then rank-ordered on their $\hat{V}$ score, and videotapes of the top and bottom 10 children were coded using a modified version of Greenspan's observation system (Greenspan & Lieberman, 1980). The data revealed significant differences in affective behavior between the top 10 and bottom 10 children. The bottom 10 children (ranked on $\hat{V}$) were more anxious and inhibited during the play session and were less cooperative during the toy-pick-up session than were the top 10 children. The top 10 infants displayed greater positive affect and were able to explore the environment independently. Thus, variations in vagal tone seem to be related not only to differences in facial expressivity but also to general affective response in a variety of social situations.

Similar work on emotion and autonomic responsivity has been reported by Kagan and colleagues (Garcia-Coll et al., 1984; Kagan, 1982). Kagan found that toddlers who were rated more inhibited across a number of social settings displayed less heart rate variability and faster heart rate while processing unfamiliar slide stimuli than toddlers who were uninhibited in their social interactions. Kagan referred to the affective state children assume when they are actively attempting to assimilate unfamiliar events as vigilance. He believes that the cardiac pattern accompanying vigilance and related to inhibition and fearfulness may index an important early individual difference dimension in emotional reactivity. It is possible that the relations between vagal tone and behavior outlined above reflect processes similar to those described by Kagan and his group.

In sum, measures of the heart rate patterning that reflect physiological differences in neural control of the heart are associated with differences in affective style. Infants with high vagal tone display more facial lability than infants with low vagal tone. They also seem to respond to mildly stressful or challenging events with less distress. Conceptually, the vagal tone measure (Porges, 1983) allows one to identify the physiological basis for these individual differences. Its advantage over other measures of heart rate variability (such as beat-to-beat variability or heart period variance) is that the Porges measure seems to reflect neural (parasympathetic) influences (McCabe et al., 1982) whereas the other measures are multidetermined.

Conclusion

The issues covered in this chapter underscore the complex and heterogeneous nature of emotion. Emotion is neither expression nor a pattern of physiological changes but is rather some complex combination of these. Progress in the understanding of the development of emotion requires that behavioral and physiological measures be used in the same study. Only in this way will we come to understand the relation between expression and the underlying physiological systems that subserve emotion. Many of the important questions regarding emotion and its development have not been addressed by contemporary research. For example, some research has documented asymmetries in brain electrical activity in the neonate in response to stimuli eliciting approach or withdrawal responses. Other research has documented differences in affect in adults as a result of unilateral brain injury. Are the asymmetries we have reported in infants similar to those documented in the adult studies? Or does the development of interhemispheric communication in the first few years of life parallel an increase in emotion blends and the decrease in pure emotion response? We can expect to obtain answers to some of these fundamental questions about the nature of emotion in future research that examines concurrent patterns of facial and physiological activity.

In this chapter we have argued for the importance of both CNS and ANS measures that reflect emotion. It is noteworthy that not one study has yet recorded both types of measures in the same experiment. Given the important role of both systems in emotion, it is imperative that future studies sample activity in both systems. The paucity of studies assessing both ANS and CNS measures in infants is paralleled by a similar deficiency of studies in adults. The tools are now available to perform these types of experiments, and they are urgently needed to begin the exploration of some of the most basic questions related to emotion. It is unclear what the differential contributions are of ANS and CNS changes to emotion. Are they differentially related to the expression of emotion? The time courses of these measures are quite different, the CNS measures having subsecond resolution and the ANS measures having a maximal resolution of roughly 1 to 2 sec. It is therefore likely that the ANS changes are more persistent than the CNS changes. The consequences of these differences are at present unclear but warrant further study. It is also of interest to explore situations where CNS and ANS measures diverge from an expected pattern. For example, if positive affect is usually associated with left frontal activation and a particular cardiac change, is there a reliably different facial expression when only one of these changes occurs in the absence of the other?

Another question of major importance to developmental research on emotion is the issue of emotional control. At some point after the first year of life, the infant begins to acquire some degree of control over affective states. Particularly important is the growing capacity to inhibit negative affect. A critical question concerning the nature of this capacity for affect inhibition is whether the expressive changes are paralleled by a dampening of the physiological signs of the target negative emotion. It may be that different types or levels of inhibition exist, with some forms associated with parallel changes in expression and physiology and other forms associated with fractionation between these systems. This area provides fertile ground for combined behavioral and physiological studies.

The growing recognition of the importance of emotional development in developmental psychology is in part a function of the increased precision afforded by physiological indices of emotion for measuring affective phenomena. With the combined use of objective systems for coding infant facial behavior and sophisticated computer-based techniques for the recording and analysis of short epochs of physiological activity, we can expect the future to bring major new advances in our understanding of emotional development.

References

Ainsworth, M. D. S., Blehar, M. C., Waters, E., & Wall, S. *Patterns of attachment: A psychological study of the strange situation.* Hillsdale, NJ: Erlbaum, 1978.

Alford, L. B. Localization for consciousness and emotion. *American Journal of Psychiatry,* 1933, *12,* 789–99.

Ax, A. F. The physiological differentiation between fear and anger in humans. *Psychosomatic Medicine,* 1953, *15,* 433–42.

Babinski, J. Contributor a l'etride des troubles mentaux dans l'hemiplegie organique cerebrale (anosognosie). *Revue Neurologique,* 1914, *27,* 845–8.

Bowers, D., Bauer, R. M., Coslett, H. B., & Heilman, K. M. Processing of faces by patients with unilateral hemisphere lesions: I. Dissociation between judgements of facial affect and facial identity. *Brain and Cognition,* 1985, *4,* 258–72.

Bryden, N. P., & Ley, R. G. Right hemispheric involvement in the perception and expression of emotion in normal humans. In K. M. Heilman & P. Satz (Eds.), *Neuropsychology of Human Emotion* (pp. 6–44). New York: Guilford, 1983.

Campos, J. J., Emde, R. N., Gaensbauer, T., & Henderson, C. Cardiac and behavioral interrelationships in the reactions of infants to strangers. *Developmental Psychology,* 1975, *11,* 589–601.

Campos, J. J., Hiatt, S., Ramsay, D., Henderson, C., & Svejda, M. The emergence of fear on the visual cliff. In M. Lewis & L. Rosenblum (Eds.), *The origins of affect* (pp. 149–82). New York: Plenum, 1978.

Campos, J., & Langer, A. The visual cliff: Discriminative cardiac orienting responses with retinal size held constant. *Psychophysiology,* 1971, *8,* 264–5.

Campos, J. J., Langer, A., & Krowitz, A. Cardiac response on the visual cliff in prelocomotor human infants. *Science,* 1970, *170,* 196–7.

Cannon, W. B. The James–Lange theory of emotions: A critical examination and alternate theory. *American Journal of Psychology,* 1927, *39,* 106–24.

Davidson, R. J. Hemispheric specialization for cognition and affect. In A. Gale & J. Edwards (Eds.), *Physiological Correlates of Human Behaviour* (pp. 128–48). London: Academic Press, 1983.

Davidson, R. J. Hemispheric asymmetry and emotion. In K. R. Scherer & P. Ekman (Eds.), *Approaches to emotion* (pp. 39–57). Hillsdale, NJ: Erlbaum, 1984a.

Davidson, R. J. Affect, cognition and hemispheric specialization. In C. E. Izard, J. Kagan, & R. Zajonc (Eds.), *Emotion, cognition and behavior* (pp. 320–65). Cambridge University Press, 1984b.

Davidson, R. J. EEG measures of cerebral asymmetry: Conceptual and methodological issues. *Psychophysiology* (Abstract), in press.

Davidson, R. J., & Fox, N. A. Asymmetrical brain activity discriminates between positive versus negative affective stimuli in human infants. *Science,* 1982, *218,* 1235–7.

Davidson, R. J., Schaffer, C. E., & Saron, C. Effects of lateralized presentations of faces on self-reports of emotion and EEG asymmetry in depressed and non-depressed subjects. *Psychophysiology,* 1985, *22,* 353–64.

Davidson, R. J., Schwartz, G. E., Saron, C., Bennett, J., & Goleman, D. J. Frontal versus parietal EEG asymmetry during positive and negative affect. *Psychophysiology,* 1979, *16,* 202–3.

Davidson, R. J., Taylor, N., Saron, C., & Stenger, M. Individual differences and task effects in EEG measures of hemispheric activation: I. Effects of reference electrode. *Psychophysiology,* 1980, *17,* 311.

Davidson, R. J., Mednick, B., Moss, E., Sason, C., & Schaffer, C. E. Self-rating of emotions are influenced by the visual field to which affective information is presented. *Brain & Cognition,* in press.

Denenberg, V. H., Hofmann, M. J., Rosen, G. D., & Yutzey, D. A. Cerebral asymmetry and behavioral laterality: Some psychobiological considerations. In N. A. Fox & R. J. Davidson (Eds.), *The Psychobiology of Affective Development* (pp. 77–118). Hillsdale, NJ: Erlbaum, 1984.

Denny-Brown, D., Meyer, S. T., & Horenstein, S. The significance of perceptual rivalry resulting from parietal lesion. *Brain,* 1952, *75,* 433–71.

Dimond, F., Farrington, L., & Johnson, P. Differing emotional response from right and left hemispheres. *Nature,* 1976, *261,* 690–2.

Donovan, W. L., & Leavitt, L. A. *Cardiac responses of mothers and securely versus insecurely attached infants.* Paper presented at the meetings of the Society for Psychophysiological Research, Minneapolis, MN, October 1982.

Duffy, E. *Activation and behavior.* New York: Wiley, 1962.

Ekman, P. Methods for measuring facial action. In K. R. Scherer & P. Ekman (Eds.), *Handbook of Methods in Nonverbal Behavior Research* (pp. 45–90). Cambridge University Press, 1983.

Ekman, P. Expression and the nature of emotion. In K. R. Scherer & P. Ekman (Eds.), *Approaches to emotion* (pp. 319–44). Hillsdale, NJ: Erlbaum, 1984.

Ekman, P., & Friesen, W. V. *Unmasking the face: A guide to recognizing emotions from facial clues.* Englewood Cliffs, NJ: Prentice-Hall, 1975.

Ekman, P., & Friesen, W. V. *The facial action coding system: A technique for the measurement of facial movement.* Palo Alto, CA: Consulting Psychologists Press, 1978.

Ekman, P., Friesen, W. V., & Ellsworth. What are the similarities and differences in facial behavior across cultures? In P. Ekman (Ed.), *Emotion in the human face* (2nd ed., pp. 128–43). Cambridge University Press, 1982.

Ekman, P., Levenson, R. W., & Friesen, W. V. Autonomic nervous system activity distinguishes between emotions. *Science,* 1983, *221,* 1208–10.

Emde, R. N., Gaensbauer, T., & Harmon, R. J. *Emotional expression in infancy: A biobehavioral study.* New York: International Universities Press, 1976.

Eppinger, H., & Hess, L. Vagatonia. *Journal of Nervous & Mental Diseases, Monograph Series, 1915,* 20.

Etcoff, N. L. The neuropsychology of emotional expression. In G. Goldstein & R. E. Tarter (Eds.), *Advances in clinical neuropsychology,* Vol. 3, New York: Plenum Press, in press.

Field, T. Gaze behavior of normal and high-risk infants during early interactions. *Journal of the Academy of Child Psychiatry,* 1981, *20,* 308–17.

Field, T. M. Individual differences in the expressivity of neonates and young infants. In R. Feldman (Ed.), *Development of non-verbal behavior in children* (pp. 279–95). New York: Springer-Verlag, 1983.

Flor-Henry, P., Koles, Z. J., Howarth, B. G., & Burton, L. Neurophysiological studies of schizophrenia, mania and depression. In J. Gruzelier & P. Flor-Henry (Eds.), *Hemisphere asymmetries of function in psychopathology* (pp. 189–222). New York: Elsevier/Holland, 1979.

Fogel, A., Diamond, G., Langhorst, B., & Demos V. Affective and cognitive aspects of the two month old's participation in face to face interaction with its mother. In E. Tronick (Ed.), *Joint regulation of behavior.* Baltimore: University Park Press, 1981.

Fox, N. A. Behavioral and autonomic antecedents of attachment in high risk infants. In M. Reite &

T. Field (Eds.), *The psychobiology of attachment* (pp. 389–414). New York: Academic Press, 1984.

Fox, N. A. Sweet–sour/interest–disgust: The role of approach withdrawal in the development of emotion. In T. Field & N. A. Fox (Eds.), *Infants' social perception* (pp. 53–72). New York: Ablex Press, 1985.

Fox, N. A., & Davidson, R. J. *EEG asymmetry in response to stranger and mother approach and maternal separation in 10 month old infants.* Paper presented at the meetings of the Society for Psychophysiological Research, Milwaukee, WI, September 1984a.

Fox, N. A., & Davidson, R. J. Hemispheric substrates of affect: A developmental model. In N. A. Fox & R. J. Davidson (Eds.), *The psychobiology of affective development* (pp. 353–82). Hillsdale, NJ: Erlbaum, 1984b.

Fox, N. A., & Davidson, R. J. Taste elicited changes in facial signs of emotion and the asymmetry brain electrical activity in human newborns. *Neuropsychologia,* in press.

Fox, N. A., & Gelles, M. Face to face interaction in term and preterm infants: Facial expression and autonomic variability. *Infant Mental Health Journal,* 1984, *5,* 192–205.

Fox, N. A., & Porges, S. W. The relation between neonatal heart patterns and developmental outcome. *Child Development,* 1985, *56,* 28–37.

Fox, N. A., Porges, S. W., & Stifter, C. *Long term continuity of vagal tone and its relation to outcome in a high-risk sample.* Paper presented at the meetings of the Society for Psychophysiological Research, Milwaukee, WI, September 1984.

Garcia-Coll, C., Kagan, J., & Resnick, J. S. Behavioral inhibition in young children. *Child Development,* 1984, *55,* 1005–19.

Gasparini, W. G., Satz, P., Heilman, K. M., & Coolidge, F. L. Hemispheric asymmetries of affective processing as determined by the Minnesota Multiphasic Personality Inventory. *Journal of Neurology, Neurosurgery, and Psychiatry,* 1978, *41,* 420–73.

Gelhorn, E. *Autonomic imbalance and the hypothalamus.* Minneapolis: University of Minnesota Press, 1957.

Goldman, P. S. Maturation of the mammalian nervous system and the ontogeny of behavior. In J. S. Rosneblatt, R. A. Hinde, E. Shaw, & C. Bear (Eds.), *Advances in the study of behavior.* Academic Press, 1976.

Goldstein, K. *The organism.* New York: Academic Book Publishers, 1939.

Goldstein, K. *Language and language disturbances.* New York: Grune & Stratton, 1948.

Graham, F. K., & Clifton, R. Heart rate change as a component of the orienting response. *Psychological Bulletin,* 1966, *65,* 305–20.

Greenspan, S. I., & Lieberman, A. F. Infants, mothers and their interaction: A quantitative clinical approach to developmental assessment. In S. I. Greenspan & G. H. Pollock (Eds.), *The course of life: Psychoanalytic contributions toward understanding personality development, Vol. 1: Infancy and early childhood* (pp. 271–312). DHHS Publication No. ADM 80-786. Washington, DC: Government Printing Office, 1980.

Heilman, K. M., Watson, R. T., & Bowers, D. Affective disorders associated with hemispheric disease. In K. M. Heilman & P. Satz (Eds.), *Neuropsychology of human emotion* (pp. 45–64). New York: Guilford, 1983.

Hiatt, S. W., Campos, J. J., & Emde, R. N. Facial patterning and infant emotional expression: Happiness, surprise and fear. *Child Development,* 1979, *50*(4), 1020–35.

Izard, C. E. *The face of emotion.* New York: Appleton-Century-Crofts, 1971.

Izard, C. E. *The Maximally Discriminative Facial Movement Coding System (Max).* Newark: University of Delaware, Instructional Resources Center, 1979.

Izard, C. E., Huebner, R. R., Risser, D., McGinnes, G. C., & Dougherty, L. M. The young infant's ability to produce discrete emotional expressions. *Developmental Psychology,* 1980, *16*(2), 132–40.

James, W. *Principles of Psychology*. New York: Holt, 1890.

Kagan, J. *Changed continuity in infancy*. New York: Wiley, 1971.

Kagan, J. Heart rate and heart rate variability as signs of a temperamental dimension in infants. In C. E. Izard (Ed.), *Measuring emotions in infants and children* (pp. 38–66). Cambridge University Press, 1982.

Katona, P. G., & Jih, F. Respiratory sinus arrhythmia: Noninvasive measure of parasympathetic cardiac control. *Journal of Applied Physiology*, 1975, *39*, 801–5.

Kelley, A., & Stinus, L. Neuroanatomical and neurochemical substrates of affective behavior. In N. A. Fox & R. J. Davidson (Eds.), *The psychobiology of affective development* (pp. 1–75). Hillsdale, NJ: Erlbaum, 1984.

Kero, P., Antila, K., Ylitalo, V., & Valimaki, A. Decreased variation in decerebration syndrome: Quantitative clinical criterion of brain death? *Pediatrics*, 1978, *62*, 307–11.

Lacey, J., & Lacey, B. The relationship of resting autonomic activity to motor impulsivity. *Research Publications Association for Research in Nervous and Mental Disease*, 1958, *36*, 144–209.

Lacey, J., & Lacey, B. Some autonomic–central nervous system interrelationships. In P. Block (Ed.), *Physiological correlates of emotion* (pp. 205–28). New York: Academic Press, 1970.

Leventhal, H., & Tomarkin, A. J. Emotion: Today's problems. In M. R. Rosenzweig & L. W. Porter (Eds.), *Annual Review of Psychology*, 1986, *37*, 565–610.

Lewis, M., Brooks, J., & Haviland, J. Hearts and faces: A study in the measurement of emotion. In M. Lewis & L. Rosenblum (Eds.), *The development of affect* (pp. 77–124). New York: Plenum, 1978.

Ley, R., & Bryden, P. Hemispheric differences in processing emotions and faces. *Brain and Language*, 1979, *7*, 126–30.

Light, K. C. Cardiovascular responses to effortful active coping: Implications for the role of stress in hypertension development. *Psychophysiology*, 1981, *18*, 216–25.

Lindsley, D. B. Emotion. In S. S. Stevens (Eds.), *Handbook of experimental psychology* (pp. 473–516). New York: Wiley, 1951.

Lindsley, D. B., & Wicke, J. D. The electroencephalogram: Autonomous electrical activity in man and animals. In R. F. Thompson & M. M. Patterson (Eds.), *Bioelectric recording techniques: B. Electroencephalography and human brain potentials* (pp. 4–86). New York: Academic Press, 1974.

Lowensohn, A. I., Weiss, M., & Hon, E. H. Heart rate variability in brain damaged adults. *Lancet*, 1977, 626–8.

Malmo, R. B. Activation: A neurophysiological dimension. *Psychological Review*, 1959, *66*, 367–86.

Mandler, G. Emotion. In R. W. Brown, E. Galanter, E. H. Hess, & G. Mandler (Eds.), *New directions in psychology* (pp. 267–343). New York: Holt, Rinehart & Winston, 1962.

McCabe, P. M., Yongue, B. G., Porges, S. W., & Ackles, P. K. Changes in heart period, variability, and spectral analysis estimate of respiratory sinus arrhythmia during aortic nerve stimulation in rabbits. *Psychophysiology*, 1984, *21*, 149–158.

Nelson, N. M. Respiration and circulation before birth. In C. A. Smith & N. M. Nelson (Eds.), *The physiology of the newborn infant*. Springfield, IL: Thomas, 1976, pp. 15–116.

Nunez, P. L. *Electrical fields of the brain*. New York: Oxford University Press, 1981.

Obrist, P. A., Gaebelein, C. J., Teller, E. S., Langer, A. W., Grignolo, A., Light, K. C., & McCubbin, J. A. The relationship among heart rate, carotid *dp/dt* and blood pressure in humans as a function of the type of stress. *Psychophysiology*, 1978, *15*, 102–15.

Obrist, P. A., Webb, R. A., Sutterer, J. R., & Howard, J. L. The cardiac–somatic relationship: Some reformulations. *Psychophysiology*, 1970, *6*, 569–89.

Panskepp, J. Toward a general psychobiological theory of emotions. *The Brain and Behavioral Sciences*, 1982, *5*, 407–68.

Perris, C., & Monakhov, K. Depressive symptomatology and systemic structural analyses of the EEG. In J. Gruzelier & P. Flor-Henry (Eds.), *Hemisphere asymmetries of function in psychopathology* (pp. 223–36). New York: Elsevier/North Holland, 1979.

Plutchik, R. Emotions: A general psychoevolutionary theory. In K. S. Scherer & P. Ekman (Eds.), *Approaches to Emotion,* Erlbaum: Hillsdale, NJ, 1984, 197–220.

Porges, S. W. Heart rate variability and deceleration as indexes of reaction time. *Journal of Experimental Psychology,* 1972, *92,* 103–10.

Porges, S. W. Heart rate variability: An autonomic correlate of reaction time performance. *Bulletin of the Psychonomic Society,* 1973, *1,* 270–2.

Porges, S. W. Peripheral and neurochemical parallels of psychopathology: A psychophysiological model relating autonomic imbalance to hyperactivity, psychopathy and autism. In H. W. Reese (Ed.), *Advances in child development and behavior* (pp. 35–65). New York: Academic Press, 1976.

Porges, S. W. Heart rate patterns in neonates: A potential diagnostic window to the brain. In T. M. Field & A. Sostek (Eds.), *Infants born at-risk: Physiological and perceptual processes* (pp. 3–22). New York: Grune & Stratton, 1983.

Porges, S. W., & Humphrey, M. M. Cardiac and respiratory responses during visual search in nonretarded children and retarded adolescents. *American Journal of Mental Deficiency,* 1977, *82,* 162–9.

Porges, S. W., McCabe, P. M., & Yongue, B. G. Respiratory heart rate interactions: A psychophysiological measure with implications for pathophysiology and behavior. In J. T. Cacioppo & R. E. Petty (Eds.), *Perspectives in cardiovascular psychophysiology* (pp. 223–64). New York: Guilford Press, 1982.

Provost, M. A., & Gouin-Decaire, T. Heart rate reactivity of 9 and 12 month old infants showing specific emotions in natural setting. *International Journal of Behavioral Development,* 1979, *2,* 109–20.

Reuter-Lorenz, P. A., & Davidson, R. J. Differential contributions of the two cerebral hemispheres to the perception of happy and sad faces. *Neuropsychologia,* 1981, *19,* 609–13.

Reuter-Lorenz, P., Givis, R. P., & Moscovitch, M. Hemispheric specialization and the perception of emotion: Evidence from right-handers and from inverted and non-inverted left-handers. *Neuropsychologia,* 1983, *21,* 687–92.

Robinson, R. G., & Szetela, B. Mood change following left hemispheric brain injury. *Annals of Neurology,* 1981, *9,* 447–53.

Safer, M., & Leventhal, H. Ear differences in evaluating emotional tones of voice and verbal content. *Journal of Experimental Psychology: Human Perception and Performance,* 1977, *31,* 75–82.

Schacter, S., & Singer, J. E. Cognitive, social, and physiological determinants of emotional state. *Psychological Review,* 1962, *69,* 379–99.

Schaffer, C. E., Davidson, R. J., & Saron, C. Frontal and parietal EEG asymmetries in depressed and non-depressed subjects. *Biological Psychiatry,* 1983, *18,* 753–62.

Schwartz, A. N., Campos, J. J., & Baisel, E. J. The visual cliff: Cardiac and behavioral responses of the deep and shallow sides at five and nine months of age. *Journal of Experimental Child Psychology,* 1973, *15,* 86–99.

Schwartz, G. E., Davidson, R. J., & Maer, F. Right hemisphere lateralization for emotion in the human brain: Interaction with cognition. *Science,* 1975 , *190,* 286–8.

Schwartz, G. E., Fair, P. L., Salt, P., Mandel, M. R., & Kleiman, G. L. Facial muscle patterning to affective imagery in depressed and non-depressed subjects. *Science,* 1976, *192,* 489–91.

Shagass, C. Electrical activity of the brain. In N. S. Greenfield & R. A. Sternbach (Eds.), *Handbook of psychophysiology* (pp. 263–328). New York: Holt, Rinehart & Winston, 1972.

Sokolov, E. *Perception and the conditioned reflex.* New York: Macmillan, 1963.

Sroufe, L. A. Socioemotional development. In J. Osofsky (Ed.), *Handbook of infant development* (pp. 462–518). New York: Wiley, 1979.

Sroufe, L. A., Waters, E., & Matas, L. Contextual determinants of infant affective response. In M. Lewis & L. Rosenblum (Eds.), *The origins of fear* (pp. 49–72). New York: Wiley, 1974.

Sroufe, L. A., & Wunsch, J. P. The development of laughter in the first year of life. *Child Development*, 1972, *43*, 1326–44.

Stifter, C. A. Individual differences in heart rate patterning and emotion expressivity in five- and ten-month-old infants. Paper presented at the meetings of the International Conference on Infant Studies, Los Angeles, CA, 1986.

Stoller, S. A., & Field, T. Alteration of mother and infant behavior and heart rate during a still face perturbation of face to face interaction. In T. Field & A. Fogel (Eds.), *Emotion and early interaction* (pp. 57–82). Hillsdale, NJ: Erlbaum, 1982.

Strauss, E., & Moscovitch, M. Perception of facial expressions. *Brain and Language*, 1981, *13*, 309–32.

Tucker, D. M., Stenslie, C. E., Roth, R. S., & Shearer, S. L. Right frontal lobe activation and right hemisphere performance decrement during a depressed mood. *Archives for General Psychiatry*, 1981, *38*, 169–74.

Vaughn, B., & Sroufe, L. A. The temporal relationship between infant heart rate acceleration and crying in an aversive situation. *Child Development*, 1979, *50*, 565–7.

Waters, E., Matas, L., & Sroufe, L. A. Infant's reaction to an approaching stranger: Description, validation and functional significance of wariness. *Child Development*, 1975, *46*, 348–56.

Wenger, M. A. The measurement of individual differences in autonomic balance. *Psychosomatic Medicine*, 1941, *3*, 427–34.

Yongue, B. G., McCabe, P. M., Porges, S. W., Rivera, M., Kelley, S. L., & Ackles, P. K. The effects of pharmacological manipulations that influence vagal control of the heart on heart period, heart period variability and respiration in rats. *Psychophysiology*, 1982, *19*, 426–32.

Part III

Facial and vocal expressions

3   Measuring change in infant emotional expressivity: two approaches applied in longitudinal investigation

Carol Zander Malatesta and Jeannette M. Haviland

When Darwin legitimized the topic of emotion for scientific inquiry with the publication of *The Expression of Emotion in Man and Animals,* he foresaw that the study of infants would lead to major advances in the field (Darwin, 1872). Infants, he thought, would provide some of the best raw data on emotion expressions in humans with which to make evolutionary inferences. Darwin, of course, presumed that the infant's naive status would guarantee "pure" forms of expression. However, what he probably did not envision was the technology that would make the study of infants' pure or raw expressions a feasible undertaking. A technology to examine these raw data of emotion has only recently become available in the form of fine-grained component analyses of facial muscle movement patterns such as Izard's Maximally Discriminative Facial Movement Coding System (Izard, 1979). Darwin might also have been impressed by the strides researchers have made in attempting to measure the structural or more enduring aspects of emotion through the use of sophisticated questionnaires of moods, traits, and temperament. Both advances have changed the field since Darwin's day, albeit in different ways. Expressive behaviors captured by videotape and preserved for detailed component analysis enable investigators to examine the overt but fleeting aspects of emotion in a behaviorally objective way; psychometrically sophisticated reporting forms permit the examination of subjective and structural components.

With the advent of the microanalytic approach of component systems, a number of questions have been generated about the mapping between analyses that decompose the parts of facial expressions to make judgments of affect and the kind of instantaneous and impressionistic judgments people make in their everyday encounters with others. Initial attempts to validate empirically the correspon-

The writing of this chapter was supported in part by an NIMH National Research Service Award (1 F32 MH08773-01) to the first author.

dence between global and component judgments so far have been encouraging (Hiatt, Campos, & Emde, 1979; Izard & Dougherty, 1980; Izard, Huebner, Risser, McGinnes, & Dougherty, 1980).

In the present chapter we consider the question once again and, in addition, examine a related one – the link between emotional expressions, on the one hand, and inferences about internal states and personality and temperament characteristics, on the other. These questions originally presented themselves to us in the course of a longitudinal investigation of the influence of maternal emotional traits and behaviors on the developmental course of affective expression in young infants. Because we were interested in mutually influential behavior, this study also engendered the development of a methodology for capturing sequential patterns of emotional–communicative behavior during dyadic interaction. The hope was to identify some of the subtle social influences mothers and babies exert on one another as they interact. Since the procedures and results of this study will be of interest to those seeking to develop dynamic models of infant emotional development, we report the study in detail. We give special attention to the specifics of doing dyadic-level analyses of emotional interaction, as well as present data that speak to the questions with which we have opened the chapter.

The study we discuss employed the two emotion measurement technologies just described, one a fine-grained microanalytic technique applied to videotape records of behavioral interactions, the second a parent rating scale – the Infant Behavior Questionnaire (Rothbart, Furby, Kelley, & Hamilton, 1977). What both measures have in common is a focus on infant socioemotional behavior. The microanalysis looks at second-to-second changes in component parts of facial–expressive behavior during a relatively brief period of dyadic interaction, whereas the latter elicits parental judgments about emotional and general temperamental behavior based on impressions accumulated over a much longer period of time. In order to examine the question of how these measures might overlap in describing expressive–communicative behavior, we must first consider what each purports to measure and how the measurements themselves are made. Thus, we shall treat measurement issues first and then proceed to a description of the investigation itself.

Measurement issues and procedures

The microanalytic approach and dyadic analysis of emotional behavior

Microanalysis. The microanalytic coding system we employed was the Maximally Discriminative Facial Movement Coding System, otherwise known as Max (Izard, 1979). The development and validation of this system can be found in

Volume I (Izard & Dougherty, 1982). Here, we simply give a brief description of the system before we report on its use for dyadic-level analyses.

Max is a theoretically based, anatomically linked, facial movement coding system designed to identify fundamental emotions and blends, based on coding movements in three regions of the face. The Max system consists of 27 codes of "appearance change" units. Six codes refer to muscle configuration changes in the brow region. Eight codes are devoted to changes in the eyes–nose–cheek region. Thirteen codes deal with changes in the mouth–lips region. Three additional codes are reserved for nonscorable, obscured, and resting-position categories. The three regions of the face are coded separately, and each region is coded independently of any change that may be occurring in the other two regions so as to maintain objectivity. The codes themselves are used in conjunction with formulas provided in a manual that comes with the videotape used in training. The formulas distinguish eight fundamental emotions – interest, joy, surprise, sadness, anger, disgust, contempt, fear, and the motive state of physical distress or pain.

In preparation for coding videotapes of experimental sessions, judges are trained in the use of the Max system by working with the training tape and manual, which consist of demonstration and practice material. Brief examples of each of the fundamental emotions and component movements associated with those expressions give coders realistic exemplars of what they will normally observe under a variety of experimental conditions. The dyadic situation of mother and young infant, however, generates unique problems, demanding practical solutions to coding facial expressions of emotion. We describe some of the problems and solutions below.

Practical considerations in the use of microanalytic systems during mother–infant face-to-face interaction. Dyadic interaction between mother and infant is highly animating for the infant, giving rise to a high density of facial changes, many of which are very fleeting and exquisitely subtle. Both mothers and infants 3 to 6 months of age show an average rate of facial expression change of about one every 8 sec (Malatesta & Haviland, 1982). Because of the high rate of change and level of subtlety, the reliability established on the Max training tape may not be preserved when one moves to the data of one's own study. Additional training and even some discretionary changes in the procedure for coding may be necessitated. Among the solutions that worked in our study were (a) renewed training with the Max tape, with special attention to known problem areas; (b) interjudge practice with samples of test tape; (c) joint sessions with immediate feedback on intercoder reliability; and (d) simplification of the coding system. The first three solutions are self-explanatory; the fourth deserves some additional comment.

In our original training sessions we observed that, of the three grand regions of the face for which there are codes, the brow region presented the least diffi-culty in achieving reliability. To a certain extent, this is attributable to the fact that this region had the fewest number of codes. As such, fewer discriminations among various alternatives were needed, and thus there was less opportunity for confusion and error. In contrast, the mouth region, having the greatest number of codes, posed the greatest obstacle to achieving reliability. With these prior observations in mind, it occurred to us that we might be able to enhance reliabil-ity with the experimental data by reducing the number of codes with which judges had to contend. In essence, this meant eliminating codes associated with emo-tions that were not of central interest to the study or those we expected to occur infrequently owing to lack of incentive conditions. The codes for various tongue movements, for example, were eliminated. By eliminating the tongue codes, we sacrificed our ability to detect the occurrence of disgust expressions in infants. However, a review of the tapes indicated that it was unlikely that disgust would have occurred in the absence of incentive conditions for the infant. That is, mothers did not attempt to feed noxious substances to their infants. In addition, mothers did not show feature changes associated with disgust even when their infants provided them with incentive events, such as spitting up. Instead of dis-playing disgust, mothers averted their heads or smiled ironically. We were will-ing to forfeit the detection of an occasional expression of disgust in the service of improving reliability. We also eliminated the codes associated with contempt and shame. We did not anticipate that these would occur. Had they in fact oc-curred we would have been hard-pressed to make sense of their occurrence, given the cognitive immaturity of our subjects. It is important to note, however, that training on all of the original Max codes reduces the likelihood of making a Type II error – that is, missing the occurrence of an unlikely expression. We knew, for example, that disgust expressions likely did not occur because a re-view of the tapes at incentive junctures showed that they were devoid of the appearance changes associated with disgust codes. Training on the codes asso-ciated with disgust thereby allowed us to rule out the occurrence of disgust in places where it was most likely to occur by rapid scanning of the tape; had a disgust face in fact occurred, its detection would still have been possible.

Another simplification of the system involved eliminating a few codes that were not orthogonal descriptors of specific affects and thus did not distinguish between one affect and another. For example, the enjoyment expression is indi-cated by the formula $EJ = 38 + 52$, where 52 represents the smile, 38 the raised cheek. Code 38, however, may occur in four other expressions and it does not discriminate among them. The smile alone, therefore, could be used to dis-tinguish the enjoyment expression (at least in the case of infants, for whom dissimulated smiles are improbable) with no loss of accuracy of detection. How-ever, we interject a caveat here. As Ekman (1982) has noted, the researcher is often forced to choose between comprehensiveness and selectivity in coding, and there are advantages and disadvantages in each case. We chose selectivity in the service of economy. However, it is worth pointing out that, as a general rule, any selectivity of simplification of the system results in the loss of some information that may or may not be critical to the goals of a particular research project. For example, because we did not code raised cheeks, we lost the opportunity to code features that theoretically encode *intensity* of expression. Since the goals of the present investigation were to detect the types and frequencies of common infant emotional expressions, we were willing to forfeit the intensity dimension for the sake of achieving much higher reliabilities for the muscle movements and emotions that we did code. This is just one example of the kinds of pragmatic considerations involved in the use of microanalytic coding systems.

A second problem inherent in coding emotion expressions in mother–infant dyadic interaction has to do with the coding of maternal expressions. The Max system provides training with infant faces only. We have found that training with adult expressions is obligatory in the dyadic context, especially if one is concerned with accurate coding of the offset phase of facial movement changes in adults. Although the primary difficulty of coding infant faces resides in the fleetingness of many expressions, the onset and offset tend to be clear when one is coding in slow time. This is not the case with maternal expressions. The onset of expression changes tends to be salient (although this varies from one region to another) and highly articulated, if not exaggerated. However, the offset of many expressions is often difficult to distinguish. Smiles are frequently graded in onset and offset, particularly in offset. A raising of the brows (of the sustained type) usually represents a clear change over baseline, but the offset typically occurs as an imperceptible fading over several seconds. One solution to the problem involved additional training on sample experimental material; that is, we familiarized ourselves with facial behavior characteristic of mothers in interaction with their infants. Another involved adopting agreed-on conventions. Our solution to the fading smile and brow problem, for example, was to adopt the convention that we consider the expression terminated 10 sec after onset or terminated with the onset of a new expression if the new expression occurs within the 10 sec.

Once these problems were solved, we achieved reliabilities ranging from 80 to 100%, depending on the infant and the region of the face. (The brow movements remained the most reliably coded signals, perhaps telling us something about the ease or difficulty infants have in reading certain emotional expressions of their caregivers.) Incidentally, Max, as a vehicle for training judges to code maternal expressions during face-to-face play between mothers and infants, is probably superior to other systems involving adult expressions, since mothers in this kind of situation tend to give very infantalized expressions; they are less likely to use the miniaturized expressions or partial versions that are more typical of adult–adult interactions (Malatesta & Izard, 1984).

The impressionistic approach and use of parental rating scales in the assessment of emotion and emotion–personality interactions

Temperament as a "macro" dimension. The macroanalytic coding system used in the present study was Rothbart's Infant Behavior Questionnaire (IBQ), which contains subscales for distress to novel stimuli (fear), distress to limitations (anger), smiling and laughter (positivity), activity, soothability, and duration of orienting. The IBQ is based on a description of temperament by Rothbart and Derryberry (1981). In their overview they write that temperament reflects "constitutional differences in reactivity and self-regulation. . . . By 'reactivity' we refer to the characteristics of the individual's reaction to changes in the environment, as reflected in somatic, endocrine, and autonomic nervous systems. By 'self-regulation' we mean the processes functioning to modulate this reactivity, e.g., attentional and behavioral patterns of approach and avoidance" (p. 37). The authors include additional hypotheses such as the supposition that temperament is a relatively enduring characteristic of an individual and that it represents the "energetic" aspect of personality rather than the "conceptual."

In this view, temperament is a constituent of personality, perhaps a core part, inasmuch as it is deemed to be a relatively enduring characteristic. This assumption is contained within most other theories of temperament as well. In comparison with other subsystems of personality, such as the affective or cognitive (Tompkins, 1962, 1963), temperament appears to be less pure in that it has multidimensional characteristics. For example, on the Rothbart temperament scale some subscales are largely affective, others more motoric or cognitive, so that overall a wide array of dispositions are tapped under the rubric of *temperament.* Presumably these add up in some way to typologies of temperament. Such typologies then become global, encompassing characteristics. Temperament scales are the psychometrician's attempt to render, scientifically, the kind of holistic, impressionistic judgments people commonly make when they interact with others. The Rothbart IBQ can be viewed as one such attempt at behavioral translation, in this case using the underlying constructs of reactivity or self-regulation. The task has been a difficult one, to judge by the controversy surrounding the issue of temperament measurement (Kagan, 1982; Plomin, 1982; Rothbart & Derryberry, 1984; Thomas & Chess, 1977) and as discussed below.

Because temperament scales are intended to describe multidimensional, transsituational, global traits, they have typically relied on self-report or parental report scales that request information about how an individual reacted across diverse situations. The Thomas, Chess, Birch, Hertzig, and Korn (1963) scales request specific information about particular situations; the Rothbart scale (1981) is also fairly specific. The Buss and Plomin (1975) scale bypasses even the specificity of reports on behavior and asks directly for global assessments of negative emotionality, activity level, impulsiveness, and sociability. In none of these cases is the person directly observed.

Most of the parent report forms require the parent to provide information germane to a given time period such as the past few weeks and ask for specific information about behavior, such as responses to bathing or feeding. A few tests ask parents to make more general statements about the infant's moods or styles of interacting in order to make judgments about behavior.

Validation of temperament report scales is just beginning. Both Bates (1980) and Rothbart & Derryberry (1981) report that there are respectable correlations between the ratings of infants made by two adults in the household, generally the parents. Product–moment correlations of mothers with fathers for the IBQ range from .45 for smiling to .69 for activity level, with a median of .60. Rothbart and Derryberry (1981) also report that there are low but significant correlations between parent ratings and home observer ratings on some of the scales. Three home observations were made for 46 subjects at ages 3, 6, and 9 months during feeding, bathing, dressing, and play. Data analysis was done on data collapsed across three observation days and correlated with the IBQ. Correlations between questionnaires and home observations were low with significant correlations for distress scales and activity level at 6 months and for fear, activity level, and smiling at 9 months. Soothability and duration of orienting could not be assessed in the home observations.

The fact that there is overlap between the definitions of temperament and affect is mentioned frequently (e.g., Buss & Plomin, 1975; Campos, Barrett, Lamb, Goldsmith, & Stenberg, 1983; Goldsmith & Campos, 1982; Izard, 1971, 1977; Plutchik, 1962; Rothbart & Derryberry, 1984; Tomkins, 1962, 1963). This overlap is only beginning to be addressed systematically.

Generally, temperament is considered to consist of the process parameters of behavior. These processes would include those applicable to affective behavior but would not be confined to them. In general, temperament seems to describe regularities and intensities, as well as onset and offset characteristics in behavior. The expectation is that the process would be observable across behavior categories and be relatively stable within a developmental period and within given environmental parameters.

Affect, however, consists of discrete types of behavior. As with any behavior sets, the interaction of various components of the set may change with an individual's age, learning, or environment, yet remain identifiable. Affects are not expected to be stable characteristics of an individual, but to be responses to events of both an external and internal nature. That is not to deny that one could learn to display a stable affect through environmental manipulation and self-manipulation.

It is possible to consider affects as analogous to types of sentences – declarative, questioning, passive, and so on. It is possible to consider temperaments as the many qualities with which the sentences are spoken. Although the complexity of a questioning sentence may change with age or learning, it should remain identifiable as a question, just as a happy affect should remain identifiable. The tendency to speak sentences of all types rapidly, as well as to accomplish other behaviors rapidly, would be more temperamental and could apply to happy expressions as readily as to questioning sentences.

It may seem, therefore, that affect and temperament can be easily separated. In practice and in theory there are problems. Theoretically, there is a chasm to be crossed in the orientation of both affect and temperament researchers toward motivation. Affect researchers such as Tomkins (1962), Izard (1977), and Ekman (1982), consider the motivational system to be primarily the affect system (see Izard, 1977, for a full explanation). The affective response directs and paces the resulting or accompanying behavior. For this reason, affect researchers seldom attend to temperamental qualities, although much can be gained by including temperament scales with affect scales, as we shall demonstrate.

In contrast, temperament researchers consider temperament to be a motivational quality influencing a variety of cognitive and affective behaviors related to affect state (e.g., Goldsmith & Campos, 1982, p. 164). This inevitably causes difficulty and leads to overlap in scaling and definition of measurements.

We are not the first to note the overlap between the temperament and affective scales. For example, Goldsmith and Campos (1982) attempt to map selected dimensions of temperament from a variety of temperament scales (Buss & Plomin, 1975; Rothbart & Derryberry 1981; Thomas et al., 1963) onto affect dimensions as defined by Ekman (1982) and Izard (1977). Both the Rothbart (1981) measure and the Buss and Plomin (1975) measure use more or less specific affect categories, including smiling, fear, emotionality (fear, anger, and distress), sociability (interest in people), and so on. The Thomas et al. (1963) measures tend to use categories that do not correspond as well to affect. These include threshold, distractibility, activity level, and regularity. Both the Rothbart and the Buss and Plomin scales also use the activity level category, and Buss and Plomin add impulsiveness. Neither of those are affect categories. Obviously, however, most temperament scales mix affect categories with temperament categories. Affect scales such as Izard's Max and Ekman's FACS do not mix temperament categories with affect categories, unless one includes completeness of an affect expression as a temperamental dimension. Even so, affect codes deal separately with intensity and type of affect.

Although both affect measures and temperament measures can vary in their levels of specificity, only temperament scales tend to mix measures of affect with temperamental qualities. Clearly, one would expect a moderate degree of overlap in the behaviors tapped by affective measure and temperament scales, not because they should be correlated in theory, but because the measures are mixed and picking up some of the same behaviors. We address these questions about the empirical relationship between the measurement systems in this chapter. First we examine the strength and liabilities of using one or the other system for different types of information.

Inherent strengths and limitations of micro- and macroanalytic assessments of infant emotion. Temperament scales offer a measure of infant affect as assessed over a broad band of functioning; this functioning is seen in contexts that are difficult to reproduce in the laboratory. Information obtained from such scales offer *distillations* of observations taken on multiple occasions in a wide variety of situations. When the report is made by a parent during the normal course of a day, there is no interference in routine behavior patterns that might occur when baby and mother are the objects of observation either at home or in an alien environment. Scales such as the IBQ, then, turn parents into ethological assistants, extending the range and sampling power of observational studies. At the same time, such measures invite potential sources of bias; typically parents are considered somewhat unreliable sources of information when it comes to their own children, although our own feeling is that this assumption is in itself a bias that should be examined more closely.

In contrast, microanalytic techniques, generally involving the coding of discrete component details of behavior, capitalize on rigor; however, because of the tremendous labor that is usually involved in coding, translating, and reducing the minutiae of fine-grained component analyses, their application is limited to relatively brief assessments under restricted environmental conditions.

This description of the strengths and limitations of the micro- and macroanalytic methods of characterizing emotion in infants would seem to recommend a judicious combination of techniques if the goal is long-range prediction of behavior. However, until we know more about how one system maps onto the other, we have little guidance as to the choices to be made in considering combinations of assessment. The present study allowed us to compare micro- and macroanalytic measures of infant affect to identify areas of overlap and discrepancy; a longitudinal follow-up 6 months after the two assessments were made afforded a means of evaluating the bases for discrepancies. (Discrepancies were indeed found.) When we began, as a general prediction, we anticipated that there would be some concordance between affect items in the Rothbart scale and affective ratings made from the Max facial affect coding system. The Max coding was based on behavior exhibited during a laboratory visit; nevertheless, we expected some overlap with the temperament trait ratings, at least on the emotion subscales, reasoning that the frequency of certain emotional expressions reflected emotional trait dispositions and that the same behaviors we were coding might in fact be the same behaviors parents use additively in making their own impressionistic judgments. If temperament traits are indeed stable and enduring aspects of personality functioning, we should be able to capture this even if our sampling is limited. For example, it does not seem unreasonable to expect a baby who is rated as having a generally positive mood to display a good deal of positive affect under laboratory conditions. On the other hand, we also anticipated some degree of discrepancy between the two measures but viewed these data as potentially informative as well.

Finally, a comparison of the two measures of affect afforded a means of examining how impressionistic judgments of affect (by parents) and those made by objective component analyses (by nonrelated adults using Max) might be related to one another. Although in previous research we had found the Max system to be satisfactory in the reliable measurement of facial movement and to be translatable into categorical affective expressions, we wanted further cross-validation of its capacity to describe what others view as emotional behavior, especially in the context of the broader domain of temperament. If we scored a 20 (raised brows) with or without a 50 (open, roundish mouth) to indicate a surprised expression, what would the naive person say we had seen? Would it be regarded as "surprise?" Furthermore, what relation would this physiognomic change (provided it is a dominant disposition for the child) have to claims that the baby was "distractible," "an alert, happy baby," "an easily aroused child," or any number of other emotion, temperament, or personality descriptions? The present study allowed us to take some tentative steps to answer these and other questions related to the measurement of affect in young infants.

The investigation

Elicitation and assessment of emotional behavior: laboratory session and microanalysis

A play, separation, and reunion session were scheduled in order to elicit a broad range of infant emotional behaviors. The session was videotaped for later sequential analysis of facial emotional behavior of infants and their mothers.

The subjects were 60 mothers and their infants, almost all of whom were white. Social class was heterogeneous but skewed toward the upper (professional/managerial) social status level. When first seen, half the infants were 3 months old, half 6 months old, equally divided between boys and girls. Follow-up data were obtained on 52 of the infants when they were 6 months older, at 9 and 12 months of age.

Mothers were asked to play with their infants as they would at home. Seated face to face with her infant, each mother was free to talk to, touch, sing to, and otherwise engage the child in play. Two cameras, one trained on each of the two partners, recorded their behaviors simultaneously. The output was fed into a special-effects generator for a split-screen image; digital time display was subsequently edited onto the tapes for timing behaviors that were to be coded.

Each mother–infant pair was taped for 15 min of play. At the end of the 15 min, the mother was signaled to leave the room, with the experimenter in the room but out of view of the infant. The mother was signaled to return and comfort her infant after a few seconds of fret crying and taping resumed for an additional minute.

At the end of the session the mothers filled out maternal and infant temperament/personality measures. These measures were subsequently used in assessing the general emotional dispositions of these mothers and infants for comparison with the microanalytic measures. The measures are described more fully in the next section. One final piece of information was collected in a follow-up contact 6 months after the laboratory session. We obtained a measure of the infant's temperament (similar to the one administered after the videotaped play session 6 months earlier) by recontacting mothers in the study and having them mail back completed temperament scales.

A microanalytic assessment of the mother and infant's emotional behavior was made in the following manner. The middle 5 min of the mother–infant play session and the 1 min of reunion were coded for instances of facial expression changes using an adaptation of Izard's (1979) Max system. The adaptation included eliminating tongue codes and all eye–cheek codes except code 37, which distinguishes the pain expression, as well as the addition of two codes for facial signals not ordinarily considered components of categorical emotions. The two additional codes were designated 24′ and 20-0. Code 24′ involves a drawing of the brows together and slightly down. Oster (1978), following Darwin (1872), designated this the knit brow; naive observers often interpret this appearance change as a puzzled, intense, concentrated look.

In Izard's Max system the 24 code is reserved for brow action involving the drawing together of the brows with no up or down movement. We rarely observed any such instances in our infants and needed a category of brow lowering that was independent of the sharply lowered brow occurring during anger (code 25). The 24′ expression usually occurs on the infant's face when he or she is examining a toy or mother's face in what appears to be a thinking or scrutinizing way; it also frequently occurs as a faint ''pre-cry'' face that subsequently dissipates. In the mother it is usually part of a worried, concerned, or puzzled expres-

Table 3.1. *Sample of joint coding sheet*

	Brow		Eyes		Mouth	
	Infant	Mother	Infant	Mother	Infant	Mother
Clock						
___	___	___	___	___	___	___
___	___	___	___	___	___	___
___	___	___	___	___	___	___
___	___	___	___	___	___	___
___	___	___	___	___	___	___
___	___	___	___	___	___	___
___	___	___	___	___	___	___

sion. (Izard has recently revised his definition of code 24 to include what we describe here as 24'.)

The code 20-0 designates the "brow flash" expression (Eibl-Eibesfeldt, 1979). This brow movement change (a rapid raising and lowering of the brow, lasting less than half a second) occurred quite commonly in 3- and 6-month-old infants. Although it involves the same configuration of brow lifting as in the Max interest expression (code 20), it appears to be functionally different. As indicated, it is of much briefer duration, often appearing as a flicker. It occurs typically during greeting with a returning mother or in response to something else she is doing or saying; it also occurs, at times, for no immediately apparent reason. In general, however, it appears to be a true greeting signal (Eibl-Eibesfeldt, 1979) and conversational or event marker (Ekman, 1979). It also seems to function as a simple agreement or acknowledgment signal in both mother and infant. It was thus considered important to distinguish between this signal and the more sustained brow raising designated by the 20 code.

Maternal and infant facial expressions were coded independently and entered onto Max coding sheets. At the completion of coding, both sets of data were entered onto a joint coding sheet (Table 3.1). In this manner we could see at a glance how maternal expression changes were related to infant facial changes. Examination of these data enabled us to confirm impressionistic judgments made earlier on the basis of informal viewing of subject videotapes to the effect that maternal behavior was nonrandom and related to the ongoing behavioral changes of the infant. Use of the data in the joint coding sheets in concert with event lag analysis (Sackett, 1979) permitted a contingency analysis of mother–infant behaviors, to be discussed shortly. Steps involved in contingency analysis include the identification of all instances where maternal expression changes occur within a second of infant facial changes; these instances are circled on the joint coding sheets and then entered into a matrix grid of frequency counts. The matrix consists of rows of maternal expression changes and columns of infant expression changes. Each instance of a particular contingent response is entered in the appropriate slot; a maternal smile given to an infant smile would be entered in one cell, a maternal brow flash given to an infant surprise expression would be entered in another, and so on. These data are then subjected to sequential lag analysis using the formulas provided by Sackett (1979) or via computer program. (See Sackett, Holm, & Henkins, 1979, for one such program.)

These procedures enabled us to identify the types and frequencies of emotional expressions exhibited by mothers and infants during what we hoped was a sample of typical interaction, perhaps somewhat intensified by the demand characteristics of the study and laboratory setup. Using the contingency analysis we were also able to describe sequential patterns of interaction occurring during the dyadic context. A summary of these results is provided in a later section.

Macroanalysis of emotional behavior: temperament scale data

During the original laboratory visit mothers filled out maternal and infant temperament/personality measures, measures chosen because they showed high loadings on affective items. The scales included the following: (a) the Infant Behavior Questionnaire, with subscales of anger, fear, duration of orienting, soothability, positivity, and activity; (b) a scaled version of the EASI Temperament Scale Emotionality Index, which provided a measure of general emotionality (Buss & Plomin, 1975); (c) the Mehrabian and Epstein (1972) Empathy Scale; and (d) the State/Trait Anxiety Inventory for a measure of trait anxiety (Spielberger, Gorsuch, & Lushene, 1970). The last three measures assessed maternal emotional traits. The first, obviously an infant scale, was administered twice – once at the first laboratory visit and again 6 months later through a mail-back procedure. We ended up with temperament evaluations at two points in time for 52 subjects. There were 13 boys and 13 girls in the younger age group (rated at 3 months and again at 9 months) and 13 girls and 13 boys in the older group (rated at 6 months and again at 12 months). Although the original purpose of the follow-up temperament sampling was to assess change in infant temperament/emotional traits as a function of maternal behaviors and emotional traits, the follow-up data became useful in making sense of why micro- and macroanalytic assessments of affect overlap in some areas and not in others. First let us examine the relationship between the two measures.

Relationship between infant emotion dispositions as judged by microanalytic coding and impressions formed by parents. In our study we employed two methods to assess emotion expression dispositions of infants – the mother's rating of her infant's temperament traits (anger, positivity, fear, etc.) and our own objective coding of frequencies of facial expressions during a play session. To recapitulate, we predicted that there would be some degree of correspondence between temperament scale and behavioral measures of infant affect but expected the correspondence to be moderate rather than strong since both methods have their own inherent limitations. Although the behavioral measure is objectively strong, it is weakened by the fact that behavior is sampled in a laboratory setting and for only a brief period of time. The temperament measure is probably somewhat biased by maternal subjectivity (Bates, 1980); at the same time, maternal judgments are informed by a broader experience with the infant. We thought that certain infant emotional behaviors might be more reliably ascertained than others and a convergence or lack of convergence on measures would indicate which behaviors could, and which behaviors could not, be readily and reliably assessed cross-modally.

We predicted overlap of measures in those areas where they appeared to be focused on the same or similar behaviors. For example, the IBQ measure of anger (called "distress to limitations" in the latest version of the IBQ) codes fussiness, crying, and distress while waiting for food, refusing food, and while being restricted or restrained (Rothbart, 1981). The laboratory measure of anger using the Max facial coding system (Izard, 1979) assesses anger by coding mouth and brow movement changes; the system codes are theoretically based and anatomically linked to inferred emotion states. Similarly, the IBQ dimension of "duration of orienting" is defined in a way that indicates it is an index of "interest" (Rothbart & Derryberry 1981). Conceivably, there should be some degree of overlap between temperament scale measures of interest and our own objective coding of eye, brow, and mouth movements associated with the emotional expression of interest–excitement (Izard, 1979). We would also expect a correspondence between a mother's rating of her infant's positivity ("smiling and laughter" scale) on the IBQ and the amount of smiling (and absence of negative affect) seen in the laboratory play session.

These predictions were tested by Pearson r statistics. We tested behavior and trait items that seem conceptually related and looked at the correlations between them. Table 3.2 presents the comparisons and indicates which associations were statistically significant. Of the nine comparisons, four were statistically significant. Of the four that were significant, three were in the expected direction, whereas one was in the opposite direction. As expected, there was a significant negative relation between the infant trait of positivity (parent impressions of the amount of smiling and laughter) and our laboratory measure of total negative affect (summed score of anger, pain, knit brow, and sad facial expressions; knit brow was included as a negative expression since it occurred so frequently as part of a pre-cry face) and a (nonsignificant) positive association between IBQ

Table 3.2. *Correlation between laboratory measures of infant affect*
(Max system) and mothers' report of infant temperament (IBQ)

Temperament traits (IBQ)	Laboratory measure (Max coding system)	Correlation coefficient	Significance level
Distress to limitations	Anger facial expressions	−.29*	.03
	Total negative facial expressions	−.18	.17
Positivity (smiling and laughter)	Anger facial expressions	−.25	.06
	Total negative facial expressions	−.32*	.02
	Joy expressions	.19	.17
Duration of orienting	Interest expressions	.004	.97
Activity	Interest expressions	.27*	.05
Soothability	Lability of facial changes	−.26*	.05
	Total negative facial expressions	−.10	.49

*Significant at $p \leq .05$.

positivity and smiling during the laboratory visit. The trait of activity was significantly related to infant interest and the trait of soothability was negatively correlated with infant emotional lability as reflected in the total amount of facial
change shown in the laboratory ($r = -.26, p < .05$). Surprisingly, there was a
significant negative correlation between the IBQ infant trait of anger (distress to
limitations) and our laboratory measure of anger, which was based on the number of angry facial expressions. This may indicate that distress to limitations was
measuring something other than trait anger, perhaps stubbornness or persistence.
It could also indicate that the laboratory measure was inadequate or unreliable;
however, the marginally significant negative correlation between the trait of positivity and the laboratory measure of anger suggests that the behavioral measure
of anger may hold some degree of validity.

The correlation coefficients for five of the nine comparisons did not reach
significance, although one was marginally significant (positivity–anger, $r = .25$,
$p = .06$) and two of the remaining four were in the expected direction. There
was no support for the expected association between the trait of duration of
orienting and our laboratory measure of interest. This is possibly because our
measure of interest is a frequency measure, whereas parental judgment may be
based on *how long* the child remains engaged with an item of interest. Our be-

havioral measure of interest was positively correlated with the mother's rating of infant activity level ($r = .27$, $p < .05$); we suspect that an interest-dominant baby may be one who, given the opportunity, explores his or her environment actively. Soothability showed a weak negative association with our measure of total negative affect, and as noted earlier there was a nonsignificant but positive association between positivity and infant smiling in the laboratory session ($r = .19$, $p = .18$).

In summing up the relationship between the temperament trait measures and laboratory measures we can say that there is a modest and, given the limited Max sampling, encouraging correspondence between the measures in some of the expected domains. This overlap suggests two important considerations: (a) Parental impressions may indeed be formed on the basis of infant expressive behavior, thus indicating a certain degree of objectivity to parental judgments; and (b) we might begin to think about the existence of emotion-dominant expressive patterns in infants as young as 3 to 6 months of age.

Micro- and macroanalytic measures of maternal emotional behaviors and the impact of maternal behavior on infant temperament

Encouraged by the correspondence obtained in the preceding analyses, we decided to see how maternal patterns of emotional behavior, as measured by Max during the laboratory play session and as reported by mothers in the form of self-report measures of personality and temperament, might affect infant behaviors and predict infant temperament change. Our sequential lag analysis had disclosed a nonrandom pattern of behavior with respect to mothers' facial expressions as they interacted with their infants in face-to-face play (Malatesta & Haviland, 1982). Infant affect was found to be very labile, as judged by the rate of expression change during mother–infant play.

Mothers made contingent facial expression changes to 25% of these infant facial expression changes, chiefly when the infant was visually engaged. The contingent responses differed subtly as a function of infant age and sex and possibly represented reaction to age- and sex-related differences in infant behavior; another possibility is that these different patterns of maternal response reflected different programs of emotion socialization based on maternal attempts to help their infants to conform to cultural expectations.

Mothers appeared to have idiosyncratic styles of interaction with their infants. We speculated that the nature of the interactions between individual mother–infant pairs represented dyad-specific adaptations of the partners to one another's emotional qualities or temperament characteristics. Although infant temperament traits generally show fairly robust stability during the first year (see Rothbart et al., 1977, as well as data from the present study presented in the next section), we expected that infants who showed extreme forms of emotional behavior would be targets of more intensive socialization efforts and might show quite dramatic changes. Presumably mothers like to have "normal" babies – not too fussy or active, but attentive, socially responsive, and developmentally appropriate; mothers' socialization goals are directed toward these ends. We anticipated that mothers with extreme emotion-dominant traits or extreme patterns of expressive behavior would cause shifts in their baby's behavior somewhat independently of the baby's original temperament. Evidence supporting these predictions was found at both group and individual levels of analysis, as reported below.

Evidence of the impact of maternal emotional behaviors on infant temperament

Infant temperament, as assessed by the Rothbart scale, is relatively stable within the first year. Although in general infants become somewhat more emotional from the third to the twelfth month, at least as rendered by maternal ratings of temperament (Fig. 3.1), there is robust intraindividual stability (Table 3.3). As indicated in Table 3.3, all correlation coefficients attain a significance level of at

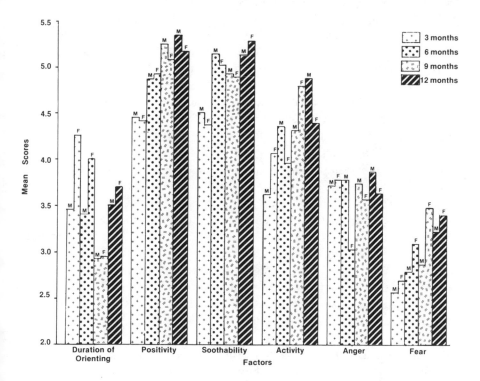

Figure 3.1. Mean scores for temperament variables for male (M) and female (F) infants at different ages.

Table 3.3. *Correlations between infant temperament traits from first time of assessment to the second time 6 months later*

Trait	Overall	Male infants (n = 26)	Female infants (n = 26)
Anger	.52	.37	.60
Positivity	.50	.49	.53
Fear	.33	.45	n.s.
Activity	.67	.72	.66
Duration of orientation	.40	.50	n.s.
Soothability	.45	n.s.	.57

Note: All correlations are significant at at least the .05 level, except where indicated.

least .05 when the sample as a whole is considered; three are significant at the .0001 level – anger, positivity, and activity level, with activity level being the most stable at .67. Recall that the temperament subscale of activity is positively correlated with frequency of interest expressions. As such, the high stability coefficients noted above would seem to suggest that (with the exception of fear) emotion traits may be *core* temperament variables.

Certain sex differences appear. In female infants, anger (or lack of it) was a more stable characteristic of temperament than fear (or lack of it), whereas the reverse pattern obtained for male infants. The reasons for these differences are not immediately apparent.

In addition to overall stability, there was marked individual stability. Infants' scores on each of the six trait scales were rank-ordered to T1 (first temperament rating) and T2 (second rating). Most infants remained in the same quartile. For anger, 31 (59%) remained in the same quartile; for positivity, the figure was 35 (67%); for fear, 28 (54%) remained the same; for activity, 37 (71%) remained the same; for duration of orienting, 30 (58%) stayed in the same group, and for soothability, 28 (54%) remained in the same quartile. Random assortment would predict only 25% remaining in the same quartile. Seven infants showed atypical patterns, with substantial gains or losses in their trait rankings. These infants and their mothers are discussed in more detail in the next section.

Infant temperament change: product of an extreme environment? Despite the overall pattern of intraindividual stability of temperament in infants during the first year, we observed infants whose pattern did not conform to the central tendency. Data on these infants are presented below. Two analyses were guided by formal hypotheses based on the developmental literature. The remaining analysis was prompted by the pattern of results suggested by the observation that seven infants showed an atypical pattern in their T1 and T2 quartile rankings.

Hypotheses. Certain findings from the original study generated two specific hypotheses that we wished to examine further. Noting that maternal facial behaviors were contingent on ongoing infant behaviors and the fact that "contingent responding," broadly defined in the earlier literature, is thought to have important emotional consequences for the developing infant (Ainsworth, 1972; Ainsworth, Bell, & Stayton, 1971; Sroufe, 1979), we expected that mothers who ranked especially high in the use of contingent responding would have infants who were easier. In fact, maternal contingency was positively correlated with infant positivity for the overall sample at T1 ($r = .20, p < .10$) and at T2 ($r = .28, p < .05$). We also predicted that infants with highly contingent mothers would show *gains* in positive emotional expressiveness over the intervening 6 months. To test this hypothesis, we classified mothers as high, medium, or low contingent responders based on their ranking on this variable (contingent responding is the percentage of infant expression changes to which the mother responded with a contingent facial change of her own). A one-way analysis of covariance of infant positivity at T2 as a function of level of maternal contingent responding (with initial differences is positivity covaried) disclosed that high contingent responding is associated with the highest positivity scores, although the difference does not reach significance [$F(2,48) = 1.70, p = .19$].

The second major hypothesis was that highly anxious mothers have babies who grow more emotionally negative with time since maternal anxiety has been linked in the theoretical and empirical literature with "negative developmental outcome" (Anders & Weinstein, 1972; Davids, 1968; Kulka, 1968). To test this hypothesis, we again classified mothers into three groups – high, medium, or low anxiety. Analysis of covariance for infant positivity as a function of maternal anxiety level was significant [$F(2,48) = 3.53, p = .04$]. Multiple comparisons of the adjusted means indicated that the positivity levels of infants having low-anxious mothers were significantly higher than that of medium-anxious mothers ($p = .04$) and high-anxious mothers ($p = .01$).

Post hoc idiographic analyses. In our sample, some trends were obscured by the large variation of the overall sample but stood out strikingly when individual dyads were examined. Following recent trends in personality research favoring a return to idiographic approaches and a parallel trend in developmental psychology recognizing that the study of single cases may be especially useful in generating developmental hypotheses (see Denenberg, 1979), we undertook two idiographic analyses. Our analyses differed somewhat from the usual idiographic approach in that we considered *dyads* individualistically. In this section we examine "atypical" mother–infant pairs in which at least one of the partners had extreme trait scores or trait change scores. First we look at selected extreme-scoring infants and then extreme-scoring mothers.

Earlier in the chapter we pointed out that the sample of infants, as a whole, was characterized by a high degree of intraindividual stability in temperament traits but that seven infants were atypical in that they shifted three quartiles in their scores on at least one trait between T1 and T2. We examined these babies' scores for the other trait dimensions and also the scores of their mothers on the three maternal emotional traits and their scores on contingency response. The patterns were quite striking. They are reported below under "Atypical infants."

In the second analysis we selected *mothers* who were atypical in their contingency responses. Within the overall sample, mothers responded contingently to 25% of all infant expression changes. In the present analysis we chose all mothers whose contingency scores were below 10%, yielding nine low-responding atypical mothers. We looked at their emotional traits as well as their infants' traits. Once again, striking patterns were evident, as described below under "Atypical mothers."

Atypical infants. The seven infants selected for a second look were atypical because their mothers reported three-quartile shifts in one or more temperament characteristics. There could be many reasons for such shifts, some of them rather trivial. A close look at the infants' mothers scores, however, suggested that their mothers had certain traits in common. Five of the seven nonstable infants were reported to become more negative or withdrawing, less positive or less active; they thus appeared to be showing increasing signs of "difficultness" (Thomas & Chess, 1977). The five mothers of these infants were all ranked medium to high on anxiety, medium to high on emotionality, medium to low on empathy, and medium to low on contingent responding. On the other hand, the two infants who were reported to become much more amenable, showing dramatic shifts in a favorable direction, had mothers who were ranked medium or high on empathy and low on anxiety. Since there was nothing remarkable in the infants' laboratory behavior, the changes reported might have been reflections of maternal feelings alone; we have no independent information to differentiate the possibility. It seems quite possible, however, that the maternal characteristics did interact with infant characteristics to produce a substantial change in temperamental qualities.

Atypical mothers. The nine low-contingent mothers who responded to fewer than 10% of their infants' affect changes were also given a second look. With one exception, the babies of these mothers were rated as difficult to soothe, not positive in mood, and either extremely active or extremely inactive. Generally, the ratings became even less positive over the 6 months, indicating at the very least a continuing decline in mother–infant ease of interacting. Seven of these eight mothers rated themselves well below the midpoint on empathy; the eighth ranked in the top quartile on empathy and anxiety.

One dyad was an exception to these general statements. A low-contingent mother whose responses to the self-report measures placed her in the top quartile on empathy and the bottom quartile on anxiety had a baby who ranked in the top quartile on positivity, soothability, activity, and duration of orienting and in the bottom quartile on anger and fear. One explanation for the dramatic difference between this baby and the other babies of low-contingent mothers is that the mother's high empathy and low anxiety offset the low facial contingency; it is also possible that this mother's contingency may have been manifest in behaviors that we did not code, such as vocal behavior.

In any case, the collective pattern of results, both the coherent eight low-responding and the ninth exception, indicate that there may be a *constellation* of maternal traits and behaviors that are associated with infant temperament changes rather than a single all-encompassing variable.

Pairs predicted to have difficulty. We can summarize the findings on atypical dyads by stating that highly anxious mothers or nonempathic mothers who reported their babies as being difficult to soothe, low on activity, and low on positive affect would likely still rate their babies low 6 months later. Two dyads satisfied all of these criteria. At T2 the babies were rated in the bottom quartile on everything, having moved down an average of 10 rank points on each temperament measure.

Similarly, "difficult" babies who had mothers high on empathy or emotionality would be predicted to show improvement. Two babies had mothers below the mean on anxiety and emotionality and well above the mean on empathy. Initially the babies were rated in the bottom quartile on activity and positivity and in the middle quartile on soothability. Six months later each had moved up two quartiles on positivity and one quartile on activity.

Summary and conclusions

In the study we described we looked at areas of overlap and discrepancy in two systems that purport to measure infant affect. A follow-up study of change in infant temperament traits allowed us to evaluate how prior measures, both micro- and macroanalytic, might be used to make predictions about developmental outcomes. We shall conclude with several observations by way of summary and integration of the findings.

First, we observed that there is a certain degree of congruency between micro- and macroanalytic measures of affect, at least among the measures used in the present study. There was not a perfect match, but this was to be expected, as we have already discussed.

Second, areas of overlap and discrepancy between the two systems gave clues to the probable relationships between certain facial behaviors and impressions of affect and temperament formed by others. Infants rated easy to soothe showed less lability of facial expression and had a slight tendency to be lower in overall negative affect expression than other infants, as observed from the pattern of correlations. Infants rated high on orienting and on activity were also high in expressing interest in the laboratory play session. Infants rated high on positivity had fewer anger expressions and less negative affect generally in the laboratory than those rated low on positivity. However, contrary to expectations infants rated high on distress to limitations showed fewer anger expressions and had a slight tendency to show less overall negative affect than infants rated low. We have suggested that this might indicate that the distress to limitations subscale might more accurately reflect persistence of stubbornness; perhaps it is simply not as pure a measure of the infant trait anger as the item pool at first suggested. Rothbart's move to change the name of the subscale from ''anger'' to ''distress to limitations'' probably reflects her awareness of this.

Third, although we confirmed that temperament ratings remain fairly stable in that most of the infants in this study retained their rank order across a 6-month period, we noted that certain infants were not rated at all similarly from one time to the next; their ratings demonstrated radical change. Those infants whose ratings changed radically could not be identified by microanalysis of their laboratory behavior at T1. However, maternal behaviors, as assessed by both micro- and macroanalytic techniques, did predict changes in infant temperament. Maternal contingent responsiveness (a laboratory-based facial measure), as well as three personality/temperament scales, in combination, did a good job of predicting which infants would show gains in positivity as well as infants who would show poorer functioning and more negative emotional traits at second evaluation.

In summary, the use of both microanalytic and macroanalytic measurement systems seems to be a good working combination. The Max microanalytic analysis seems best suited for analyzing sequences of dyadic behavior within situations. In addition, it may be useful for identifying parents who have difficulty interacting with their infants, infants who may be at risk for developing maladaptive patterns of emotion expression. However, caution is advised in undertaking such a task because a mother's low contingency response score may be offset by other maternal traits not captured by the microanalytic facial behavior analysis, such as contingent affect carried by the voice or an empathic disposition. The IBQ may be a better instrument than Max coding for assessing long-term dyadic interaction patterns because it uses a constellation of variables rather than single variables. Max coding, even extended to a wider assortment of situations, probably cannot encompass the kaleidoscope of family events that parents are automatically privy to. The Rothbart scale draws on such constellations of events in a summative, holistic way. Together, the micro and macro systems allow an in-depth study of the multifaceted dimensions of early socioemotional development.

References

Ainsworth, M. D. S. Attachment and dependency: A comparison. In J. L. Gewirtz (Ed.), *Attachment and dependency* (pp. 97–137). Washington, DC: Winston, 1972.

Ainsworth, M., Bell, S., & Stayton, D. Individual differences in strange situation behavior of one-year-olds. In H. Schaffer (Ed.), *The origins of human social relations* (pp. 17–57). Academic Press, 1971.

Anders, J. F., & Weinstein, P. Sleep and its disorder in infants and children: A review. *Pediatrics,* 1972, *50,* 312–24.

Bates, J. E. The concept of difficult temperament. *Merrill–Palmer Quarterly,* 1980, *26,* 299–319.

Buss, A. H., & Plomin, R. *A temperament theory of personality development.* New York: Wiley, 1975.

Campos, J. J., Barrett, K. C., Lamb, M. E., Goldsmith, H. H., & Stenberg, C. Socioemotional development. In P. Mussen (Ed.), *Carmichael's manual of child psychology* (pp. 783–915). New York: Wiley, 1983.

Darwin, C. *The expression of the emotions in man and animals.* New York: D. Appleton & Company, 1872 (reprinted Chicago: University of Chicago Press, 1965).

Davids, A. A research design for studying maternal emotionality before childbirth and after social interaction with the child. *Merrill–Palmer Quarterly,* 1968, *14,* 345–54.

Denenberg, V. H. Paradigms and paradoxes in the study of behavioral development. In E. B. Thoman (Ed.), *Origins of the infant's social responsiveness* (pp. 251–89). Hillsdale, NJ: Erlbaum, 1979.

Eibl-Eibesfeldt, I. Human ethology: Concepts and implications for the sciences of man. *Behavioral and Brain Sciences,* 1979, *2,* 1–57.

Ekman, P. About brows: Emotional and conversational signals. In M. von Cranach, K. Foppa, W. Lepenies, & D. Ploog (Eds.), *Human ethology* (pp. 169–99). Cambridge University Press, 1979.

Ekman, P. Methods for measuring facial action. In K. R. Scherer & P. Ekman (Eds.), *Handbook of methods in nonverbal behavior research.* Cambridge University Press, 1982.

Goldsmith, H. H., & Campos, J. J. Toward a theory of infant temperament. In R. N. Emde & R. J. Harmon (Eds.), *The development of attachment and affiliative systems* (pp. 161–93). New York: Plenum, 1982.

Hiatt, S. W., Campos, J. J., & Emde, R. N. Facial patterning and infant emotional expressions: Happiness, surprise and fear. *Child Development,* 1979, *50,* 1020–35.

Izard, C. *The face of emotion.* New York: Appleton-Century-Crofts, 1971.

Izard, C. *Human emotions.* New York: Plenum, 1977.

Izard, C. The Maximally Discriminative Facial Movement Coding System (Max). Newark: University of Delaware, 1979.

Izard, C. E., & Dougherty, L. M. A system for identifying affect expressions by holistic judgments (Affex). Newark: University of Delaware, 1980.

Izard, C. E., & Dougherty, L. M. Two complementary systems for measuring facial expressions in infants and children. In C. E. Izard (Ed.), *Measuring emotions in children* (pp. 97–126). Cambridge University Press, 1982.

Izard, C. E., Huebner, R. R., Risser, D., McGinnes, G. C., & Dougherty, L. M. The young infant's ability to produce discretè emotional expressions. *Developmental Psychology,* 1980, *16,* 132–40.

Kagan, J. Heart rate and heart rate variability as signs of a temperamental dimension in infants. In C. E. Izard (Ed.), *Measuring emotions in infants and children* (pp. 38–66). New York: Cambridge University Press, 1982.

Kulka, A. M. Observations and data on mother–infant interaction. *Israel Annals of Psychiatry and Allied Disciplines,* 1968, *1,* 70–83.

Malatesta, C. Z., & Haviland, J. M. Learning display rules: The socialization of emotion expression in infancy. *Child Development,* 1982, *53,* 991–1003.

Malatesta, C. Z., & Izard, C. E. Facial expressions of emotion: Young, middle-aged and older adults. In C. Z. Malatesta & C. E. Izard (Eds.), *Emotion in adult development* (pp. 253–73). Beverly Hills, CA: Sage, 1984.

Mehrabian, A., & Epstein, N. A measure of emotional empathy. *Journal of Personality,* 1972, *40,* 525–43.

Oster, H. Facial expression and affect development. In M. Lewis & L. Rosenblum (Eds.), *The development of affect* (pp. 43–75). New York: Plenum, 1978.

Plomin, R. Childhood temperament. In B. Lahey & A. Kazdin (Eds.), *Advances in clinical child psychology* (Vol. 6, pp. 45–92). New York: Academic Press, 1982.

Plutchik, R. *The emotions.* New York: Random House, 1962.

Rothbart, M. Measurement of temperament in infancy. *Child Development,* 1981, *52,* 569–78.

Rothbart, M. K., & Derryberry, D. Development of individual differences in temperament. In M. E. Lamb & A. L. Brown (Eds.), *Advances in developmental psychology* (Vol. 1, pp. 37–86). Hillsdale, NJ: Erlbaum, 1981.

Rothbart, M. K., & Derryberry, D. Emotion, attention and temperament. In C. E. Izard, J. Kagan, & R. Zajonc (Eds.), *Emotion, cognition and behavior.* Cambridge University Press, 1984.

Rothbart, M. K., Furby, L., Kelley, S., & Hamilton, J. S. *Development of a caretaker report temperament scale for use with 3-, 6-, 9-, and 12-month-old infants.* Paper presented at the biennial meeting of the Society for Research in Child Development, New Orleans, April 1977.

Sackett, G. P. The lag sequential analysis of contingency and cyclicity in behavioral interaction research. In J. D. Osofsky (Ed.), *Handbook of infant development* (pp. 623–49). New York: Wiley, 1979.

Sackett, G. P., Holm, C. C., & Henkins, A. Computer technology: A FORTRAN program for lag sequential analysis of contingency and cyclicity in behavioral interaction data. *Behavior Research Methods and Instrumentation,* 1979, *11,* 366–78.

Spielberger, C. C., Gorsuch, R. L., & Lushene, R. E. *Manual for the state-trait anxiety inventory.* Palo Alto, CA: Consulting Psychologists Press, 1970.

Sroufe, L. A. Socioemotional development. In J. D. Osofsky (Ed.), *Handbook of infant development* (pp. 462–516). New York: Wiley, 1979.

Thomas, A., & Chess, S. *Temperament and development.* New York: Brunner/Mazel, 1977.

Thomas, A., Chess, S., Birch, H. G., Hertzig, M., & Korn, S. *Behavioral individuality in early childhood.* New York: New York University Press, 1963.

Tomkins, S. *Affect, imagery, consciousness: Vol. I. The positive affects.* New York: Springer, 1962.

Tomkins, S. *Affect, imagery, consciousness: Vol. II. The negative affects.* New York: Springer, 1963.

4 Judgments of emotion from facial expression and situational context

Linda A. Camras

Recent studies (Borke, 1971; Camras, 1980; Felleman, Barden, Carlson, Rosenberg, & Masters, 1983; Green & Ekman, 1973; Izard, 1971; Reichenbach & Masters, 1983) have consistently shown that young children can identify emotions with significant accuracy on the basis of either facial expressions or descriptions of emotion-inducing events. However, research attempting to determine whether children preferentially rely on situational context or expressive cues when judging emotion has not yielded consistent results. Although several investigators (Burns & Cavey, 1957; Gove & Keating, 1979; Uberg & Docherty, 1976) report that reliance on facial information increases with age, the results of other studies (Gnepp, 1983; Greenspan, Barenboim, & Chandler, 1976; Kurdek & Rodgon, 1975; Reichenbach & Masters, 1983) point to precisely the opposite conclusion. Substantial differences in methodology may be responsible in part for some disagreement among studies. However, rather than dismiss such differences as merely sources of measurement error, in this chapter I argue for their conceptual significance. In particular, some methodological differences may reflect real-world variability that alters children's preference for facial or situational cues. In addition, methodological decisions often reflect conceptual assumptions that influence research findings and their interpretation.

With regard to facial versus situational cues to emotion, many studies (Greenspan et al., 1976; Iannotti, 1978; Kurdek & Rodgon, 1975; Uberg & Docherty, 1976) have considered their conceptual focus to be the development of empathy and/or nonegocentric thinking. These studies have been concerned with determining when a child becomes capable of understanding what another person is feeling when the person's feelings are different from those of the child. In these experiments, children typically are presented with a story and/or drawing representing a situational context (e.g., a child's puppy dies) and a facial expression (e.g., smile) representing the story character's affective state. It is presumed that subjects' own emotional response will reflect situational context, whereas the story character's "true" emotional response is represented by his or her facial expression. Given these assumptions, investigators (Iannotti, 1978; Kurdek &

Rodgon, 1975) have sometimes been surprised to discover that children's reliance on the contextual information presented in their study actually increased with age. Interpreted within their conceptual framework, such a finding implies that egocentric thinking increases and empathy decreases as children get older.

Perhaps their results would have seemed less paradoxical had developmental researchers been familiar with earlier studies of facial versus situational emotion cues involving adult subjects (Fernberger, 1928; Frijda, 1969; Goldberg, 1951; Goodenough & Tinker, 1931; Munn, 1940). Rather than focusing on empathy, these studies were directly concerned with the relative influence and accuracy of facial expression versus situational context. The general conclusion investigators reached was that situational context is the more important source of information used by adults. Although contextual dominance has since been discredited as a comprehensive generalization (Ekman, Friesen, & Ellsworth, 1982), clearly developmental psychologists cannot always assume that choosing facial expression over context is the ontogenetically mature response.

On purely a priori grounds, there are reasons to argue for the importance of both facial expression and contextual information in observers' affect judgments. On the one hand, recent emotion theories (Ekman, 1977; Izard, 1971; Tomkins, 1963, 1982) have emphasized the special role of facial expressions, leading one to hypothesize that they might provide a focal point for people attempting to make affect judgments in real-life situations. On the other hand, emotion theorists (Ekman, 1972) have also developed such concepts as "display rules," that is, rules that dictate the suppression, modification, and/or deceptive substitution of emotional expressions in certain social situations. If facial expressions cannot always be relied on in real-life settings (due to the operation of display rules), then individuals may be predicted to sometimes depend more on other factors such as the situation itself. However, problems in judgment will also be encountered if one relies completely on situational context. Since many situations evoke different emotions in different people, context alone often will not provide unambiguous emotion cues. In sum, both facial expression and situational context are legitimate sources of emotion information for observers but neither is completely reliable.

These considerations suggest that the use of facial and situational affect cues should vary depending on the circumstances in which an emotion judgment is being made. By the same token, some disagreement among developmental studies may reflect appropriate differences in subjects' use of emotion cues. That is, methodological features of an investigation may lead subjects to give more weight to one or another source of emotion information. More important, these features might parallel critical or influential characteristics of real-life settings. Given this possibility, it is of interest to review briefly a number of material and procedural features of emotion judgment studies and consider their possible influence on experimental data and their possible parallels in real-life situations.

Methodological features of emotion judgment studies: a selective and critical review

Some potentially differences among past studies of facial versus contextual emotion cues have been the type, quantity, and quality of stimulus materials presented to subjects. Facial expressions have been presented in the form of drawings (Burns & Cavey, 1957; Gnepp, 1983; Gove & Keating, 1979; Kurdek & Rodgon, 1975; Uberg & Docherty, 1976), still photographs (Reichenbach & Masters, 1983), and videotapes of live actors (Deutsch, 1974; Greenspan et al., 1976). Similarly, contextual cues have been presented in the form of videotaped scenarios (Deutsch, 1974; Greenspan et al., 1976), narrated stories (Reichenbach & Masters, 1983), drawings of an event or situation (Gnepp, 1983), or some combination of narration and visual illustration (Burns & Cavey, 1957; Gnepp, 1983; Gove & Keating, 1979; Iannotti, 1978; Kurdek & Rodgon, 1975; Uberg & Docherty, 1976).

The effect that differences in stimulus type and quantity may have on subjects' responses to emotion cues was demonstrated by Gnepp (1983). Gnepp varied her presentation of situational context, using a narrative story in one condition and a line drawing plus narrative story in a second condition. Results showed that subjects gave more weight to situational context in the second condition. Furthermore, the addition of drawings to the verbal narration had a greater impact on first- and sixth-grade subjects than on preschoolers. These findings suggest that the influence of a cue source (face or situation) depends in part on its strength (i.e., number and quality of the individual emotion cues the source provides). In addition, older children may show a greater preference for the stronger cue source, perhaps because of their greater information-processing capacity.

At first blush, Gnepp's findings appear to challenge the ecological validity of experimental studies that have presented emotion cues in forms other than those occurring in vivo. That is, one might argue that we can draw no conclusions from these studies because they do not reflect the relative strength of facial versus situational cues as experienced in real-life situations. Furthermore, one might assert that future research should utilize only the most realistic stimulus materials (videotaped scenarios or even live presentations) to determine the "true" impact of facial expression versus situational context.

Such an argument, however, implicitly rests on a questionable assumption about real-life situations. That is, it presupposes a consistent balance between facial and situational cues in the real world that must be accurately reproduced in the laboratory. In contrast to this assumption, the relative influence of different emotion cues probably varies in real-life situations just as it varies in experimental studies. Thus, even if one presented completely lifelike stimulus materials to subjects in an experimental setting, one would probably find the impact of facial expression and situational context to differ depending on the facial expressions and situations involved.

A number of factors may contribute to variability in the influence of facial expression versus situational context on observers' judgments of emotion. For purposes of discussion, many of these can be grouped together and referred to as factors affecting cue "strength." These include number, duration, magnitude, intensity, and salience of the individual elements serving as emotion indices. With respect to facial expression, cue strength would thus depend on the frequency, intensity, and duration of the muscle movements involved in producing the emotional facial expressions. With respect to situational context, cue strength would depend on the number, duration, and salience of situation elements associated with the emotion. In addition, cue strength would depend in part on the observer's beliefs about the probabilistic relationship between the emotion cue and the indicated affect. For example, an observer may believe that lowered brows are a virtually certain indicator of anger or that they indicate the slight possibility of this emotion. An emotion cue may also be perceived as having a weak equiprobable relationship to several feelings (e.g., lowered brows indicating the possibility of anger, puzzlement, or determination). Furthermore, perceived probabilistic relationships between emotions and emotion cues are likely to differ across individuals and also change during the course of development. That is, as children learn more about both affect and affect display rules, their degree of confidence in particular emotion cues as accurate and reliable indices of an emotion may undergo modification.

If the influence of contextual versus expressive cues depends on all these factors, investigators probably should not be greatly concerned about their affect cues' verisimilitude per se. That is, researchers need not completely abandon procedures involving factitious stimulus materials but instead should exploit the opportunity they provide for systematically varying cue strength and studying its effect on subjects' judgments. One means of doing so (as suggested by Ekman et al., 1982) would be to evaluate situational context and facial expression separately by presenting them independently to subjects and obtaining emotion judgments. Subsequently, the two sources of information might be presented together, and inferences regarding their relative importance would take into account their independent values. Studies such as this would shed light on the relationship between the strength of cues provided by an information source and observers' reliance on the source when making inferences about affect. Other studies might investigate the contribution of the various factors discussed above (e.g, number, duration, intensity of individual cues) to the total "strength" of the emotion cues provided by a source of information.

Given their conceptual focus on empathy, most past developmental studies have failed to include conditions where facial expressions and situational contexts are judged separately for emotion content. However, Reichenbach and Masters (1983) did collect such judgments for the stimuli they used. They found that their facial stimuli (photographs) were judged "correctly" about 50% of the time, whereas their situation stimuli (stories) were judged "correctly" 73% of the time. When noncongruent combinations of situation and facial expression were presented, third-grade subjects chose the emotion represented in the story situation more than 70% of the time. In contrast, nursery school children showed no significant preference for either face or context, although there was a nonsignificant tendency to choose the emotion shown by the face.

Reichenbach and Masters concluded that children's reliance on situational context increases with age. However, their data are also consistent with the alternative hypothesis that older children give more weight to whichever cue source is the strongest (i.e., provides the strongest emotion cues). Future studies might compare these alternatives by including face–context combinations in which the facial expression is judged to be a better source of information than the situational context. Without such studies, one cannot determine whether Reichenbach and Masters' third-grade subjects were responding to the source or the strength of the emotion cues.

Social features of the situational context: display-rule situations

As indicated in the preceding section, the existence of display rules in our culture (e.g., "Big boys don't cry") suggests that facial expressions do not always accurately reflect the emotional state of the expresser. Thus, observers may sometimes legitimately choose to reject facial information when attempting to infer another person's emotional response. Research by Saarni (1979, 1982) and Cole (1983) suggests that even preschool children have some awareness of cultural display rules. This awareness can be expected to influence children's emotion judgments when they are presented with display-rule situations and conflicting facial cues.

The possible effect of display-rule knowledge can be seen in a study by Greenspan et al. (1976). In this study, children were shown videotapes in which two boys arm wrestled and one of them lost. In one version of the videotape, the losing boy displayed what was considered to be an appropriate congruent emotional response. His facial expression, tone of voice, and posture all were intended to show sadness. In a second version of the videotape, the loser displayed what was considered to be a noncongruent emotional response (described by the investigators as "amused nonchalance"). Subjects in this study were asked a general open-ended question about the losing boy (i.e., "How does he feel?") and were also questioned specifically about his facial expression. In response to the open-ended question, both first- and third-grade subjects said that the losing boy was feeling bad even when he displayed "nonchalance" on the videotape. In response to the specific question about facial expression, first-grade subjects also identified the facial expression as negative. However, most third graders correctly identified the expression as a positive one. These data suggest that the third-grade children recognized but discounted the losing child's positive emotional expression as a socially dictated display rather than a genuine affective response.

Several studies besides that of Greenspan et al. have utilized situational contexts in which display rules for emotional expression may operate. For example, scenarios involving an unpleasant medical procedure (e.g., receiving an injection) have been presented by several investigators (Burns & Cavey, 1957; Gnepp, 1983; Uberg & Docherty, 1976). In these studies, the injection recipient is shown with a positive facial expression (i.e., a smile). In order to be credited with an accurate emotion judgment or empathic response, subjects must report the smiling injectee to be genuinely happy. However, during the course of development, children may learn a display rule that dictates the masking of negative responses to inevitable (and presumably beneficial) medical procedures. If so, one might expect older children to make emotion judgments based on the unpleasant situation but younger children to take the patient's smile at face value. Consistent with this hypothesis, two studies in which injection scenarios were presented to preschoolers (Burns & Cavey, 1957; Uberg & Cocherty, 1976) found empathy (i.e., responses to facial expression) to increase over the age range examined (3 to 5 or 6 years), whereas a third study with older children (Gnepp, 1983) found reliance on facial expression to decrease with age. Although these results cannot be attributed solely to the operation of display rules (since other stories were also used), the findings suggest that display-rule knowledge is acquired during childhood and influences emotion judgments.

The extent to which display-rule knowledge has affected the results of past studies is difficult to ascertain. In many research reports, the specific stories or situations presented to the subjects have not been described. Thus, one does not know the proportion of scenarios that may have involved display-rule situations. Furthermore, responses to the individual stories are not treated separately in data analysis. Thus, even if the number of display-rule situations were known, one could not determine whether subjects responded differently to display-rule and non-display-rule scenarios. Finally, since relatively little research has been conducted in this area, one often cannot be certain whether a particular situation involves the operation of a display rule and when knowledge of this rule is acquired by children. Nonetheless, it is clear that display rules may have an important influence on emotion judgments by children and adults presented with conflicting facial and situational information. A more extensive exploration of their development and influence would be a fruitful area for future research.

Form of subject's response

Research on emotion recognition by adults has demonstrated that the type of response required from subjects may have an important influence on findings. In many early studies (Gates, 1923; Landis, 1924; Sherman, 1927), subjects were asked to produce their own verbal labels for various emotion stimuli. The experimenter then decided whether the words produced by different individuals (e.g., *fear* and *terror*) were synonyms or represented different emotions. Thus, depending on whether the experimenter was a "lumper" or a "splitter," he or she might conclude that subjects either agreed or disagreed about the emotion represented by the stimulus.

Studies requiring children to produce verbal labels are subject to the same problems that characterized such studies with adults. That is, in research on facial versus contextual cues, the child may be scored as responding to the face, the context, or neither depending on which words are accepted as accurate labels for the emotion. However, perhaps an even greater problem with emotion-labeling studies lies in the task demands they place on younger subjects. Such studies require the spontaneous production of emotion words as opposed to a recognition response. Since spontaneous production (i.e., recall memory) makes more cognitive demands on subjects than does recognition, it is considered a less sensitive measure of a child's knowledge. An additional problem with spontaneous production measures arises if the experimenter wishes to determine whether children choose either facial expression or situational context significantly more often than would be expected by chance. When subjects are free to produce any emotion label as a response to the stimulus, it is difficult to determine what should be considered chance performance.

Despite these potential problems, many developmental studies (e.g., Burns & Cavey, 1957; Deutsch, 1974; Kurdek & Rodgon, 1975) have asked open-ended questions (e.g., "How does this child feel?") rather than provide subjects with a choice of verbal labels. In these studies the abilities of younger children may have been underestimated due to difficulties in recalling emotion terms. Although even 18-month-old infants sometimes use emotion words (Bretherton & Beeghly, 1982; Ridgeway, Waters, & Kuczaj, 1985), a study by Izard (1971) specifically showed that children's ability to supply verbal labels for emotion stories lags behind their ability to choose (i.e., recognize) the appropriate facial expression for the story character. This suggests that studies with young children probably should be utilizing recognition response measures.

Of course, procedures involving a recognition response (e.g., forced-choice procedures) have their own potential difficulties. Most important, the experimenter must be certain that children correctly comprehend the emotion words offered during the experimental procedure. However, if the investigator can assume that the emotion labels are understood, the advantages of using a recognition response are substantial.

In order to determine the age at which children can correctly comprehend emotion labels, Camras and Allison (1985) conducted a study in which the subjects' ability to recognize affect words and their ability to recognize emotional facial expressions were compared with one another and with chance. In this study, preschool, kindergarten, and first- and second-grade children were told 12 stories describing emotion-inducing events. Two stories were presented for each of six emotions: happiness, sadness, anger, fear, disgust, and surprise. After each story, the subjects were presented either with three emotion labels (e.g., "happy," "sad," "surprised") or with facial expressions of three emotions. Subjects were asked to choose the label or expression appropriate for the story character.

The facial expressions used in this study were described by Ekman and Friesen (1975, 1978) and are considered universal expressions for the six emotions. Stimulus materials consisted of 5 × 7 in. black and white photographs, each showing a child model posing one of the facial expressions. The verbal labels employed by the investigators were selected on the basis of informal observations of children's emotion vocabulary. The labels were "happy," "sad," "surprised," "angry and mad," "afraid and scared," and "disgusted and yucky."

Data analysis showed that all facial expressions and all verbal labels were recognized with significant ($p < .01$) accuracy, even by the youngest subjects. However, children's performance did improve with age. For preschoolers, the proportion of correct responses was 80% for facial expressions and 82% for verbal labels. For second graders, the proportions were 90% for facial expressions and 97% for emotion words. Although performance was high on both response measures, recognition of the verbal labels exceeded that of the facial expressions. However, the advantage of using labels over facial expressions appeared to be substantial for only two emotions: disgust and fear.

Camras and Allison's findings suggest that procedures involving recognition of emotion words are viable even in studies with 4-year-old children. Of course, this conclusion cannot be generalized beyond the emotion terms employed in their experiment. Nevertheless, their results, along with those obtained by Izard (1971) in his study of expression recognition and emotion-label production, indicate that response measures involving a choice among emotion words are preferable to those involving open-ended questions such as "How does this child feel?"

Single versus multiple emotion responses

Previous studies comparing facial expression and situational context appear to rest on an assumption that only one emotion is experienced in a particular situation. Thus, subjects are presented with cues for two different affects but are required to choose only one as the "true" response. In reality, however, multiple or blended emotional responses may occur in many circumstances (e.g., sadness and anger when another child takes one's toy). Furthermore, research by Harter (1982; Harter & Buddin, 1983) suggests that by 6 years of age children believe that two emotions can be experienced at the same time as long as they are both positive or both negative in valence. Harter has also found that 10-year-olds understand that some situations evoke both a positive and a negative emotional response. Thus, in studies of facial versus situational cues, subjects may often perceive themselves as being asked to make a choice between two affects that they believe are both being experienced.

Although future research may explicate children's preferences when choosing among cue sources is required, important information about emotion judgments might be obtained in studies allowing subjects to report the presence of two emotions. Camras and Brusa (1983) gave children this option in order to explore their ability to integrate information provided by both facial expression and situation. In this study, subjects were presented with compatible combinations of situational and facial cues. That is, situations were presented in which more than one emotional response would be plausible (e.g., anger or sadness or both). In addition, some subjects were presented with facial expressions representing either of the two plausible emotions.

The subjects were 18 male and 18 female kindergarten children (mean age 5.9 years). Each subject was presented with nine stories describing situations in which two emotional responses might occur. The following are examples of these stories and their target emotions:

1. Sadness–disgust: "My friend's puppy got very sick one day. While she was holding the puppy, it threw up and it got all over her. Then, the puppy died in her arms."
2. Surprise–fear: "One day my friend went to the refrigerator to get a glass of milk. When she opened the door she saw a lion inside."
3. Sadness–anger: "My friend hurried home from school one day because she wanted to have a cherry popsicle from her freezer. But when she got home, her sister was eating the last one and she was not able to have any at all."

Subjects were assigned to one of three groups, which differed in terms of the facial cues with which they were provided. Subjects in Group 0 were shown no facial expressions at all in conjunction with the stories. Subjects in Groups 1 and 2 were shown a photograph of one of the target emotions with each story. The photographs were the same as those used in Camras and Allison's (1985) emotion-labeling experiment. In the present study, a line drawing depicting the story situation was also shown to subjects as each story was told.

Each subject received nine trials in which a story was presented (with or without an expression photograph), and the subject was asked about the main character's emotional response. For each story, the subject was asked about the presence of each target emotion. That is, for each target emotion, the experimenter asked, "Do you think my friend was [emotion X] or not [emotion X]?" If the subject indicated that the emotion was present, the experimenter also asked, "Do you think my friend was a little [emotion X] or very [emotion X]?" In addition, the subject was asked about the presence of a third (distractor) emotion. The emotion chosen as a distractor for each story was predicted to be an unlikely response to the situation described.

Subjects were given three scores for each story which represented their judgments about each of the three emotions queried: 0 ("not [emotion X]"), 1 ("little [emotion X]"), or 2 ("very [emotion X]"). Scores were summed across the nine stories to yield three total scores per subject: one for the distractor emotion (emotion 0), one for target emotion 1 (i.e., the target emotion whose picture was shown to Group 1 subjects), and one for target emotion 2 (i.e., the target emotion whose picture was shown to Group 2 subjects).

Scores were subjected to an analysis of variance with two fixed factors (Child's Sex and Group) and one repeated measure (response to each of the three emotions queried). The results showed that subjects attributed both target emotions to story characters much more often than they did the distractor emotion. In addition, the children's judgments were influenced by the facial expression they were shown. That is, the subjects judged the facially displayed target emotion to be experienced more intensely than the nondisplayed target emotion. Also, the target emotion was judged to be more intense when its expression was shown as opposed to when no facial expression was shown to the subjects (i.e., Group 0 subjects). To summarize, children tended to attribute both target emotions to story characters but judged the target emotion shown in the face to be experienced more intensely than the target emotion for which no facial cues were presented.

One limitation of this study is that facial expression and situational context were not independently evaluated, as suggested in the preceding review of past research. However, data obtained in Camras & Allison's (1983) study of emotion recognition suggest that facial cues were slightly stronger than situational cues in the present investigation. Using the same photographs employed here, Camras & Allison found that kindergarteners identified the emotional expressions with an overall accuracy of 88%. In the present study, Group 0 subjects (who were given only contextual cues) judged the target emotions to be present 82% of the time. Nevertheless, facial expression did not completely dominate the kindergarteners' judgments; the subjects provided with both facial and situational cues reported the presence of both target emotions.

In sum, Camras and Brusa's findings demonstrate that children as young as 5 years of age can systematically utilize both facial expression and situational context when making emotion judgments. When given both contextual and facial information, the children in this study did not choose one information source and reject the other. Instead, their situation-based attributions (as indicated by Group 0 subjects) were modified to reflect the addition of further (facial) cues for one of the situationally indicated affects. Thus, even kindergarten children were shown to respond in terms of cue strength and not merely to show a preference for one or the other source of information.

A developmental hypothesis

The preceding discussion of methodological features and their implications suggests that requiring subjects to choose among emotion cues may not always be justified. Nonetheless, sometimes a choice will be made, especially when children see cues for two emotions they believe are incompatible. With regard to children's preferences in such situations, the inspection of data from several studies suggests a developmental hypothesis that differs somewhat from those proposed by previous investigators. In the past, investigators have tended to conclude that children prefer either facial expression or context and that this preference may or may not be modified as development proceeds. However, the data are also consistent with the hypothesis that children first develop a bias toward facial information but subsequently come to prefer whichever cue source provides the strongest emotion cues. In three studies involving preschool children (Burns & Cavey, 1957; Gove & Keating, 1979; Uberg & Docherty, 1976), preference for facial information increased over the age range studied (3 to 5 or 6 years). However, studies that have compared preschool or kindergarten children with older subjects (Gnepp, 1983; Greenspan et al., 1976; Kurdek & Rodgon, 1975; Reichenbach & Masters, 1983) have tended to reveal an increasing preference for contextual information. In those studies that examined each cue source separately, the response of older children corresponded to the stronger cue source. For example, as indicated above, Reichenbach and Masters (1983) presented contextual cues that were considerably more powerful than facial ones. They found third graders to show a definite preference for contextual cues. However, nursery school subjects showed no significant preference for either facial expression or context, although there was a nonsignificant tendency to prefer the facially displayed affect. This suggests a bias for facial expression in younger children that may partly overwhelm even stronger contextual cues.

The results of Gnepp's (1983) study are also consistent with the proposed developmental hypothesis. In one condition of her study, Gnepp presented facial and situational cues that did not differ significantly when evaluated independently. Gnepp found a substantial preference for facial expression by nursery school children and first graders, whereas sixth graders showed only a slight, nonsignificant preference for the face. In her second condition, Gnepp increased the strength of her situational cues. This depressed preschool children's preference for facial expression, although the facially displayed affect was still chosen 73% of the time. Both first- and sixth-grade subjects now showed a slight (though nonsignificant) tendency to choose the affect indicated by situational context. Thus, Gnepp's findings are also consistent with the hypothesis that younger subjects are biased in favor of facial expressions whereas older children respond to cue strength.

Clearly, these few studies do not provide sufficient evidence for either of the two alternative hypotheses (i.e., the development of a preference for contextual information versus the development of a preference for the stronger cue source). Further research is needed in which the independent values of the two sources are determined and systematically manipulated. In particular, children's responses to strong facial cues and weaker situational cues should be examined.

Summary and conclusion

A number of tentative but potentially important inferences were drawn in this chapter from an analysis of previous research. First, the conflicting results of past studies suggest that children may not consistently rely on *either* facial expression or situational context when the two are in apparent contradiction. Younger children may have a bias toward utilizing facial expression when making affect judgments. However, older children may prefer whichever information source provides the strongest cues – except perhaps when knowledge of display rules leads children to discount the person's facial expression immediately. A second inference is that emotion judgments often involve the systematic integration of cues from both facial expression and situational context rather than the complete rejection of information from one of these sources. Furthermore, children (and adults) may judge a person to be experiencing more than one emotion simultaneously – both the affect indicated by the facial expression and the affect suggested by the situation.

Taken together, these rather narrow inferences carry implications that have considerably broader significance. Given the difficulties that have arisen in attempting to determine children's preference for one or another source of emotion cues, perhaps a basic shift in orientation to the problem is necessary before further progress can be made. Past studies of facial expression versus situational context have basically taken a stimulus-oriented approach to emotion judgment. Stimuli from various sources (e.g., face or situation) are seen as impinging on observers, who may be more responsive to information from some sources than from others. An alternative approach, implied in much of this chapter's discussion, would involve an observer-oriented treatment of the problem. That is, the observer's task of making emotion judgments would provide the starting point for investigation. Research would focus on determining the processes by which observers obtain and utilize information to be used in making such judgments. The result would be a process model describing the apperception and integration of emotion cues from various sources. Such a model might more easily accommodate case-by-case differences in observers' use of facial expression versus contextual information. Thus, a process-oriented model might provide a conceptual framework within which the apparent contradictions among past studies might be more easily interpreted.

References

Borke, H. (1971). Interpersonal perception of young children: Egocentrism or empathy? *Developmental Psychology, 5*, 263–9.

Bretherton, I., & Beeghly, M. (1982). Talking about internal states: The acquisition of an explicit theory of mind. *Developmental Psychology, 18*(6), 906–21.

Burns, N., & Cavey, L. (1957). Age differences in empathic ability among children. *Canadian Journal of Psychology, 11*, 227–30.

Camras, L. A. (1980). Children's understanding of facial expressions used during conflict encounters. *Child Development, 51*, 879–85.

Camras, L. A., & Allison, K. (1985). Children's understanding of emotional facial expressions and verbal labels. *Journal of Nonverbal Behavior, 9*(30), 84–94.

Camras, L. A., & Brusa, J. (1983). *Children's judgments of emotion from face and context.* Unpublished manuscript.

Cole, P. (1983, April). *Preschoolers' emotional display rules: Grin and bear it?* Paper presented at the meeting of the Society for Research in Child Development, Detroit, MI.

Deutsch, F. (1974). Female preschoolers' perceptions of affective responses and interpersonal behavior in videotaped episodes. *Developmental Psychology, 10*, 733–40.

Ekman, P. (1972). Universals and cultural differences in facial expression of emotion. In J. Cole (Ed.), *Nebraska Symposium on Motivation, 1971* (pp. 207–83). Lincoln: University of Nebraska Press.

Ekman, P. (1977). Biological and cultural contributions to body and facial movement. In J. Blacking (Ed.), *Anthropology of the body* (pp. 39–84). London: Academic Press.

Ekman, P., & Friesen, W. V. (1975). *Unmasking the face.* Englewood Cliffs, NJ: Prentice-Hall.

Ekman, P., & Friesen, W. (1978). *Facial action coding system: A technique for the measurement of facial movement.* Palo Alto, CA: Consulting Psychologists Press.

Ekman, P., Friesen, W., & Ellsworth, P. (1982). What are the relative contributions of facial behavior and contextual information to the judgment of emotion? In P. Ekman (Ed.), *Emotion in the human face* (2nd ed, pp. 111–27). Cambridge University Press.

Felleman, E. S., Barden, R. C., Carlson, C. R., Rosenberg, L., & Masters, J. (1983). Children's and adults' recognition of spontaneous and posed emotional expressions in young children. *Developmental Psychology, 19*(3), 405–13.

Fernberger, S. (1928). False suggestion and the Piderit model. *American Journal of Psychology, 40*, 562–8.

Frijda, N. H. (1969). Recognition of emotion. In L. Berkowitz (Ed.), *Advances in experimental social psychology* (Vol. 4, pp. 167–233). New York: Academic Press.

Gates, G. (1923). An experimental study of the growth of social perception. *Journal of Educational Psychology, 14*, 449–61.

Gnepp, J. (1983). Children's social sensitivity: Inferring emotions from conflicting cues. *Developmental Psychology, 35*, 805–14.

Goldberg, H. (1951). The role of "cutting" in the perception of motion pictures. *Journal of Applied Psychology, 35*, 70–1.

Goodenough, F., & Tinker, M. (1931). The relative potency of facial expression and verbal description of stimulus in the judgment of emotion. *Journal of Comparative Psychology, 12*, 365–70.

Gove, F., & Keating, D. (1979). Empathic role-taking precursors. *Developmental Psychology, 15*, 594–600.

Green, J., & Ekman, P. (1973). *Age and the recognition of facial expressions of emotion.* Unpublished manuscript.

Greenspan, S., Barenboim, C., & Chandler, M. (1976). Empathy and pseudoempathy: The affective judgments of first and third graders. *Journal of Genetic Psychology, 129*, 77–88.

Harter, S. (1982). Children's understanding of multiple emotions: A cognitive–developmental approach. In W. Overton (Ed.), *The relationship between social and cognitive development* (pp. 147–95). Hillsdale, NJ: Erlbaum.

Harter, S., & Buddin, B. (1983, April). *Children's understanding of the simultaneity of two emotions: A developmental acquisition sequence.* Paper presented at the meeting of the Society for Research in Child Development, Detroit, MI

Iannotti, R. J. (1978). Effects of role-taking experiences on role-taking, empathy, altruism, and aggression. *Developmental Psychology, 14*, 119–24.

Izard, C. E. (1971). *The face of emotion.* New York: Appleton-Century-Crofts.

Kurdek, L. A., & Rodgon, M. (1975). Perceptual, cognitive and affective perspective taking in kindergarten through sixth grade children. *Developmental Psychology, 11*, 643–50.

Landis, C. (1924). Studies of emotional reactions. II. General behavior and facial expressions. *Journal of Comparative Psychology, 4*, 447–509.

Munn, N. L. (1940). The effect of knowledge of the situation upon judgment of emotion from facial expressions. *Journal of Abnormal and Social Psychology, 35*, 324–38.

Reichenbach, L., & Masters, J. (1983). Children's use of expressive and contextual cues in judgments of emotion. *Child Development, 54*, 993–1004.

Ridgeway, D., Waters, E., & Kuczaj, S. (1985). The acquisition of emotion descriptive language: Receptive and productive vocabulary norms for ages 18 months to six years. *Developmental Psychology, 21*(5), 901–8.

Saarni, C. (1979). Children's understanding of display rules for expressive behavior. *Developmental Psychology, 15*(4), 424–9.

Saarni, C. (1982). Social and affective functions of nonverbal behavior: Developmental concerns. In R. S. Feldman (Ed.), *Development of nonverbal communication.* New York: Springer-Verlag.

Sherman, M. (1927). The differentiation of emotional responses in infants. I. Judgments of emotional responses from motion picture views and from actual observation. *Journal of Comparative Psychology, 7*, 265–84.

Tomkins, S. S. (1963). *Affect, imagery, and consciousness* (Vols. 1 and 2). New York: Springer.

Tomkins, S. S. (1982). Affect theory. In P. Ekman (Ed.), *Emotion in the human face* (2nd ed., pp. 353–95). Cambridge University Press.

Uberg, K., & Docherty, E. M. (1976). Development of role-taking skills in young children. *Developmental Psychology, 12,* 198–203.

Part IV

Mother–infant interactions

5 Sharing emotionality and sharing knowledge: a microanalytic approach to parent–infant communication

Hanuš Papoušek, Mechthild Papoušek, and
Lynne Sanford Koester

Perhaps much of the recent and persisting fascination with the study of human emotional expression is the result of its particularly elusive quality, which in fact seems to have led some to dismiss the area of inquiry altogether as an "epiphenomenon." Yet, as Murphy (1983) notes, emotions in infancy may have survival-related value as signals of needs as well as reinforcement of the behavior of others. Izard (1978) has stressed the key assumption that emotions emerge as they become adaptive in the life of the infant and in the infant–caregiver and infant–environment relationships. The fact that emotional states are by nature internal, and therefore not directly or easily accessible to others, of course requires that researchers and caregivers alike infer the likely cause and meaning of an infant's particular affective signal. Lewis & Michalson (1982) state that "emotional experiences are public only insofar as emotional expressions are made available and insofar as the socialization process permits both a correct attribution, that is, an attribution that matches the internal feeling of another person, or an empathic response that is accurate" (pp. 181–2).

When investigating or discussing the affective life of infants, we are further constrained by their preverbal stage of development, which therefore precludes any attempts at self-report measures. However, expressions of feeling states by infants may be more overt and observable at this stage simply because they have yet to be as strongly influenced by a socialization process that typically introduces some elements of shame, disguising one's feelings, or expressing them in

The authors express their sincere appreciation to Betty Harris, Monika Haekel, and Michael Theile for their invaluable assistance in the preparation of this manuscript. We also thank Lucia Harzenetter for help with data analysis and Dr. Gerhard Dirlich for statistical consultation. This research was funded in part by grants from the Die Deutsche Forschungsgemeinschaft, which we greatly appreciate. The opportunity for the third author to participate in this effort was made possible by a research fellowship from the Alexander von Humboldt-Stiftung, Federal Republic of Germany; this support is also gratefully acknowledged.

93

more socially acceptable ways. Methodologically, then, the study of infant emotions is characterized primarily by extensive efforts to document physiological correlates (e.g., Field, 1981; Kagan, 1982; Lewis, Brooks, & Haviland, 1978; Schwartz, 1982) and facial configurations of infants in various emotional states (see Fogel, 1977; Izard, 1971; Izard & Dougherty, 1982; Oster, 1978).

Theoretical efforts are directed primarily toward linking the affective realm of development with cognitive events and/or ontogeny, with a psychoevolutionary approach, or in some instances with a socialization or social learning interpretation of emotional development. As Izard indicated in Volume I (Izard, 1982), we have arrived at the increasingly accepted view that emotional processes fall into three broad classes and can therefore be examined according to their biological, behavioral, and experiential manifestations. It is clear that emotions are of fundamental importance to humans and that their communicative and social value as signals and as reinforcers cannot be overlooked in any comprehensive view of optimal (or pathological) development.

It is not the purpose of this chapter to summarize or review the literature in this area, one that has attracted much attention and labor in the past decade; for such reviews, the reader is referred to those by Izard (1982) and Sroufe (1979). Rather, it is our intent to focus on a few narrow aspects of emotional development, namely, the early, preverbal period of the developmental process, the interrelationship between emotionality and integrative processes, and that part of emotionality characterizing the interactions of infants with the social environment. Such a concentration necessarily brings increased attention to one of the potential continua of emotionality, that of pleasure and displeasure.

Several premises fundamental to our concept of emotions in infancy should be stated at the outset. The first is that emotions are neither phenomena existing separately from others nor merely on–off phenomena that are either present or absent for certain periods of time but that otherwise lie dormant awaiting elicitation. Rather, we view emotions as one aspect of behavioral states showing fluctuations under the influence of both innate and universal control mechanisms, on the one hand, and of adaptive processes of integration involved in interactions between the individual and the ecology (including human enculturation), on the other. There is clear evidence for both kinds of influence dating back to Darwin's (1872) hypothesis of the innateness and universality of certain emotional expressions, which has been substantiated by a robust body of empirical evidence. However, the increased variability and individual differences observed by the second and third years of life are also indicators of the influence of social and cultural forces. In more subtle forms, such indicators can be detected much earlier, of course.

The mechanisms underlying such regulation deserve further attention in an effort to determine what might be the most fundamental process. Various authors have stressed the primacy of either emotions (e.g., Izard, 1978) or cognitive processes (e.g., Kagan, 1978; Sroufe, 1979). H. Papoušek and M. Papoušek (1979) have proposed the role of integrative processes, including information processing and the organization of adaptive behavioral responses. This is seen as the most general and most fundamental mechanism, without which no behavioral interaction with one's environment can take place. The evidence that non-social learning events as such can elicit changes in behavioral state and emotionality (as elaborated in this chapter) corresponds to this view (H. Papoušek, 1967, 1977). Since the involvement of such integrative processes is common to both social and nonsocial interactions with the environment, we assign it more fundamental significance, although this is not intended to imply an underestimation of the importance of the social environment.

Hardly discernible integrative processes, which have still not attracted sufficient scientific attention, occur very soon after birth; for example, neonates are born with innate programs for circadian physiological cycles that deviate from the usual 24-hour periods and must therefore be adjusted postnatally to the real environmental periodicity. This process of consolidation and synchronization generally lasts 6 to 8 weeks (Hellbrügge, Lange, Rutenfranz, & Stehr, 1964; Stratton, 1982), although it can also be disturbed by environmental factors, even including climatic fluctuations. H. Papoušek and M. Papoušek (1984) compared local reports on irregularities in biospheric conditions (provided by an agency of medical meteorology, Der Deutsche Wetterdienst, Wetteramt München) with a systematic, longitudinal, chronobiological diary of a newborn infant. In this detailed case study, an obvious coincidence occurred between biospheric irregularities and temporary desynchronizations of the infant's sleeping and waking cycles. There was concurrent evidence of increased periods of unexplainable fussiness, sometimes referred to as "colic cries," characterizing the infant's emotional state.

The infant activates in various degrees its capacities to collect, process, and integrate information through sensory organs or from memory when exposed to environmental events; through this activation, the infant succeeds in its cognitive and behavioral adaptation to such events. When this effort toward adaptation strains the integrative mechanisms without leading to an effective solution, such as in problematic situations, the infant shows signs of displeasure. Successful adaptation can conversely elicit pleasant feelings, at least as indicated by vocal or facial expressions.

Although the same process is evident in social interactions, it acquires additional dimensions. The parent, for instance, stimulates the infant in a way that requires various integrative capacities, such as identification of the partner, prediction of the outcome of stimulation, and so forth. Signs of infantile difficulties connected with coping with parental stimulation often lead parents to modify their stimulation in ways that facilitate the infant's cognitive adaptation. Signs of pleasure in the infant, elicited by successful adaptation, not only satisfy the parent's need to know the degree to which the baby "is with him or her," but also call forth intuitive empathic matching by the parent. The infant's smile (perhaps the result of a cognitive event) is followed by the parent's smile, and mutual matching provides continued pleasure in the evolving social interaction. Thus, in many ways the interconnection between cognitive and emotional processes becomes particularly meaningful in the context of the infant's interaction with his or her social environment.

We focus primarily on the signs of pleasure–displeasure as one continuum of emotional expression deserving special attention due to the early appearance of these signs and their role in parent–infant communication. As originally conceptualized (H. Papoušek & M. Papoušek, 1979), these signs may attest to the function of some intrinsic rewarding system that motivates infants in their efforts to adapt cognitively. However, such signs of intrinsic reward quickly take on quite another meaning, as they become extrinsic pointers and motivators for caregiving. We propose that one of the fundamental prerequisites for parental care is to understand what the infant likes or dislikes, when the infant has difficulties and needs help, and which caregiving behaviors – both material and didactic – are most effective.

The role of emotions in behavioral regulation: their relations to integrative processes and motivation

Earlier studies by the first author were concerned with complex adaptive behaviors in neonates and the coordination of behavioral changes over time (H. Papoušek, 1961, 1967, 1977). In addition to shedding light on specific processes of conditioning, these efforts led to increased understanding of intrinsic/extrinsic motivation, behavior regulation, and the integration of experience in infancy. To accomplish this in the framework of the learning experiments, systematic records were kept of infant motor behavior, respiration and heart rate, vocalizations, and facial expressions. As was stated then, the most important question is not what or when a child learns, but how; therefore, the roles of motivational, cognitive, social, and biological factors must all be acknowledged and included in any analysis of early experience.

Conditioning methods used in the previous studies allowed infants to obtain a biologically relevant reward as a result of their own activity (H. Papoušek, 1961); in one case, for example, head turns to the left following an auditory signal were reinforced with a portion of milk. Further investigations with the same healthy, full-term newborns included procedures of extinction, reconditioning of the head turn, differentiation between two acoustic signals paired with different reinforcement, for example, sweet versus bitter solutions (H. Papoušek, 1967), and reversals of these differential responses. Of particular relevance to the present chapter are the patterns of affective behavior that accompanied the progression of learning and adaptation to the demands of these experimental situations.

During the initial "integration phase" of learning, the infants often became fussy and inexplicably distressed. With perseverance, however, the final phase in which the conditioned responses were correctly and predictably performed was no longer accompanied by signs of discomfort; rather, there was a noticeable shift toward quiet pleasure, as indicated by vocal and facial expressions. When procedures requiring the extinction of these learned responses were introduced, the same emotional pattern was seen, this time in reverse sequence. In newborns, however, a unique state change was also observed when they responded as usual to a previously conditioned stimuli only to find that their behavior was no longer reinforced; there was a sudden and dramatic shift from Waking State IV (agitation, distress) to Waking State I (eyes open, no movement or vocalization). It appeared that the difficult adaptation process in this case overextended the capabilities of these very young subjects, leading to a sudden inhibition or withdrawal during which the newborn stared motionlessly, breathing deeply as if sleeping with its eyes open (H. Papoušek, 1969).

Throughout the conditioning experiments, changes in facial and vocal expressions associated with the learning process followed a predictable pattern: "Difficulties in the integration of adaptive behavior called forth unpleasant feelings, whereas successful adaptation elicited joy" (H. Papoušek, 1977, p. 88). Thus, both adaptation and avoidance came to be viewed as part of a fundamental cognitive regulatory system, implying a close connection between cognition, autonomic and state regulation, and socioemotional behavior.

This experimental evidence, even with children under 6 months of age, led to a conceptual interpretation that is basically congruent with Kagan's assumption (1978) regarding the primacy of thought in relation to the effects of incentive events on state changes in older children. Kagan suggested that "incentive events are accompanied by an evaluation of the individual's ability to understand, assimilate, or instrumentally deal with the incentive situation and the resulting state change. When there is uncertainty over assimilation or action, a change in emotional state is most likely" (pp. 36). In young infants, however, the opposite was regularly observed as well, that is, changes of state occurring as a result of successful adaptation. Nevertheless, it would be questionable to assert that thought processes as complex as those described by Kagan would already be functional in early infancy.

In a further attempt to operationalize more specifically the emotional reactions of infants, subjects were first conditioned to differentiate between a bell and a buzzer (H. Papoušek, 1967); correct head turns were then rewarded with either milk or a weak, bitter solution, respectively. At the ages of 88 to 102 days, infants quickly responded with different emotional reactions: After the bell, we saw quiet, contented, sucking babies; after the buzzer, we saw babies who grimaced, were agitated, and used aversive tongue movements. The next phase involved a simple reversal of signals. Surprisingly at the time, the infants responded initially with maladaptive behavior, that is, by continuing to respond to the acoustic signal rather than the reward itself. For example, infants continued to drink the bitter solution when it was suddenly paired with the bell and did not show the expected signs of displeasure that accompanied their earlier exposure to the same solution. It appeared that the conditioning signal itself, which elicited the behavior initially, had a more enduring effect than that of the reinforcement. However, when the infants had mastered the reversal paradigm, they again displayed what were considered to be more appropriate emotional responses to the pleasant or unpleasant tastes of the two reinforcement solutions. In the context of this chapter, this is an important point in that it is related to the conditionability of emotional behavior and its potential significance for the emotional development of the child within the social environment.

The role of incongruity and familiarity

In the studies just described, it was observed that the amount and quality of the infants' orienting behaviors, the exploratory behaviors of the older infants, and their communication attempts varied not only in accordance with the properties of the stimulation provided; in addition, there seemed to be intrinsic factors related to their prior experience or exposure to a particular stimulus. It was found that, from the very beginning of postnatal learning, an infant's adaptive behavior is influenced by the degree of prior familiarity with an external event and by the degree to which the event is in some way contingent on the infant's own behavior. Both familiarity and contingency, though linked to external events or their representations, can thus be viewed as intrinsic variables that are closely tied to motivation, cognition, and emotion. Infants, in fact, behave very much like our adult colleagues when faced with a problem-solving situation: Their facial expressions register signs of puzzlement, confusion, even displeasure or satisfaction, varying according to the expected successfulness of their efforts. Oster (1978) also found patterned facial expressions of emotionality strikingly similar to those in adults when she studied elementary units of facial expressions in infants. The fact that these indicators of emotional state are visible before the actual behavioral response (e.g., head turing in infants) leads us to believe that they reflect internal anticipatory and motivational processes.

Piaget, for example, noted the motivational function of discrepancy when he proposed that moderate incongruities between external perceptual events and internal schemata indeed facilitated cognitive advancement. He also acknowledged, however, that too great a discrepancy between these two might elicit fear or avoidance rather than the active approach necessary particularly during sensorimotor development (Piaget, 1952).

Motivation theorists such as Hebb (1949) and Hunt (1965) have similarly stressed the important function of the pleasure that results from recognition of the familiar or from encounters with variations mildly discrepant but still within the cognitively assimilable framework of the familiar. In observing infants in particular, one often sees clear expressions of delight accompanying the reappearance of or reencounter with the familiar; it was this impression that led to a previously stated belief that "the infant is as strongly pulled by the expectation of pleasure connected with successful cognitive operations as the infant is pushed by unpleasant feelings resulting from incongruity, dissonance, or failure in adjustment" (H. Papoušek & M. Papoušek, 1981, p. 142).

The role of expectancy and contingency

It seems obvious now that, even for infants, motivation to solve problems, to find solutions in rather complex learning situations, occurs quite apart from the satisfaction of visceral needs such as hunger or thirst. For example, infants continue to exert maximal effort in response to signals in learning experiments with appetitional reinforcement even when satiated and show the same concurrent pleasure when adaptive responses have been successful even though they may refuse intake of the reinforcement (H. Papoušek, 1967). Thus, the act of performing the correct response may be a more compelling and enduring motivator than an extrinsic factor such as visual stimulation or even food. Once infants have learned to expect that a particular outcome will result from their own behavior, then successfully achieving this outcome again elicits positive emotional responses. A lack of congruence between this anticipation and the result, however, may produce temporary distress, which can lead to further attempts, exploration of new possibilities, and eventual adaptation. Infants appear to be just as attracted to the expectations of a pleasurable outcome that accompanies success as they are motivated to avoid the negative affect experienced with too much incongruency, dissonance, or the inability to discover the contingencies and adjust their own behavior accordingly. This has been referred to as the "congruence between the intended outcome (Soll-Wert) and the real outcome (Ist-Wert)" (H. Papoušek & M. Papoušek, 1977, p. 15), which in itself produces a pleasurable and thus self-reinforcing internal state and therefore must be considered an important part of intrinsic motivation. In terms of infants' interactions within the social environment, as seen in numerous recently filmed observations of parent–infant dyads, the same pattern occurs: Pleasurable responses on the part of the infant are elicited by the infant's apparent expectation that an event will be repeated or the anticipation that his or her own activity will succeed in eliciting a particular event.

The importance of contingency learning and of contingent responsiveness by caregivers has been elaborated convincingly by such researchers as Watson (1972) and Goldberg (1977). However, we would like to reiterate the relationship between this and emotional development by an additional illustration that brings us back to the earlier studies demonstrating neonatal conditioning (e.g., H. Papoušek, 1965, 1967, 1977). Since that time, there has been considerable debate about the issue of operant as opposed to classical conditioning in infants. Why should the former be so much more effective during the early postnatal stage of human learning? Sameroff's (1971) interpretation was based on differential cognitive abilities, with the assumption that classical conditioning actually requires the more sophisticated process of integrating perceptions from several modalities – abilities that may not exist in the first month of life. An equally compelling interpretation, however, is that the recognition of behavioral contingencies (possible in newborns and necessary for operant conditioning) is perhaps the critical factor in this form of learning. Again, this is integrally related to both motivation and emotions; once infants form expectations about the consequences of their own actions, the repetition of these actions and fulfillment of their anticipations elicit positive affect. "Such pleasant emotional experiences represent effective mechanisms for inner reward, an important component of intrinsic motivation" (H. Papoušek, 1977, p. 16). Furthermore, the sooner the newborn discovers relevant environmental events that occur contingent on his or her own behavior, the more likely it is that learning will occur and that the pleasure accompanying this feat will help elicit and sustain further successful problem-solving.

It is acknowledged, of course, that attempts at adaptive responses can be either successful or unsuccessful and may therefore lead to either intrinsic "reward" or "punishment" (i.e., pleasant or unpleasant feelings). Although it is understood that the process of cognitive development is one that basically progresses from the unknown to the known (and vice versa), this must be within limits, and perhaps fairly narrow ones for the tiny, immature infants we choose to study: Too much uncertainty or incongruity leads not to curiosity but to fear and distress, whereas too little leads beyond familiarity to boredom. As discussed in a later section, the roles of the caregiver and the social environment take on particular significance in this instance, being necessary to protect the infant from boredom and/or stress by monitoring and modulating the exposure to external stimulation.

Interactional expressions of emotionality

Under naturalistic ecological circumstances, most events functioning as potential incentive events are delivered by the infant's social environment, in which both sides interact on different levels. The classification of social interactions is fraught with definitional ambiguities. Elsewhere (H. Papoušek & M. Papoušek, 1982) we have tried to approach this problem from the view of a general systems theory and have defined "any conspecific interaction as social and any behavioral unit as indexing social behavior inasmuch as it occurs in the context of social interchange" (p. 151). Due to symbolic capabilities, humans can use almost any observable behavioral unit (a word, a number, a movement, or even a pause in movement) as a means of social communication. Human communication exemplifies the programmatic structure of social interactions and can make them context and culture specific, particularly due to the development of language. This circumstance, however, does not exclude the participation of genetic factors, particularly during the preverbal period of infancy.

Before speech develops, infants may depend to a critical degree on various nonverbal means of communication because of the protracted period of helplessness and dependency on caregivers. Caregivers, however, are typically adults capable of using rather differentiated means of communication. The distance between communicative capacities on both sides of the interacting parent–infant dyad has been compensated for by various forms of adaptation favored during the process of human evolution.

On the infant side, the most important contribution is obviously the precocity in integrative capacities, unparalleled in the animal world. Learning, cognitive, and symbolic capacities enable the infant to develop concepts, acquire skills and rules, and utilize abstractions to a degree that makes possible the use of first words within a year. Moreover, typical features of babyishness make the infant attractive so as to offer some protection from potential social hostility. On the parental side, it seems possible that certain biologically determined, perhaps innate, universal parental capacities facilitate the fulfillment of caregiving responsibilities. Moreover, various cultural traditions and institutions multiply those parental capacities by experience collected and transmitted across generations and cultures. Our interest is in examining the role of emotionality in the interactional process for both parents and infants.

Early motor responses in newborns have been characterized as "overexaggerated," "generalized," and "uneconomical" but gradually becoming more specific, precise, and efficient as the infant develops (H. Papoušek, 1961; H. Papoušek & M. Papoušek, 1984). We have mentioned, for example, the protective "biological fuse" that is operative in neonates, in which the infant responds to overstimulation by retreating into a sudden sleeplike condition, thus changing behavioral states entirely (H. Papoušek, 1969). In contrast, the older infant is able to use a more specific, refined behavioral change such as gaze aversion in response to stimulation that is overwhelming. In the sequence of learning in the first 2 months, we have seen that conditioning stimuli usually evoke nonspecific changes in general body movement and vocalization, whereas from the eleventh week on the infant exhibits responses more appropriate to the given experimental situation. In fact, in terms of emotional expression it appears that these later reactions are more similar to those that one might label in adults as indicative of joy, indecision, or uncertainty.

This phenomenon is similar to a trend noted by Sroufe (1979) and earlier by Werner (1948) in which the developing organism proceeds from a state of global diffuse behavior to one of increasingly specific coordinated acts. Sroufe uses the example of the general activity of a young infant, often accompanied by smiling and cooing, in comparison with that of the older infant, who is able to replace this nonspecific motor response with focused attention and anticipatory quieting.

As can be seen in many skills that develop during infancy, there is a progression from the early precursor activity (often accompanied by increased general motility and signs of autonomic activation in the form of heart rate and respiratory changes) to fast, smoothly executed, and efficiently coordinated acts; one need only consider the acts of directed reaching and grasping or early toy manipulation to find examples of this phenomenon. Through such a process, the infant develops more accurate, finely tuned adjustments of behavior to meet specific environmental circumstances with less expenditure of energy.

This developmental increase in motor coordination, on both the cortical and subcortical levels, may be somewhat analogous to the shift from "tonic" to "phasic" types of motor responses to electrical brain stimulation, which Bergström (1969) considers typical of the developing brain functions in early ontogeny. "Tonic" responses correspond to the relative prevalence of the reticular core in the maturing animal or human brain and show diffuse time relations between the stimulus and a gradually increasing response intensity. "Phasic" responses characterize the input–output relationships in the parallel structures that develop later in the peripheral areas of the brain. Such responses are faster and more precisely adjusted to the parameters of the stimulation in both time and intensity. The adaptive differentiation of the behavioral coordination does not occur uniformly in all behavioral categories. Tonic responses prevail in the autonomic system, whereas phasic responses are more evident in deliberate, intentional acts such as those seen in the motor components of communicative skills. Because expressions of emotion include both autonomic and voluntary elements, it is interesting to explore their developmental differentiation further.

Study I: dynamics of general expressions of emotionality

Attempts to study the communicative value of emotionality are accompanied by difficult problems both in the assessment of particular expressions and in the categorization of interactional contexts for the purpose of interpreting their potential meaning. Other major difficulties in the developmental approach to interactional emotionality are related to the selection of situations that are comparable across age groups and to the analysis of individual variability as it occurs in each partner of the dyad. We attempted to cope with these difficulties and to derive at least preliminary information about the communicative aspects of infant emotions from a follow-up observational study of mother–infant dyads spontaneously interacting in a homelike laboratory setting (M. Papoušek & H. Papoušek, unpublished data).

Methods. Mothers were informed of our interest in the development of their infant's preverbal vocalization, facial expressions, and gestures. They were asked to enjoy one of the infant's diurnal periods of waking at our laboratory in the same way they would do so at home. Since our intention was to focus on emotions in an interactional context, we disregarded situations in which the infant's affective state was obviously related to other factors such as hunger, sleep, or defecation. Three- to 15-min samples of the remaining interactional situations were recorded for a detailed analysis of emotional behaviors. This was accomplished with microanalytic techniques involving audiovisual recording equipment that combined the picture of interacting partners with a visual oscillographic display of voice and a visual digital display of the time base from a quartz clock in 0.01-sec intervals (M. Papoušek & H. Papoušek, 1981b).

With these techniques, we analyzed the dynamics in episodes of infant emotionality during the recorded samples of interactions in 10 mother–infant dyads observed at infant ages of 2, 7, and 10 months. Within each interactional sample, the existence of 15 different infant behavioral items was coded every 0.1 sec. These items included visual behavior (eyes open, visual contact with object of directed activity), upper extremities ("dialogue gestures," closed fists, droopy extremities, object-directed activities), general motility (rhythmical movements, increased poorly coordinated motility, hypertonic body posture), vocalization (quiet signs of pleasure, laughter or joyful squeal, fuss, cry), and facial expression (smile, signs of displeasure). The presence and combinations of individual items were interpreted as indicators of the infant's behavioral–emotional state and used for distinguishing either a neutral emotional state or two types of emotionality: pleasure and displeasure. In each type, two degrees of intensity were differentiated according to the number of observed signs of emotionality: partial intensity (if one or two congruent items from different behavioral categories suggested the same kind of emotionality) and maximal intensity (if three or more congruent items did so). For computation of emotional dynamics, we report only those episodes in which maximal expression of emotion was coded at least once. The vast majority of episodes appeared to be separated from one another by periods of at least 10 sec of undifferentiated (i.e., neutral) behaviors; therefore, a minimum interepisodic interval of 3 sec was chosen a priori for the purpose of defining termination of individual periods of emotionality.

Results. The German mothers participating in these observations were all of middle-class socioeconomic level and engaged in behaviors that we interpreted as typical supportive, attentive parental care. (Notes recorded by the observers offered potential confirmation of the communicative significance or interpretations of the infant emotions and were also confirmed by our recording of maternal "baby talk" in the same contexts.) These behavioral strategies, however, changed with the age of the infants. With 2-month-old infants, the primary maternal behaviors were attempts to soothe a distressed child or to elicit vocalization or a smile. With the 7-month-olds, there was a predominant tendency to offer toys or to engage in ritualized games, often culminating in gentle teasing in conjunction with nursery rhymes or similar repetitive utterances. In the 12-month-old group, there was a richer, more diverse repertoire of maternal interventions; however, the strategies now included some prohibitive tendencies, such as attempts to discourage the baby from leaving the infant chair.

It was somewhat surprising that the frequency with which infants showed periods of emotionality did not decrease, but rather increased with age. In the 2-month-old group, we found no discernible episodes of pleasure in 3 of 10 infants or of displeasure in 5 of 10 infants; by 12 months, episodes of pleasure were observed in all 10 subjects, and displeasure in all but 1. The range of emotional expressivity, as measured by a number of coded items, also increased with age. Similarly, the frequency of laughter and cry increased with age; although each was noted only once in all episodes with 2-month-olds (i.e., laughter in 8.33% and cry in 10% of the pleasure–displeasure episodes, respectively), laughter was found in 80.77% of the pleasure episodes with 7-month-olds and 55.88% with 12-month-olds. Cry, during episodes of displeasure, occurred in 21.43% of the episodes with 7-month-olds and 16% of these episodes with 12-month-olds.

In general, episodes of intense interactional emotionality appeared to be brief, and their duration did not change significantly with age. Episodes of pleasure lasted an average of 4.22 sec at 2 months, 4.05 sec at 7 months, and 4.13 sec at 12 months. Episodes of displeasure showed a slight but nonsignificant tendency to increase in length with age, lasting an average of 6.67, 4.79, and 7.79 sec in each of the corresponding age groups, respectively.

The vast majority of the episodes we observed began with a short period of partial intensity in all three age groups (0.71, 0.29, and 0.67 sec of transition into episodes of pleasure, beginning with 2-month-olds; 1.11, 0.39, and 0.60 sec building up to episodes of clear displeasure). Similarly, the episodes subsided with a final period of partial intensity, lasting 1.42, 0.60, and 1.31 sec in each respective age group after episodes of pleasure, and 1.16, 0.44, and 2.22 sec after displeasure. Vocal signs of pleasure or displeasure typically accompanied the transitions from partial to maximal intensity of emotional expression; these rising and falling oscillations generally occurred between one and four times within each episode, across subjects. In only two instances of displeasure episodes, both in 7-month-olds, did as many as seven peaks occur within a single episode of emotionality.

Thus, the most striking developmental changes seen in the periods of partial intensity, and in the faster transition phase signaling the end of a particular episode, indicated an increasing flexibility and adaptiveness in the infant's control of emotionality. The shorter these phases are, the more "phasic" is their course and the better is their adaptation to the course of interaction in terms of time and intensity parameters. Although statistically significant (one-way ANOVAs resulted in probabilities at the 5% level in all cases and at the 1% level in all but one case), we are cautious in interpreting these analyses due to the interactional context of the observations, which contributes to a high degree of heterogeneity, as mentioned above. Mothers were far from passive in relation to their infant's expressions of emotions, and they used categorically different strategies when soothing as opposed to encouraging an infant. Furthermore, infants may learn, over time, to utilize the consequences their emotional expressions elicit in caregivers to control the course of social interchange. Reliable categorization of the determinants of interactional emotional expression seems to remain beyond the grasp of empirical investigation.

Another interesting developmental change can be seen in the presence of both types of emotionality – pleasure and displeasure – in the same episodes. Such mixed episodes were found only in 12-month-old infants and on the whole in 10 episodes in 5 of the 10 subjects. Periods of pleasure within those episodes lasted on the average 0.61 sec ($n = 11$), and periods of displeasure 1.53 sec ($n = 12$); the transitions from one type of emotionality to another lasted only 0.35 sec and did not include a general decrease in emotionality. Such fast transitions concerned mainly changes in facial and vocal expressions of emotionality.

We are keenly aware of the difficulty of disentangling all aspects of emotionality in situations as complex as social interactions; however, we believe there is more than speculative support in our data for the conclusion that those observable expressions of emotionality – facial and vocal in particular – that play an important role in interactional communication, and sooner or later develop into intentional skills, become ready to serve these purposes around the age of 1 year. We assume that together with the first words, also appearing at this age, the newly developed flexibility in the control of infantile emotionality signals to parents that the main gate for sociocultural adjustment has opened. This is also the age at which the human symbol system provides a new avenue for the differentiation of self and others; however, it is not possible to elaborate here this subtle but central process in early communication patterns.

The fact that interactional incentive events can so easily terminate one form of emotionality and elicit a different one perhaps does not facilitate evaluation of emotionality but deserves attention in a theoretical interpretation, Kagan (1978, p. 37), for instance, considers the ease with which an affect state can be altered by new information as perhaps the best support for the statement that affect is dependent on cognitive beliefs and processes.

Only rather exceptionally (i.e., in only one episode in the 12-month-olds) did we find expression of both pleasure and displeasure occurring simultaneously. This sign of inconsistency and other irregularities in the integration of emotional expressions can be considered arguments against the preadaptedness of fundamental patterns in behavioral regulation. Yet other authors (Izard & Malatesta, in press) see signs of a greater adaptiveness among human beings in the relative infrequency of fixed incentive–emotion sequences. The fact that a given incentive event produces emotion but not the same one in all individuals indicates the flexibility necessary for person–environment adaptation, according to Izard and Malatesta.

In other analyses of intuitive forms of parental care, we have raised the question of interrelations between developmental milestones on the infantile side and changes in caregiving tendencies on the parental side. We suggest that evolution has favored certain didactic forms of parental interventions that maximize the cognitive potential of the developing infant (H. Papoušek & M. Papoušek, 1983). Considering the significance of infant emotional expressions from this perspective, we find it intriguing that ritualized games (peek-a-boo, nursery rhymes ending with tickling, etc.) do not typically appear in the parental repertoire before the development of laughter in the infant. Because our observations can encompass only a small fraction of daily parent–infant interactions, it is of course difficult to speculate which comes first in this sequence or what the detailed interrelationships between games and laughter (as one example) might actually look like. It is interesting, however, to focus attention on those signs of progress in infant development that may elicit new strategies in parental efforts to facilitate that development. We have had an opportunity to derive some information about this aspect of infant emotionality from data reported in the following study on vocal expressions of emotionality.

Study II: microanalysis of infant vocal expressions

Looking at the general patterns of interactional emotionality in infants, we realized that vocal expressions might be the most useful category for further detailed analysis. The voice is considered to be an especially sensitive indicator of emotional states because of its close relationship to breathing and vegetative functions. Nevertheless, emotional states become manifest in rather complex ways through acoustic signals, which include the domains of fundamental frequency, intensity, temporal structure, and spectral characteristics (Crystal, 1973; Jürgens & Ploog, 1976; Scherer, 1982a,b). In pursuing this, however, we were confronted with the problem of finding an objective assessment system that would allow analyses of analogous or comparable aspects of expression in both infants and parents; the vocalization of these two members of the dyad appeared at first glance to be extremely different. (Similar difficulties may have discouraged others in the past, since the most frequently reported aspects of parent–infant vocal exchange appear to be those related to temporal sequencing.)

On the basis of our preliminary experience (M. Papoušek & H. Papoušek, 1981a), we decided to pay more attention to the prosodic elements of vocal communication, with particular emphasis on musical elements. The availability of sonagraphic technology for evaluating the fundamental frequency (F_0) even in a high-pitched voice, the dynamics of amplitudes, and the power spectrum in ad libidum–selected parts of vocalization combined with computer analyses has substantially facilitated and improved former auditory analyses, although it has not outdated them completely. In spite of this, studies including detailed analyses of prosody require major investments of time and effort; in this presentation, we therefore report only on 2- and 3-month-old infants.

Technological advances have not yet been matched by the development of adequate systems for the assessment of infant vocalization. In our human cultural heritage, labels applied to individual patterns of vocalization have long been associated with inferences about emotionality; therefore, it is now difficult to describe vocalizations and remain neutral as to the question of whether emotions exist as relatively discrete and independent phenomena. Thus, authors frequently describe infant vocalizations as comfort, distress, or pleasure sounds, even in reports otherwise unrelated to issues of emotionality.

One of the most important attempts to utilize polygraphic and spectographic documentation to analyze functional relations between discrete patterns of cry and non-cry vocalizations was made by Wolff (1969), although he made only a few specific references to emotionality. His recommendation to include infant state as a nonspecific codeterminant of vocal sounds and his attention to interrelationships between vocalization and cognitive processes represent a valuable approach, one that we find applicable to analyses of emotionality as well. Similar principles led us to earlier analyses of learning and cognitive processes, including such parameters as behavioral state and facial and vocal expressions; at the time, however, adequate electronic technology was not available (H. Papoušek, 1961).

Rather specific typologies of vocalizations have, of course, been developed by phoneticians and linguists, although many of these concern primarily the mechanisms of speech production (see Crystal, 1973; Ferguson & Garnica, 1975; Lieberman, 1967; Martin, 1981; Oller, 1980). Only rarely have these categorizations included the earliest non-cry sounds or relationships to regulatory processes in other than vocal behaviors; in fact, only recently have functional relations to later language development been considered (Oller, 1980; Stark, 1978; Stark, Rose, & McLagen, 1975). Thus, most of the phonological progress to date has provided technological rather than conceptual help to those interested in functional connections between vocalization and emotionality.

Scherer (1982a) provides a comprehensive survey of the present state of the art, covering recent studies devoted to early vocalization (including aspects of emotionality) and carefully explaining modern techniques. M. Papoušek and H. Papoušek (1981a) discuss the role of prosody and musical elements in parent–infant interactions and stress the intimate interrelations among integrative processes, behavioral state, and emotionality in infants. They also draw attention to the didactic aspects of parental interventions. Both reports make evident that much more attention has been paid to cry categories than to non-cry categories and that acoustic data on non-cry vocalizations that are comparable to those on cry vocalizations are still lacking. Scherer stresses the danger of reading too much into an infant's vocalization in attempts to interpret emotional expressions and urges comparisons between vocal and other behavioral indicators of emotionality in designs using independent, objective measures for both.

Sample selection. Following the above suggestions, we analyzed acoustic parameters in vocal sounds elicited in twelve 2-month-old infants during interactions with their mothers. The interactions were recorded in a homelike laboratory setting under conditions similar to those in Study I; in this case, however, we wanted to explore whether and how far some acoustic features of vocal sounds alone characterize infant emotionality along the continuum of maximal pleasure–partial pleasure–emotional neutrality–partial displeasure–maximal displeasure.

The states of pleasure and/or displeasure were assessed independently of vocalizations, based on facial expressions, hand and body movements, visual behavior, and interactional context recorded with a videotape recorder during laboratory sessions. The lexical content of baby talk in which mothers commented on the infant's state was used as an additional criterion for assessing pleasure or displeasure.

Infant vocalizations were selected from an original sample of 500 sounds so as to eliminate reflexive sounds (such as cough and hiccough), voiceless sounds, and sounds impaired by simultaneous maternal utterances or poor recording quality. The remaining 108 infant sounds, isolated from behavioral and contextual cues, were auditorily assessed by three trained evaluators. The evaluators were asked to assign each sound to one of four categories of infant emotionality. Laughter, squeals, and pleasure cry were to be categorized as maximal pleasure, relaxed vowel-like sounds or precursors of cry as partial displeasure, and cry as maximal displeasure. The average inter-rater agreement reached 79.3%. On the whole, 75 vocal sounds (69.4%) unanimously classified by all three evaluators were then compared with the videotaped records of observable behaviors. Auditorily assessed categories of emotionality appeared to be in full agreement with categories derived from observable and contextual cues. Further selection was made so as to include at least two sounds from each infant and to have sufficient distribution of sounds in each of the four categories. Thus, our final sample for evaluation was reduced to 70 examples, as shown in Table 5.1.

Techniques. Analyses of infant vocalizations were performed by the use of a Digital Sona-Graph TM 7800 (Kay Elemetrics), which allowed narrow-band (45-Hz) and broad-band (500-Hz) spectrograms, sound wave displays, and power spectrum at selectable points. (That is, power spectrum analyses were produced at the point of maximum pitch; at this point the distribution of energy across the spectrum and its peak were assessed.) Specifically, power spectrum measurements included peak amplitudes in eight spectral bands ranging from 0 to 16 Hz; data were proportional rather than absolute, in that they were in relation to the corresponding amplitude of the fundamental frequency for each sound ($F_0 = 1$).

Spectrograms were also used for the measurement of duration and for qualitative evaluations corresponding to those parameters described and used by Sirviö & Michelsson (1976) and by Stark et al. (1975) (e.g., quality and type of fundamental frequency contours, subharmonic break, vibrato, vocal fry, and glottal stop). Additional auditory analyses included voice quality, pitch (analysis of maximal pitch by a musically trained person), and loudness (5 degrees).

Results. The representation of episodes of partial or maximal pleasure in interactions of 2-month-old infants basically challenges the traditional impression that infants mainly cry or use precursors of crying at this age. Table 5.1 summarizes the data on the main acoustic parameters: fundamental frequency, loudness, duration, and distribution of energy (*E*) across the harmonic spectrum. These

Table 5.1. *Acoustic measures of vocalizations* (N = 70) *in twelve 2-month-old infants during interactions with mothers: relation to infant emotionality assessed by trained observers*

Acoustic measure	Behavioral–emotional state				One-way analysis of variance	
	Maximal pleasure (n = 6), $\bar{X}$	Partial pleasure (n = 22), $\bar{X}$	Partial displeasure (n = 28), $\bar{X}$	Maximal displeasure (n = 14), $\bar{X}$	F(3,66)	p <
Pitch F_0 (Hz)	806.6	311.1 *	466.2	479.2	32.02	0.01
(in musical note)	g″–g″ sharp	e′ flat	b′ flat	b′ flat–b′		
Loudness (degrees 1 to 5)	4.3	2.9	3.0	4.9	31.84	0.01
Duration (msec)	683	468	559 *	1,254	8.92	0.01
Frequency at the peak of spectral energy	1,245.0	622.3	880.0	2,094.0	14.64	0.01
E_{peak}/E_{fund} in spectral bands						
0–1 kHz	0.95	1.05	1.23	1.12	2.12	n.s.
1–2 kHz	1.69	0.78	1.18 (*)	1.59	9.59	0.01
2–3 kHz	0.96	0.55	1.03	1.33	8.13	0.01
3–4 kHz	0.95	0.30 *	0.77	1.11	7.13	0.01
4–6 kHz	0.92	0.34 *	0.83	0.99	5.67	0.01
6–8 kHz	0.65	0.23	0.59 (*)	0.97	8.93	0.01
8–12 kHz	0.14	0.00	0.14 *	0.52	22.86	0.01
12–16 kHz	0.13	0.00	0.10	0.23	4.42	0.01

Note: E_{peak}/E_{fund} is an energy ratio computed as (peak amplitude in spectral band)/(amplitude at fundamental F). The Wilcoxon matched-pairs signed-ranks test was used as an additional procedure for making comparisons between classes of emotionality in cases where vocal samples were available from the same subjects in more than one category, i.e., between partial pleasure and partial displeasure (n = 6), and partial displeasure and maximal displeasure (n = 7). For criteria of emotionality see text.
*p < 0.05; (*) p < 0.1. Asterisks between two columns indicate a comparison of the two numbers in those columns.

data suggest continuous changes in all measured parameters along the transition from the state of partial pleasure toward either maximal pleasure or maximal displeasure. According to Scherer (1979), these changes may reflect nonspecific changes in general emotional arousal.

During the state of partial pleasure, infants were found to vocalize in the lowest pitch in the shortest utterances and with minimal loudness. Correspondingly, the peak of energy in the power spectrum was positioned in the lowest frequencies. The average pitch reached its peak in the state of maximal pleasure, and the second highest level in the state of maximal displeasure. The continuous changes in individual parameters are obviously not quite parallel and are not accompanied by parallel changes in the distribution of spectral energy, most of which is invested in the upper harmonics above 2,000 Hz in the displeasure sounds, as compared with 1,245 Hz in the state of maximal pleasure.

Several other authors have also advocated the notion of continuity in various acoustic parameters of infant vocalizations (Stark, 1978; Stark et al., 1975; Wolff, 1969). We cannot rule out the possibility that humans perceive such continuities categorically, just as in the case of color perception in the continuum of wave frequencies of daylight, and that the search for objective categorical criteria may therefore not be fruitful. Nevertheless, it is necessary to consider the potential existence of distinct vocal patterns consisting of additional finer parameters before calling off the search altogether.

Thus, in addition to changes in measured acoustic parameters during transitions from partial pleasure to either maximal pleasure or maximal displeasure, we also found evidence of some potential specific phenomena, although not proportionally across categories. Aside from patterns of energy distribution across harmonics, it may particularly be an aperiodicity in sound waves and the signal-to-noise ratio that make possible the auditory discrimination of vocal expressions of pleasure and displeasure (Scherer, 1982b). Elaboration of the methodological approach to these phenomena is required, however. The shift of spectral energy to higher frequencies of upper harmonics is usually interpreted as a consequence of increased tension in the vocal tract and thus changed resonance factors, auditorily perceived as a "tense voice" (Laver, 1980; Scherer, 1982b).

In order to illustrate the changes in vocal sounds occurring along the continuum of pleasure–displeasure in 2-month-old infants, we include four typical sonagrams in Figure 5.1. Expressions of maximal pleasure are rare and heterogeneous in this age group; they are represented by a squeal in Figure 5.1A but may include pleasure cries and laughter as well. These sounds have distinct sonagraphic characteristics but are commonly differentiated from other categories by their higher average pitch.

Cry representing maximal displeasure (Figure 5.1D) is characterized by auditory and sonagraphic signs of hyperphonation, tense and/or harsh voice, segments of vocal cry, and voiced ingressive elements. The most common sonagraphic pattern includes irregular intensity in the fundamental frequency, vibrato, or subharmonic breaks. Cries are often distal cues and therefore appear less frequently in face-to-face interactions; when they do occur, they usually elicit caregivers' interventions, which in effect interrupt or terminate the face-to-face interaction.

Vocal signs of partial pleasure or partial displeasure are relatively common during interactions. The example illustrating partial pleasure (Figure 5.1B) is a vowel-like sound, the musical timbre of which is usually perceived as pleasing, relaxed, and euphonic. Approximately one-half of these sounds in our sample are combined with consonantal elements. The early differentiation of vowel-like

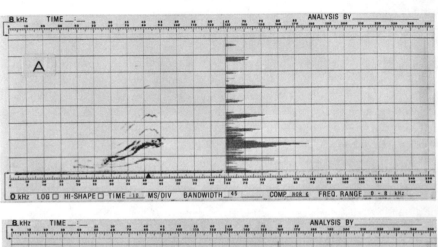

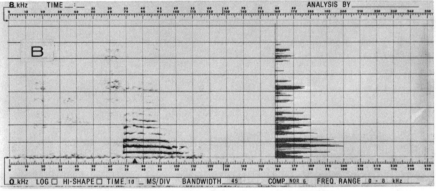

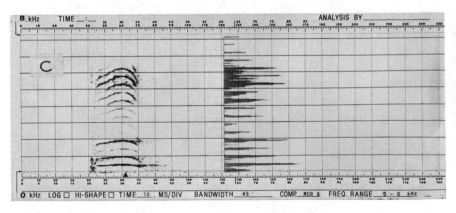

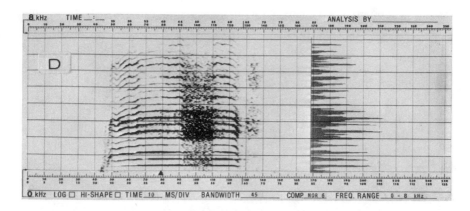

Figure 5.1. Sonagraphic examples of infant vocalizations at 2 months during mother–infant interactions. Narrow-band sonagrams (45-Hz bandwidth) with power spectrum at indicated points of maximum pitch (see black triangles); frequency range 0 to 8 kHz; time scale 10 msec per division. (A) During maximum pleasure: high-pitch squeal with a continuous rising pitch contour; F_0 830.6 Hz; peak spectral energy at 1,650 Hz. (B) During partial pleasure: vowel-like nasalized sound with a continuous falling pitch contour; F_0 349 Hz; peak spectral energy at 698 Hz. (C) During partial displeasure: vowel-like nasalized and tense sound with a continuous rise–fall contour; F_0 466.2 Hz; peak spectral energy at F_0. (D) During maximum displeasure: cry sound with a discontinuous rise–fall pitch contour and with a harsh voicing and a voiceless friction noise in the intermediate section; F_0 392 Hz; peak spectral energy at 3,200 Hz.

and consonantlike sounds in 2-month-old infants together with the first pitch modulations made possible by a prolongation of expiration bring about changes typical of "cooing." These new features occur with increasing frequency and variability in vocal exploration and vocal play (Lenneberg, 1967; M. Papoušek & H. Papoušek, 1981a; Stark, 1978). Melodic contours in these partial pleasure sounds are typically smooth and continuous, and subharmonic breaks seldom occur. In contrast, sounds produced during partial displeasure (Figure 5.1C) include a harsh or tense voice and frequent glottal stops. Contours in fundamental frequency are fragmented, their intensity is irregular, and vibrato and subharmonic breaks occur similarly but not as frequently as in the cry. As can be seen from these examples, the potential patterns of vocal sounds are of such complexity as to allow not only fine-grained communication of internal feelings, but also a display of interindividual variability and a means of identifying others in the social environment.

So far, our data suggest that some acoustic parameters in infant vocalizations (e.g., frequency, loudness, duration) do reflect the degree of nonspecific emotional arousal and that others (e.g., distribution of spectral energy) in combination with qualitative auditory or sonographic features are more distinctly related to the pleasure–displeasure continuum. These cues may assist the caretaker in making an appropriate guess about the infant's level of arousal, emotional state, and readiness for interaction.

Study II: microanalysis of parental vocal expressions

In spite of the widely accepted assumption that social coexistence in general, and parent–infant bonding in particular, have been favored during human evolution, adequate attention to parental preadaptedness in support of this evolutionary process has developed only recently with the advent of microanalytic techniques for the study of parent–infant interactions. In previous articles, we have argued that, in addition to protecting the infant against environmental risk and acting as a base for emotional attachment, parents also provide didactic support to the cognitive potential of the developing infant (H. Papoušek & M. Papoušek, 1978, 1982), although they may do so intuitively without conscious awareness of their didactic capacities.

With the same techniques, we have also shown that some of these parental tendencies (viewed as vague signs of increased emotionality in former approaches) can be better interpreted as specific adjustments, seemingly innate and universal (H. Papoušek & M. Papoušek, 1983), which allow communicative interchange and transmission of elementary knowledge to the infant.

As stressed in earlier reports (M. Papoušek & H. Papoušek, 1981a), evidence for a similar interpretation can be seen not only in facial or gestural behaviors but also – and in a particularly interesting form – in the prosodic and musical elements of vocal interchanges. Since these elements are available to both the parent and the preverbal infant, they deserve full attention not only as expressions of emotionality but also as potential means of preverbal communication in both members of the interacting dyad.

Mothers and fathers alike use simple enhanced melodic contours at a higher average pitch and at an extended pitch range when addressing 3-month-old infants. Moreover, the parental prosodic repertoire is restricted to a limited set of distinctive, prototypical contours that recur with a high degree of similarity (M. Papoušek, H. Papoušek, & M. Bornstein, 1985). These contours do not occur randomly but depend on changes in infant vocalizations, facial expressions, visual behavior, hand gestures, and/or general motility. For instance, as shown in Table 5.2, vocal expressions of pleasant excitement in 3-month-old infants elicit a majority of rising contours in parental vocalizations, whereas vocal expressions of fussiness elicit a majority of falling contours (M. Papoušek et al., 1985).

In so responding to the infant's increased emotionality, however, parents do not merely increase their own affect, perhaps in the sense of sharing emotionality, but may also try to influence the infant's behavioral–emotional state and to restore or maintain states that are didactically meaningful. Rising contours may

Table 5.2. *Effects of state in 3-month-old infants on melodic contours in parental baby talk*

Parental melodic contour	Vocal expression of state in infants			Statistics[a]	
	Pleasant excitement (*n* = 15), $\bar{x}$	Fussiness (*n* = 13), $\bar{x}$	Others (*n* = 54), $\bar{x}$	K–W ANOVA $p \leq$	M–W *U* test $p \leq$
Level	3.77	6.61	6.44	n.s.	0.04
Rise	27.45	18.45	28.15	0.03	0.02
Fall	22.13	34.46	16.53	0.0002	0.035
Rise–fall	21.31	8.86	14.32	0.002	0.001
Sinusoidal	13.53	6.54	9.69	0.04	0.02

Note: Data based on 14 mother–infant and 14 father–infant interactions. In pleasant excitement, frequency of vocal signs of pleasure: minimum of 4 per minute and twice as high as that of other sounds; frequency of fussy sounds: maximum of 1 per minute. In fussiness, frequency of cry or its precursors: minimum of 4 per minute and twice as high as that of other sounds.
[a] Abbreviations: K–W ANOVA, Kruskal–Wallis one-way analysis of variance; M–W *U* test, Mann–Whitney *U* test between pleasant excitement and fussiness.

well be interpreted as encouragement, and falling contours as soothing forms of communication. In former studies of learning in infants under 6 months of age (H. Papoušek, 1969), we observed that the active waking state was correlated with the quickest and most accurate learned responses. When this state cannot be easily sustained or reinstated, parents tend to resort to the alternative of facilitating transition to quiet sleep in the infant.

Thus, changes elicited in parental vocalization seem to imply both emotionality and purposeful intervention, and the melodic contours in parental baby talk are interesting as potential attention-getting, encouraging, praising, and soothing mechanisms serving the purposes of didactic guidance.

It is interesting that the distribution of melodic contours shown in Table 5.2 was affected equally in both parents by the vocal expressions of emotionality in the infants. This fact, together with our finding that the overall distribution of melodic contours in parental baby talk is almost identical in both mother and father (M. Papoušek et al., 1985), raises the question of the universality of parental behaviors interpretable as intuitive didactic guidance. It is very difficult to prove the concept of preadaptedness of didactic tendencies in human caregiving. However, at least supportive evidence for their preadaptedness might be seen in the intuitive quality and prevalence of such tendencies across ages, sex, and cultures. The reported universality across parental sex is sufficient justification for future comparative studies.

Table 5.3. *Distribution of maternal melodic contours in utterances with semantic content distinctly interpreting interactional situations*

Melodic contour	Semantic content			
	Praising (n = 190), %	Soothing (n = 80), %	Encouraging vocalizations, etc. (n = 210), %	Appeal for eye-to-eye contact (n = 262), %
Level	2.1	1.3	5.7	1.9
Two-level	0	0	5.2	56.9
Rise	2.6	0	29.5	7.6
Fall–rise	1.0	0	18.1	8.4
Fall	31.6	80.0	11.9	12.6
Rise–fall	36.3	13.8	20.0	7.3
Sinusoidal	26.3	4.4	9.5	5.3

Note: This involved 36.2% of all utterances in 21 mothers talking to 2-month-old infants; n = 742. Chi-square analyses comparing the distribution of melodic contours between every possible pair of categories of semantic content indicated highly significant differences ($p < 0.001$).

The materials from Study II offered an opportunity for a closer look at the potential role of parental melodic contours in the sense of intuitive didactic guidance. This time we analyzed primarily the semantic content of maternal utterances recorded during interactions with 2-month-old infants and selected four predominant categories of interactional context: appeal for visual contact with the infant, appraisal or confirmation of the infant's behavior, soothing, and encouragement of a vocalization or of a continuation or repetition of other behaviors (Table 5.3). Evaluation of the videotaped nonvocal behaviors served as additional evidence for this purpose. The meaning of the situations could thus be identified in 742 cases, or 36.2% of a total of 2,084 maternal utterances from 21 mothers.

The results indicate that the prosody of parental vocalizations does depend on interactional contexts and maternal tendencies to intervene supportively. Each of the four contextual categories is characterized by a different maximum frequency of melodic contour as well as by a different distribution pattern in the remaining contour categories. Thus, expressions of emotionality in maternal vocalizations also reveal features of intentional, albeit not consciously and rationally controlled, didactic interventions.

The analysis of melodic contours has still attracted relatively little attention in infancy research, and there is to date no standardization of categories employed by those authors who do undertake such analyses. Nevertheless, Stern, Spieker, and MacKain (1982) reported a similar maximum of rise–fall ("bell-shaped") and sinusoidal contours in interactional situations with 2-, 4-, and 6-month-olds, comparable to our own observations of pleasant excitement. Ryan (1978) found an increased frequency of rising contours in invitations to vocal contributions to a dialogue, although in this case the vocalizations were addressed to 1-year-old infants. Neither Stern and colleagues nor Ryan included the two-level contours in their categories that accompanied appeals for visual contact in our observations.

Realizing the interrelations between emotions and integrative processes in infants as we discussed earlier in this chapter, we shall now consider further interrelations between parental emotions, meanings of interactional situations, and parental tendencies to give didactic support to the infant's integrative processes. While responding to the infant's expressions of emotionality, parents in the same vein seem to be responding to signals as to the course of integrative processes, fluctuations in behavioral states, and resulting internal feelings in the infant. Moreover, parental responses seem to be influenced by tendencies to give adequate support to the infant's integrative capacities.

Melodic contours in parental responses can hardly be seen as mere expressions of the consequences of emotionality. Both the interactional context and the content of baby talk clearly indicate tendencies to facilitate the infant's cognitive adaptation and to restore his or her state of wakefulness and emotionality to one that is most conducive to this adaptation. Demonstrating the effectiveness of such interventions, however, remains an important task for further research. In addition, future interactional analyses should take into account the possibility that infants may learn that the forms of their own vocalizations elicit differential and meaningful vocal responses from caregivers. The sharing of emotionality is intrinsically related to the sharing of knowledge.

The significance of emotionality in interpreting infant–caregiver relations

As indicated in earlier sections, expressions of affect are not necessarily inextricably linked with social events or interactions. Both positive and negative emotions certainly can occur in social isolation, even though the cognitive process eliciting them may be one involving mental representation or anticipation of a particularly pleasing or distressing social event. For the infant, causing the repetition of a familiar stimulus, discovering the effects of his or her own actions on the physical environment, or experiencing a novel and interesting phenomenon that can then be assimilated into previous schemata may all be accompanied by vocal and facial indicators of enjoyment. The presence of another person to appreciate these emotional displays adds another complex dimension that may influence the continuation and dynamics of future expressions by the infant, perhaps functioning in much the same way as the more systematically produced experimental rewards. Although this perspective is consistent with much of the available empirical literature in the area of infant emotions, it still basically treats the infant's emotional state as the dependent variable.

It is important to direct attention to early expressions of emotion as they influence others; it is hardly possible to imagine a social situation in which at least some degree of emotion would not be present, and surely the affective behavior of others often plays a major role in determining one's own feelings. With the current shift toward recognizing the reciprocal nature of parent–infant relations and the role of the infant as elicitor as well as recipient of caregiving behaviors (Bell, 1968; Lewis & Rosenblum, 1974), it is necessary to address the influence of infant displays of pleasure or displeasure as they affect parenting behaviors.

As Klinnert, Campos, Sorce, Emde, and Svejda (1983) have indicated, there has been a recent shift toward treating emotions as independent variables. The process referred to as social referencing involves the ways in which emotions influence the behaviors of others but primarily concerns the ways in which an individual (e.g., the infant) seeks from other people (e.g., the caregiver) cues that might help the individual to interpret or determine appropriate responses in a novel situation. Following this model, for example, Klinnert (1981; cited in Klinnert et al., 1983) studied the effect of mothers' emotional reactions on infants' responses to a somewhat frightening toy; similarly, Sorce, Emde, Klinnert, and Campos (1981; cited in Klinnert et al., 1983) investigated effects of maternal responses when infants approached a visual cliff. Both studies showed striking evidence of the impact of the mothers' facial expressions on the infants' approach or avoidance in these novel situations. Thus, although these studies treated the caregivers' emotional expressions as independent variables, they still viewed the infant responses as being regulated or influenced by those of the adult. We would suggest another avenue of approach to this issue, which essentially places social referencing in a more reciprocal context. The question then becomes, How do infants' emotional expressions elicit, modify, or sustain optimal caregiving responses from significant others in their social world?

Microanalytic techniques applied to filmed observations have led to an awareness that there are many complex parental behaviors that, although often carried out without conscious intent or control, are nevertheless appropriately adjusted to the capabilities and perceptual–cognitive needs of the human infant. These intuitive parenting behaviors appear to be precisely orchestrated – through repetition, exaggeration, imitation, and other means – to facilitate the development of infant competence even at a stage when parents often doubt the presence of such capabilities in one so young.

More pertinent to the issue at hand, however, is the fact that these same methods have enabled us to analyze and gain some insights into the close relationships between parental and infant behaviors. In addition to vocalization patterns, we have also found that the temporal structure of parent–infant interactions depends on both the situational context and the emotional state of the infant. Turn taking, for example, is an important feature of any effective dyadic communication; however, the absence of turn taking may also have particular significance in relation to infants. For example, Stern, Jaffe, Beebe, and Bennett (1975) reported more turn taking in serious, instructional types of parent–infant interactions than in other types of parent–infant interactions and more concurrent vocalizations when the dyad was expressing positive affect than when it was expressing negative affect. We observed that mothers stopped giving turns to infants during vocal interchanges and drowned out infants' vocal sounds as soon as the infants started fussing or crying.

It has also been shown that an infant's emotional state influences the emotional and physiological reactions of attending adults, in some cases mobilizing the adults' readiness to respond in an effort to alter the infant's state (when aversive) or to sustain it (when pleasurable). Frodi et al. (1978) showed parents videotapes of crying and smiling infants and rated parental mood changes, blood pressure, and skin conductance level. They reported negative moods, increase in blood pressure, and increase in skin conductance associated with infant crying but not with smiling. It seems evident that expression of either pleasure or displeasure by the infant serves as a message to the social environment that corresponds to differential reactions and behaviors by those who subsequently interact with that infant.

Of course, as mentioned before, the expression of any emotion may occur essentially in a social vacuum and may be elicited by distinctly nonsocial stimuli. However, even in the case of a smile that occurs in the course of learning, there may be social significance if another person per chance observes it and can also detect the contingencies on which this pleasurable response was based. Such cues may be vital for helping parents to predict what situations are novel, familiar, incongruent, or challenging in the infant's perceptual framework. For the infant, particularly the neonate who is less capable of generating his or her own sources of novel stimulation, this emotional expression may become an instrumental act in itself, the goal of which is to elicit more or less of a given stimulation or parental behavior.

Early in the postnatal period, we find highly consistent, homogeneous patterns of parental communication to infants, with a shift toward increasing variability and heterogeneity by the end of the first year. As postulated elsewhere (M. Papoušek et al., 1985), this early uniformity may be more dependent on biological determinants, whereas the latter differentiation shows more the effects of enculturation. By the same logic, infant expressions of emotions become more differentiated, more situation specific, and more consciously controlled over time, resulting in vastly increased variability across infants. Thus, the entire nature of parent–infant interactions, viewed as an evolving and dynamic process, becomes highly individualized as each responds differentially to the emotional behaviors of the partner as the relationship develops.

We would concur with Emde (1980, cited in Murphy, 1983) that the study of parent–infant affect must be viewed as a reciprocal reward system: Just as infants are rewarded by the nurturant expressions of parental affection, enabling them to develop the trust necessary for later independence, so are the parents reinforced by the positive affect expressed by their infant and therefore continue their efforts to provide for the infant's needs.

In addition, we would stress the close relationship between emotionality and integrative processes, one that may have deep psychobiological roots and may have played a significant role in the evolution of specific human adaptiveness. To some, this additional dimension of emotionality may represent another aspect increasing the complexity of present concepts. To others, whom we join, it may point to a passable research avenue that may contribute to the elucidation of one crucial aspect of emotionality and thus eventually reduce the present complexity of such a difficult problem.

References

Bell, R. Q. A reinterpretation of the direction of effects in studies of socialization. *Psychological Bulletin*, 1968, *75*, 81–95.

Bergström, R. M. Electrical parameters of the brain during ontogeny. In R. J. Robinson (Ed.), *Brain and early behaviour: Development in the fetus and infant* (pp. 15–37). New York: Academic Press, 1969.

Crystal, D. Non-segmental phonology in language acquisition: A review of the issues. *Lingua*, 1973, *32*, 1–45.

Darwin, C. The expression of emotions in man and animals. London: Murray, 1872 (reprinted by University of Chicago Press, 1965).

Emde, R. N. Emotional availability: A reciprocal reward system for infants and parents with implications for prevention of psycho-social disorders. In P. M. Taylor (Ed.), *Parent–infant relationships* (pp. 87–115). New York: Grune & Stratton, 1980.

Ferguson, C. A., & Garnica, O. K. Theories of phonological development. In E. H. Lenneberg & E. Lenneberg (Eds.), *Foundations of language development: A multidisciplinary approach* (Vol. 1, pp. 153–80). New York: Academic Press, 1975.

Field, T. Infant arousal, attention, and affect during early interactions. In L. P. Lipsitt & C. K. Rovee-Collier (Eds.), *Advances in Infancy Research* (Vol. 1, pp. 58–100). Norwood, NJ: Ablex, 1981.

Fogel, A. Temporal organization in mother–infant face-to-face interaction. In H. R. Schaffer (Ed.), *Studies in mother–infant interaction* (pp. 119–51). London: Academic Press, 1977.

Frodi, A. N., Lamb, M. E., Leavitt, L. A., Donovan, W. L., Neff, C., & Sherry, D. Fathers' and mothers' responses to the faces and cries of normal and premature infants. *Developmental Psychology*, 1978, *14*, 190–8.

Goldberg, S. Social competence in infancy: A model of parent–infant interaction. *Merrill–Palmer Quarterly,* 1977, *23*(3), 163–77.

Hebb, D. O. *The organization of behavior.* New York: Wiley, 1949.

Hellbrügge, T., Lange, J. E., Rutenfranz, J., & Stehr, K. Circadian periodicity of physiological functions in different stages of infancy and childhood. *Annals of the New York Academy of Sciences,* 1964, *117*, 361–73.

Hunt, J. MV. Intrinsic motivation and its role in development. In D. Levine (Ed.), *Nebraska Symposium on Motivation* (Vol. 13, pp. 189–282). Lincoln: University of Nebraska Press, 1965.

Izard, C. E. *The face of emotion.* New York: Appleton-Century-Crofts, 1971.

Izard, C. E. On the ontogenesis of emotions and emotion–cognition relationships in infancy. In M. Lewis & L. A. Rosenblum (Eds.), *The development of affect* (pp. 389–413). New York: Plenum, 1978.

Izard, C. E. (Ed.). *Measuring emotions in infant and children.* Cambridge University Press, 1982.

Izard, C. E., & Dougherty, L. M. Two complementary systems for measuring facial expressions in infants and children. In C. E. Izard (Ed.), *Measuring emotions in infants and children* (pp. 97–126). Cambridge University Press, 1982.

Izard, C. E., & Malatesta, C. Z. A developmental theory of emotions. *Behavioral and Brain Sciences* (in press).

Jürgens, U., & Ploog, D. Zur Evolution der Stimme. *Archiv für Psychiatrische Nervenkrankheiten,* 1976, *222*, 117–37.

Kagan, J. On emotion and its development: A working paper. In M. Lewis & L. A. Rosenblum (Eds.), *The development of affect* (pp. 11–41). New York: Plenum, 1978.

Kagan, J. Heart rate and heart rate variability as signs of a temperamental dimension in infants. In C. E. Izard (Ed.), *Measuring emotions in infants and children* (pp. 38–66). Cambridge University Press, 1982.

Klinnert, M. D., Campos, J. J., Sorce, J. F., Emde, R. N., & Svejda, M. Emotions as behavior regulators: Social referencing in infancy. In R. Plutchik & H. Kellerman (Eds.), *Emotion: Theory, research, and experience* (Vol. 2, pp. 57–86). New York: Academic Press, 1983.

Laver, J. *The phonetic description of voice quality.* Cambridge University Press, 1980.

Lenneberg, E. *Biological foundations of language.* New York: Wiley, 1967.

Lewis, M., Brooks, J., & Haviland, J. Hearts and faces: A study in the measurement of emotions. In M. Lewis & L. A. Rosenblum (Eds.), *The development of affect* (Vol. 1, pp. 77–123). New York: Plenum, 1978.

Lewis, M., & Michalson, L. The measurement of emotional state. In C. E. Izard (Ed.), *Measuring emotions in infants and children* (pp. 178–207). Cambridge University Press, 1982.

Lewis, M., & Rosenblum, L. A. (Eds.), *The effect of the infant on its caregiver.* New York: Wiley, 1974.

Lieberman, P. *Intonation, perception, and language* (Research Monograph No. 38). Cambridge, MA: MIT Press, 1967.

Martin, J. A. M. *Voice, speech, and language in the child: Development and disorder.* New York: Springer-Verlag, 1981.

Murphy, L. B. Issues in the development of emotion in infancy. In R. Plutchik & H. Kellerman (Eds.), *Emotion: Theory, research, and experience* (Vol. 2, pp. 1–34). New York: Academic Press, 1983.

Oller, D. K. The emergence of the sounds of speech in infancy. In G. H. Yeni-Komshian, J. F. Kavanagh, & C. A. Ferguson (Eds.), *Child phonology* (Vol. 1, pp. 93–112). New York: Academic Press, 1980.

Oster, H. Facial expression and affect development. In M. Lewis & L. A. Rosenblum (Eds.), *The development of affect* (Vol. 1, pp. 43–75). New York: Plenum, 1978.

Papoušek, H. *Conditioned alimentary motor responses in infants* (Vol. 409). Prague: Thomayerova Sbírka Přednášek, 1961 (in Czech).

Papoušek, H. The development of higher nervous activity in children in the first half-year of life: European research in cognitive development. *Monographs of the Society for Research in Child Development*, 1965, *30*(2, Serial No. 100), 102–11.

Papoušek, H. Experimental studies of appetitional behavior in human newborns and infants. In H. W. Stevenson, E. H. Hess, & H. L. Rheingold (Eds.), *Early behavior: Comparative and developmental approaches* (pp. 249–78). New York: Wiley, 1967.

Papoušek, H. Individual variability in learned responses in human infants. In R. J. Robinson (Ed.), *Brain and early behavior* (pp. 251–63). New York: Academic Press, 1969.

Papoušek, H. Entwicklung der Lernfähigkeit im Säuglingsalter. In G. Nissen (Ed.), *Intelligenz, Lernen, und Lernstörungen* (pp. 75–93). Berlin: Springer-Verlag, 1977.

Papoušek, H., & Papoušek, M. Mothering and the cognitive head-start: Psychobiological considerations. In H. R. Schaffer (Ed.), *Studies in mother–infant interaction* (pp. 63–85). London: Academic Press, 1977.

Papoušek, H., & Papoušek, M. Interdisciplinary parallels in studies of early human behavior: From physical to cognitive needs, from attachment to dyadic education. *International Journal of Behavioural Development*, 1978, *1*(1), 37–49.

Papoušek, H., & Papoušek, M. The infant's fundamental adaptive response system in social interaction. In E. Thoman (Ed.), *Origins of the infant's social responsiveness* (pp. 175–208). Hillsdale, NJ: Erlbaum, 1979.

Papoušek, H., & Papoušek, M. How human is the human newborn, and what else is to be done? In K. Bloom (Ed.), *Prospective issues in infancy research* (pp. 137–155). Hillsdale, NJ: Erlbaum, 1981.

Papoušek, H., & Papoušek, M. Infant–adult social interactions, their origins, dimensions, and failures. In T. M. Field, A. Huston, H. C. Quay, L. Troll, & G. A. Finley (Eds.), *Review of developmental psychology* (pp. 148–63). New York: Wiley, 1982.

Papoušek, H., & Papoušek, M. The psychobiology of the first didactic programs and toys in human infants. In A. Oliverio & M. Zappella (Eds.), *The behavior of human infants* (pp. 219–39). New York: Plenum, 1983.

Papoušek, H., & Papoušek, M. Qualitative transitions in integrative processes during the first trimester of human postpartum life. In H. F. R. Prechtl (Ed.), *Continuity of neural functions from prenatal to postnatal life* (pp. 220–44). London: Spastics International Medical Publications, 1984.

Papoušek, M., & Papoušek, H. Musical elements in the infant's vocalization: Their significance for communication, cognition, and creativity. In L. P. Lipsitt (Ed.), *Advances in infancy research* (Vol. 1, pp. 164–225). Norwood, NJ: Ablex, 1981a.

Papoušek, M., & Papoušek, H. Musikalische Ausdruckselemente der Sprache und ihre Modifikation in der "Ammensprache." *Sozialpädiatrie in Praxis und Klinik*, 1981b, *3*, 294–6.

Papoušek, M., Papoušek, H., & Bornstein, M. H. The naturalistic vocal environment of young infants: On the significance of homogeneity and variability in parental speech. In T. M. Field & N. Fox (Eds.), *Social perception in infants* (pp. 269–97). Norwood, NJ: Ablex, 1985.

Piaget, J. *The origins of intelligence in children*. New York: International Universities Press, 1952.

Ryan, M. L. Contour in context. In R. N. Campbell & P. T. Smith (Eds.), *Recent advances in the psychology of language* (pp. 237–51). New York: Plenum, 1978.

Sameroff, A. J. Can conditioned responses be established in the newborn infant? *Developmental Psychology*, 1971, *5*, 1–12.

Scherer, K. R. Nonlinguistic vocal indicators of emotion and psychopathology. In C. E. Izard (Ed.), *Emotions in personality and psychopathology* (pp. 495–529). New York: Plenum, 1979.

Scherer, K. R. The assessment of vocal expression in infants and children. In C. E. Izard (Ed.), *Measuring emotions in infants and children* (pp. 127–163). Cambridge University Press, 1982a.

Scherer, K. R. Methods of research on vocal communication: Paradigms and parameters. In K. R.

Scherer & P. Ekman (Eds.), *Handbook of methods in nonverbal behavior research* (pp. 136–98). Cambridge University Press, 1982b.

Schwartz, G. E. Psychophysiological patterning and emotion revisited: A systems perspective. In C. E. Izard (Ed.), *Measuring emotions in infants and children* (pp. 67–93). Cambridge University Press, 1982.

Sirviö, P., & Michelsson, K. Sound spectrographic cry analysis of normal and abnormal newborn infants: A review and a recommendation for standardization of cry characteristics. *Folia phoniatrica,* 1976, *28,* 11–173.

Sroufe, L. A. Socioemotional development. In J. Osofsky (Ed.), *Handbook of infant development* (pp. 462–516). New York: Wiley, 1979.

Stark, R. E. Features of infant sounds: The emergence of cooing. *Journal of Child Language,* 1978, *5,* 379–90.

Stark, R. E., Rose, S. N., & McLagen, M. Features of infant sounds: The first eight weeks of life. *Journal of Child Language,* 1975, *2,* 205–21.

Stern, D. N., Jaffe, J., Beebe, B., & Bennett, S. L. Vocalizing in unison and in alternation: Two modes of communication within the mother–infant dyad. *Annals of the New York Academy of Sciences,* 1975, *263,* 89–100.

Stern, D. N., Spieker, S., & MacKain, K. Intonation contours as signals in maternal speech to prelinguistic infants. *Developmental Psychology,* 1982, *18,* 727–35.

Stratton, P. Rhythmic functions in the newborn. In P. Stratton (Ed.), *Psychobiology of the human newborn* (pp. 119–45). New York: Wiley, 1982.

Watson, J. S. Smiling, cooing, and "the game." *Merrill–Palmer Quarterly,* 1972, *15,* 323–40.

Werner, H. *Comparative psychology of mental development.* New York: International Universities Press, 1948.

Wolff, P. H. The natural history of crying and other vocalizations in early infancy. In B. Foss (Ed.), *Determinants of infant behaviour* (Vol. 4, pp. 81–109). London: Methuen, 1969.

6 Capturing the wider view of attachment: a re-analysis of Ainsworth's Strange Situation

Klaus E. Grossmann, Karin Grossmann,
and Anna Schwan

1. Introduction

1.1. Karl Bühler's conception as a generalized model

A conceptual basis for empirical research in early infant development (as well as in communication research) was provided by Karl Bühler in Vienna in the 1920s (K. Bühler, 1925, 1930). Bühler argued that three levels of adaptation existed in human development: (a) adaptation through reflexes and instincts, (b) playful selection of appropriate actions through reward, and (c) insightful intellect. Charlotte Bühler, Karl's wife, concentrated on affective development and cooperation (*Zusammenspiel;* C. Bühler, 1962, chap. 4). The Bühlers' approach was amazingly modern and integrative. However, it did not become influential because of the political upheavals that eventually forced them out of their country and also, perhaps, because of the difficulties implicit in any approach that uses more than one level at a time.

Nonetheless, Karl Bühler's theory eventually led to a better understanding of communication processes. It differentiated among symptoms, signals, and representations. Symptoms are behaviors that can be objectively studied on the level of the individual. Behavioral psychology concentrates mainly on symptoms (K. Bühler, 1927/1965).

Signals are behaviors that carry meaning for at least one other individual. The effect of signals can be studied on a functional level. Objective identification of behavior on the symptom level is a prerequisite. However, it does not translate directly to the level were one individual influences another individual by the use of signals. Ethologists used the signal level for their evolutionary approach. (K. Lorenz took part of his orals for his second doctorate with Karl Bühler.) System theorists introduced the concept of intention as a decisive criterion for functional analyses of mutual influences by means of signals (e.g. MacKay, 1972). Func-

Empirical work was generously supported by Deutsche Forschungsgemeinschaft, grants Gr 299/9 and Gr 299/11.

124

tional psychology concentrates mainly on (intended) effects (K. Bühler, 1927/1965).

Bühler's third level was concerned with interpretation, with meaning per se. Data without interpretation are useless. Communication without (phylogenetically or ontogenetically determined) intention is also useless. The meaning, in the theoretician's mind, is purposive in the sense of Tolman. If an infant has a sad face and cries (symptom) he may get his mother or father to console him (signal) in order to overcome his stress and reestablish happiness and exploratory spirits (purpose linked to theoretical interpretation).

1.2. A bridge between Bühler's theory and Ainsworth's standardized observation

The method presented here uses all three levels at once. On the symptom level it first identifies "actions" shown by infants (§ 2.2). Similar actions, however, may lead to different consequences, and different actions may lead to comparable consequences. Therefore, on the level of signals, the method is designed to evaluate the functional effects of infants' signals on their mothers or fathers (§ 2.4). The interval between the onset of an action and the identification of a consequence is called a sequence (§ 2.3). The sequence defines the basic unit of analysis. During a sequence the infant may show expressive behaviors, which may (signal) or may not (symptom) affect the person present (§ 2.5). With the present method an attempt is made to identify gestures (§ 2.5.1), facial expressions (§ 2.5.2), vocalizations (§ 2.5.3), as well as overlapping modes of expression (§ 2.5.4).

We are convinced that any observational method in the area of social communication has an implicit meaning. A method is usually inspired by a certain theory – for example, that any emotional expression may become a signal that together with its elicit response is imbedded in the meaning or quality of a given relationship. Consequently it is tailored to fit a certain purpose. The "meaning" behind our method is presented in § 2.6, where Karl Bühler's influence may perhaps be most clearly noticeable.

The purpose of the present method was to achieve a better understanding of what happens between infants and their attachment figures in Ainsworth's so-called Strange Situation (§ 1.5). We concentrated particularly on those episodes where reunion took place between infants and their mothers after two brief separations from the mothers. In one of our studies we were forced to label about two-thirds of forty-nine 12-month-old infants as "insecurely attached" (§ 1.6). Therefore, we re-analyzed attachment research (§ 1.3) in terms of its narrow view and its wider view (§ 1.4). This, in turn, led to a reconsideration of Ainsworth's Strange Situation. The purpose was to capture the wider view of attachment (§ 1.7). Our results are encouraging. We were able to show, using our method, that some infants not only avoided parents physically when they were emotionally most insecure, but also stopped communicating with them as a consequence of separation stress. The breakdown of showing and communicating inner conflicts may perhaps be another step toward understanding the development of relationships (§ 3 and 4).

1.3. Attachment research

The Strange Situation (Ainsworth, Blehar, Waters, & Wall, 1978) was developed as a validating instrument for extended observations of 23 mother–infant dyads throughout the first year of life. The observations were based on Bowlby's (1969, 1973) theory of attachment. One basis of the attachment concept is the emphasis on its phylogenetic origin. It is considered to be a need of any infant to become attached to some figure(s). As a consequence of Ainsworth's influencial research, attention has shifted from nonattached infants under severe social deprivation (Harlow, 1971; Spitz, 1945) to the quality of attachment as a developmental result of the attachment figure's behavior in response to the infant's signals.

Ainsworth's first comprehensive observations were made in Uganda. The reports revealed a wealth of data gathered in the best tradition of ethology. Complex observational data, however, do not fit easily into meaningful patterns. The difficulty of integrating the many detailed observations was documented in Ainsworth (1967). Nonetheless, there was, at the end, an impressive working basis, which eventually became very influential in infancy research.

The main consequence of Ainsworth's heuristic conceptualization of her observations of infant–mother interactions was the now famous Baltimore study (Ainsworth, Bell, & Stayton, 1971). Observations in 23 families were made every 3 weeks throughout the first year, 4 hours each time (i.e., 64 hours in each case). No ready method for capturing the essence of interaction was available then. Ainsworth's ethologically oriented research was aimed at the discovery of organizational concepts. The meaning of different styles of togetherness had to be teased out of the narrative reports written about the Baltimore observations. One robust aspect of the infant–mother relationship became clear: the infants' signals "as related to the mothers' responses." The resulting descriptive assessment system was called "sensitivity versus insensitivity to the babies' communications" (Ainsworth, Bell, & Stayton, 1974).

There were, of course, many noticeable aspects other than maternal sensitivity or insensitivity. Something important, however, is to be learned from the conceptualization of this overriding concept. It is a global variable, indeed. It assesses the ability of a mother to notice her infant's communications, to interpret them correctly, and to respond to them appropriately and promptly.

Noticing a baby's signals has two aspects. The mother must be available to the infant before she has an opportunity to notice his signals. If she is available, she may either ignore intentionally some specific communications, or she may, in general, have a high threshold and respond only to very obvious signals and not to the more subtle ones.

The ability to interpret an infant's communications correctly has three essential components: the mother's attention to the baby's communications, her ability to see the communications without distortions, and her empathy. *Empathy* means to see and to feel states and intentions from the baby's point of view. Frequently a certain egocentrism on the mother's part may lead to remote intellectual reactions instead of empathy with the baby's emotions (Ainsworth et al., 1974, pp. 127ff).

Grossman (1977, pp. 96ff) introduced Ainsworth's assessment system of sensitivity to a German readership. He explained that this was not a scale in the traditional sense, but a careful description of complex behavioral events for each of the five anchor points. The scale, in fact, contained everything important for those who had already carefully worked through the existing material. The scale was the result of a great effort to conceptualize a large number of qualitative descriptions of complex forms of interactions and relationships.

There have already been descriptions of and diaries about infants, such as those of Pestalozzi and Jean Paul, as well as E. Willard in Boston. The most famous one, by Tiedemann, was published in 1787. By about 1800 the movement had lost its impetus. According to C. Bühler and H. Hetzer (1929) the most likely reason was that no one knew how to use the observational information. The art of introducing order into a multitude of facts is not easy. Any meaningful interpretation places even heavier demands on the creative scientific mind (Grossmann, 1983a; Grossmann & Grossmann, 1984). In this light, Ainsworth's convincing conceptualization of sensitivity to the baby's signals was a real breakthrough.

1.4. Attachment and interaction: a narrow and a wider view

Attachment behavior occurs when the attachment system is activated. Through sensitive responses the infant learns that his signals are understood, that the attachment figure is reliable and predictable and a source of easing emotional distress, particularly through bodily proximity when this is most needed by the infant. Sensitivity is defined by perception, correct interpretation, and prompt and appropriate response to the baby's signals (Ainsworth et al., 1974).

Attachment theory conceptualizes the emotional consequences to the infant when the primary attachment figure is insensitive, unavailable, and uncooperative. The narrow view concentrates on infants' responses to separation. Securely attached infants seek tender bodily closeness during reunion; insecurely attached infants, in contrast, show avoidance or ambivalence (§ 1.5). The narrow view of attachment looks at the symptoms in Karl Bühler's sense (§ 1.2), whereas a wider view of attachment attempts to explore the full spectrum of interactions that characterizes a relationship. It concentrates on the quality of mutual signals and control (Bowlby, 1969, chap. 13).

The narrow view of attachment as a hypothetical construct is based on Bowlby's conception that the phylogenetic origin of attachment is the mother's protection of the infant. Inge Bretherton (1980), in her discussion of young children in stressful situations, calls it Model II, in which attachment is mediated by interaction and is concerned with protection and close bodily contact. It is often seen in a stressful context where one attachment figure, usually the mother, is of highest priority to the baby. Smith (1980), however, found no biological evidence for the assumption that a special bond to only one significant other is the phylogenetically selected way of accomplishing protection from predators. To him it appears to have been rather a group enterprise: A limited number of significant others with different degrees and qualities of significance usually protect the infants as well as the mothers. Psychologically the parents, however, do much more. The psychological parental investment has been aptly analyzed from an inclusive fitness point of view within the frame of sociobiology, recently by Porter & Laney (1980).

Parental investment into the psychological development of the child via a dynamic stability of growing relationships is a necessity for survival in the social group. The social and psychological fitness of the child as a human being depends utterly on the messages carried within relationships. The Swiss biologist Adolf Portmann (1956) named the infant's psychological prematurity during the first year of life the "extrauterine prematurity" (*Extrauterines Frühjahr*). At the end of this period, when infants finally reach the maturity that other primates have already reached at birth, the child has acquired three specifically human abilities: standing upright, the fundamentals of social communication, and the beginnings of goal-oriented thinking, encapsulated in Piaget's notion of object permanence. The infant is physiologically born too early, because the infant's brain growth does not permit any later birthdate, but instead of simply waiting outside the uterus to reach physiological maturity, the infant learns intensively to communicate. This is called Model I by Bretherton (1980), in which attachment is conceived as interaction, and interactions can vary qualitatively and in terms of contents across situations and between partners.

Infants learn rules (Bruner, 1972, 1978); they learn social signals (Ainsworth

& Bell, 1974). The wider view of the attachment concept has to do with those aspects of signal interchanges that develop into relationships of certain qualities. The basis of our attempts to understand relationships (Hinde, 1979) is the interactors' expressive behaviors and the message they carry.

The wider view of the attachment concept provides an observational orientation as well as an empirical conceptualization, which is the actual major breakthrough of Mary Ainsworth's work. It has established a certain confidence that such complex ongoings as "sensitivity" (§ 1.3) can be reliably observed, recognized, and qualified. This level of orientation, which owes much to a number of outstanding ethologists, provides the frame for searching for the contents of the wider attachment concept – without losing sight of the narrow attachment concept – by using measurement strategies of emotional expression.

1.5. Attachment and the Strange Situation

The validity of the effects exerted by more or less sensitive mothering was assessed by a standardized observational procedure called the Strange Situation (Ainsworth & Wittig, 1969). The Strange Situation consists of eight episodes designed to show infants' use of their attachment figures under increasing separation stress – in particular, infants' abilities to use their mothers as a secure base for exploration and play and as a haven of security when they are distressed. The Strange Situation procedure also reveals the differences between mothers and strange persons in their success in consoling emotionally distressed infants. Each of the eight episodes is 3 min long, but if the infants are under noticeable distress, an episode may be curtailed. The sequence of episodes is as follows: (1) The attachment figure (mother) and infant are introduced by the researcher into a nicely furnished playroom. (2) The researcher leaves, and the mother and infant stay together for a while. (3) A friendly, but unknown person enters and slowly attempts to establish contact with the mother and infant. (4) The mother then tries to leave the room without interrupting the infant's ongoing behavior. (5) She returns and the unfamiliar playmate leaves the room. (6) The mother and infant stay together. (7) The mother leaves again and her infant remains alone. (8) The mother then returns, and the second reunion is observed.

Infant behaviors are traditionally coded on the basis of 7-point scales as follows: proximity-seeking behavior, proximity-maintaining behavior, resistance to proximity, avoidance of proximity. In our experience, the application of the avoidance scale is to be learned very carefully by anyone applying this procedure.

Infants' behavior patterns are traditionally classified as follows. Those who tend to avoid their attachment figures, particularly during reunion in Episodes 5 and 8, have been labeled A. Those who easily establish contact and tender bodily proximity have been termed B. Those who show ambivalent behavior and alternate in an unpredictable manner between approach and resistance have been termed C. After the introduction of video recording techniques, Main (1981) found a number of infants who did not fit into the three main patterns. They were termed NTC (not to classify) by Main and Weston (1981) and 0 by us. We strongly emphasize that this is not a classification of the infant per se, but of the infant's interactive and relationship patterns toward a specific attachment figure in the Strange Situation. Independent data have shown that different patterns are usually shown by the same infants toward their mothers and toward their fathers (Grossmann, Grossmann, Huber, Wartner, 1981; Main & Weston, 1981).

The Strange Situation, in our view, focuses more on the narrow view of the attachment concept than on the wider view. The Baltimore observations during the first year, in contrast, do not (Ainsworth 1971). Maternal sensitivity was observed at home during the first year. Quality of attachment was classified in the Strange Situation in Ainsworth's study on the basis of the infants' tendencies to seek and to maintain close, tender bodily proximity after mild separation stress. The correlation between high maternal sensitivity in the first year and the mothers' function as a secure base validated the Strange Situation as a research instrument. This correlation, however, has so far been demonstrated only for infants whose mothers differed greatly in their ability to notice their infant's signals and to respond to them appropriately as well as promptly (Grossmann, Grossmann, Spangler, Suess, & Unzner, 1985). The Strange Situation, in our view, does not automatically qualify as a suitable instrument for assessing the wider view of the attachment concept. It is neither a test nor an experiment (Grossmann et al., 1981). It is one of a number of research tools designed to help us understand the inherent emotional and social qualities experienced by infants during their primary socialization. When carefully used, the Strange Situation has been shown to produce meaningful data in a variety of contexts.

We believe, however, that the Strange Situation should be used cautiously as a "method," a research tool, as if it were "the operationalization" of attachment sui generis. The Strange Situation per se is neither a representation of the attachment concept in general nor a representation of all aspects of the mother–infant relationship. Any new research perspectives must eventually produce suitable assessment methods. Attachment research and its ethological orientation, however, are still much more suitable than other approaches to the discovery and construction of a more complete picture of a wider concept of attachment.

1.6. Some unexpected findings

In our North German study, we classified a high percentage (about two-thirds) of infants as "insecurely attached" using the original Ainsworth criteria. Although superficially this result may confirm certain prejudices about a stern German way of child rearing, there was actually no basis for such an interpretation. First, in another sample of 50 mother–child pairs in southern Germany most infants at 12 months (almost 60%) were classified as "securely attached" on the basis of the same criteria. Second, in our North German sample (Grossmann et al., 1985) maternal sensitivity scores for mothers whose infants showed the A relationship in the Strange Situation were not nearly as low as for the mothers in Ainsworth's study. The overall difference in sensitivity scores, although significant, was not quite as impressive as in Ainsworth's research. In addition, in infants 10 months of age, maternal sensitivity was no longer significantly related to the attachment classification of the infants. Therefore, it was our intention to widen the set of criteria used for assessing the infants in the Strange Situation.

1.7. Consequences: capturing the wider view

The fact that at 10 months of age maternal sensitivity did not correlate with the way infants behaved in the Strange Situation according to Ainsworth's classification criteria called for an explanation. We offer two. The first is that maternal expectations for a child of 10 months are different from those at 2 and at 6 months (for a discussion of this explanation see Grossmann et al., 1985). The other explanation concerns the nature of the encounters between infants and their mothers at 12 months and fathers at 18 months. What did they actually do, particularly if so many of them were classified as "insecurely attached" on the basis of Ainsworth's criteria (§ 1.5). We asked ourselves, How do infants who initially avoid their parents after brief separations reestablish interaction?[1]

We concentrated, first, on the expressions or signals of the infants. Gestures, facial expressions, and vocalizations are central to the interactions. We have already indicated that we were guided by Karl Bühler's model of communication. Bühler's (1927/1965) differentiation into *symptoms* (the expression of inner states of feelings), *signals* (the attempt to excert control and social interaction), and, after language development, *symbols* is helpful here (§ 1.2). To repeat, any behavior can, in principle, be a symptom of an internal state or state changes such as feelings. Symptoms become signals if they convey a certain meaning for others; if this happens they are usually responded to by others. Karl Bühler spoke of mutual control as early as 1927. Signals become symbols if they stand for something else and if they develop a special meaning for the people involved in such interactions and communications.

The 12-month-olds in Ainsworth's Strange Situation were judged to be insecurely attached if they failed to establish and maintain close bodily proximity with their primary attachment figure. However, some expressive behaviors may have become distal signals for togetherness and psychological security. Tinbergen & Tinbergen (1972, p. 50) have criticized the tendency to underrate the bond-maintaining effects of fleeting and distant contacts that we observed in many children of our study when their mothers or fathers returned after brief separation in Episode 5 or 8 of the Strange Situation.

The task of the measurement of emotions in infants and children, then, is a multiplex and multileveled enterprise:

1. What do infants feel in the Strange Situation? How can we identify their emotional expressions and in what way should they be interpreted?
2. What is the effect of infants' expressive behavior under the circumstances studied? How do infants' expressed emotions correspond to their orientations as expressed by their gestural activities?
3. Is close bodily contact after stress the only indication for a secure relationship? Ainsworth has clearly shown that in the Strange Situation avoidance amounts actually to a child's tendency to withhold expressive signals from the attachment figure (i.e., to put on a poker face). Can this in a different culture be compensated for by more distant forms of communication?
4. Does "suppression" or absence of facial or vocal signals in itself serve as a signal for the attachment figure (or any other interactor for that matter)?

These are only some of the complexities that confronted us when we tried to measure infants' expressive behavior in the Strange Situation. Ethology, however, gave us some means of probing infants' expressive behavior by reexamining a well-founded incompatibility in infants' behavior: If they are psychologically insecure, they do not explore or play as well as when they feel well. Ainsworth's data, Mary Main's work (1977, 1981), as well as our own research show a clear decrease in exploration and play as the stress increases with succeeding episodes in the Strange Situation, particularly during the absence of the attachment figure.

For the purpose of preparing the reader for the complexities of our procedure a brief look at Episode 5 of the Strange Situation (§ 1.5) might be helpful. The mother returns after a maximum of 3 min absence. The strange person leaves on the mother's entrance. The mother and child stay together for 3 min, after which the mother leaves again after reassuring her infant that she will be back soon. The traditional difference between securely and insecurely attached children is whether or not the infants establish close bodily contact with their mothers as they reenter at the beginning of the episode. If the mother is a secure base for the child, the child is securely attached to her. She removes the psychological insecurity that gave rise to the activation of the attachment system. Thereby the exploratory system, which was inhibited by the excitation of the attachment system, can express itself again.

Consequently, we concentrated on finding symptoms of insecurity, stress, or well-being under the assumption that the Strange Situation does not actually stress all children equally and that under mild distress distal communications may be sufficient for reestablishing security. Admittedly, quite often as we sat before the video screen, we had to rely on the mind's capacity to integrate a complex set of signals into a meaningful gestalt (Izard & Dougherty, 1980).

Some mothers seemed to prefer contact via distance signaling; their vocalizations were as friendly as those of the other mothers. We do not yet know whether any lack of facial expression is characteristic of an identifiable group of German mothers, as Main, Tomasini, and Tolan (1979) have found for U.S. mothers. Some mothers easily establish a joint attention structure with their children on objects. Facial expression, under these conditions, is often neutral; that is, there are no codable facial movements. The voice, however, is often animated, commentating, and less often soothing. Our tentative impression, initially, was that we may be dealing with two intermingling interactive processes: the role of the mother as a secure base and the role of the mother in focusing the infant's attention on extradyadic events.

2. Method for evaluating infants' communications to their attachment figures after two brief separations in Ainsworth's Strange Situation

The method to be introduced here was developed for a sample already reported in the literature (Grossmann et al., 1981). Our main interest in developing the method was instigated by our finding that only 16 of 49 German children had been classified B on the basis of Ainsworth's original criteria. This was only 33%, as compared with the usual range of 60% and 70% in various U.S. samples. In contrast, 24 infants (49%) were classified A, 6 classified C (12.2%), and 3 classified 0 (6.1%). Our attempt to assess the wider view of the attachment concept resulted in the questions and measures listed below.

2.1. Questions and measures: an overview

The following questions were to be answered by our re-analysis of Episodes 2, 5, and 8 of the Strange Situation:

1. How do infants reestablish interaction after two brief separations?
2. What role does the mother (parent) play in initiating new behavior sequences?
3. How are objects used in this situation?
4. What role does the infant's expressive behavior play in reestablishing contact?
5. What kind of interaction actually occurs?
6. Is there a relationship between what the child does, the social consequences, and the expressive behavior of the child?
7. Is the interactive process of children classified avoidant different from that of children classified nonavoidant?

The method involves keeping a continuous descriptive account of three converging measures called actions, sequences, and consequences. The activity of an infant is observed until there is a consequence brought about by this action. The consequence defines the end and the length of a sequence. When the action of the infant changes and/or when there is a new consequence, a new sequence starts. Each of these behavioral units, called a sequence, is categorized according to the kind of social interaction the pair is having. Five categories emerged: (1) direct communication, (2) joint action with an object, (3) joint attention structure, (4) unsuccessful approaches, and (5) parallel attention structure. In analyses other than those reported here we subdivided category 3 into two, depending on who was active and who was only passively onlooking. In still another analysis we subdivided category 4 into clear avoidance and disorientation of the infant, and we noted in category 5 whether the infant was monitored while both infant and adult maintained their independent parallel attention structure (§ 2.45). Such adaptations of the method follow the material available and the questions to be answered.

An additional measure, expressive behavior, is designed to assess the emotional quality of the interaction during a given sequence. This measure is derived from a number of sources. Emotional expression has been asserted to ''represent complex systems of organized functioning inherent in the human person which are useful to the individual and by implication, advantageous to the species'' (Emde & Gaensbauer, 1981). Emotional expression is undoubtedly complex, and a number of factors come into play, but since this is a descriptive method, we concentrated on obvious overt expressions in the child. Three kinds of emotional expression or lack of it were assessed: facial expressions, vocalizations, and bodily gestures.

The measure of facial expressions were derived from the Maximally Discriminative Facial Movement Coding System (Max) of Izard (1979) and a system for identifying affect expressions by holistic judgments (Affex) developed by Izard & Dougherty (1980). With open observational procedures such as the Strange Situation many of the carefully developed patterns of facial expression analysis systems, however, are simply not applicable. Any method such as ours, therefore, has to strive to make the best of what is actually given. Therefore, only clear facial expressions were identified.

2.2. Actions[2]

At each moment the child is occupied in some way. This activity is coded. Gestures, facial expressions, and vocalizations are an additional information source and are noted separately (see § 2.5).

Two general categories of action are distinguished: The child is either oriented or unoriented. Orientation can be toward an object, mother, father, or the stranger. The following descriptions of the codes explain how the actions have been differentiated and noted in the presence of the mother.[3]

2.2.1. Orientation toward mother[4]

OM 0 (OM 0): *to turn away/to avoid*

The child clearly turns away from the mother without a change of location. He turns his head in another direction, goes away, crawls around (but does not locomote), leans away, looks away, and so on. Turning away or avoiding should be clearly identifiable as a solitary action. There should also be the impression that the child wants no contact with the parent or that he clearly wants to avoid the parent. The child does not reorient from one thing to another; rather he is first occupied with turning away.

OM 1 (OM 1): *to turn toward without moving toward; no eye contact*

The infant looks in the direction of the parent but does not change his own location. There is no eye contact between infant and mother. When it is impossible to determine whether the mother looks at the infant or whether there is eye contact because of technical reasons, this forced omission is noted.

OM 1* (OM 1*): *to turn toward without moving toward; eye contact*

The child is oriented toward the mother for longer than 3 sec, and within this time eye contact is established. This eye contact may be shortly interrupted by moving of the head or something else.

OM 2 (OM 2): *to turn and move toward*

The child is oriented toward the parent and, through a change in position, tries to reach the parent. Actions intended here include walking, crawling, or sliding to the parent.

OM 3 (OM 3): *to touch*

The infant orients toward the mother and shortly establishes body contact with his hands. The infant touches the mother's arm or leg.

OM 4 (OM 4): *body contact*

The infant's objective is to establish body contact, and he maintains the contact for a longer time, for example, in order to be comforted. The infant could cling to the legs of the mother because he wants to be picked up.

BC (KK):   *body contact not initiated by the infant*

Body contact is noted when the mother initiates contact, for example, when she takes the infant's hand or when the infant looks at a toy while sitting on the mother's lap. When the mother physically helps her infant to a goal, this action is distinguished from body contact. Body contact can sometimes occur by accident, for example, when the mother touches her infant while he plays intensively.

EC (AK):   *eye contact*

When there is eye contact during a sequence for less than 3 sec, it is noted along with the ongoing action.

2.2.2. Orientation to an object

OO 0 (OG 0):   *to turn away/to avoid*

The infant turns away from an object without being immediately reoriented. This turning away should clearly be seen as an action in itself. Such actions could include pushing or throwing an object away or turning and going away from an object. (Throwing a toy can also be an interesting game by the infant and would be appropriately coded as OO 5. This is an easy distinction to make.)

OO 1 (OG 1):   *to turn toward/to look*

The infant is oriented toward an object, for example, a toy, door, camera, or table. The criterion is the direction of the infant's gaze. The position of the infant is unchanged, and the action is defined by the infant turning or bending his head forward.

OO 2 (OG 2):   *to look and move toward*

The infant is oriented toward an object and changes his position in order to reach the object. For example, he walks, runs, crawls, or slides to the object.

OO 3 (OG 3):   *to touch, to seize, to grasp*

The infant is oriented toward an object and somewhat hesitantly touches or takes the object into his hand without handling it. Perhaps the infant picks up an object and carries it to another place but does not play with or handle the object.

OO4 (OG 4):   *simple handling*

The infant grasps an object and handles it without becoming absorbed in the play. The infant does not look very long at the object. He explores the object – for example, shakes a toy, puts it in his mouth, pushes it around, and so on.

OO 5 (OG 5): *play manipulation*

The infant plays intensely with an object and looks at it constantly. The difference between simple handling and manipulation should be seen by the increase and intensification of handling in manipulation. This difference is often difficult to determine. A deciding factor for manipulation is steady, concentrated optomotor coordination.

2.2.3. Orientation toward mother with an object

SO M (ZG M): *to show an object*

The infant holds an object high toward the mother and wants her to pay attention to it.

GO M (GG M): *to give an object*

The infant gives an object to the mother, and she takes it. It is important to note that this action begins when both infant and mother are oriented to the object and ends when the mother has taken the object.

TO M (NG M): *to take an object*

The infant takes an object from the mother. The beginning and end of this action are treated as in GO M.

HO M (HG M): *to help the infant*

The infant has a goal, for example, getting out of a rocking horse or getting on a toy car. The object or goal is the center of attention, and the mother is a helper. Body contact is not noted separately, because this action is included in the assistance.

2.2.4. No special orientation. When an infant is unoriented, his behavior is coded through the following actions:

LA (US): *to look around*

The infant looks around and is undirected. He searches for a new orientation or surveys his surroundings. The infant may turn his body by stretching or sitting down, but he does not change his standing place. The infant shows no goal-oriented behavior but is not absolutely passive. When the infant looks around for longer than 3 sec, this is considered a sequence (see § 2.3). When the infant looks around 3 sec or less, this action is noted in the ongoing sequence.

WA (UG):   *to walk or crawl around*

The infant not only looks around, but changes his position. He is not yet directed toward a new goal; rather he searches for a new goal. There is often the impression that the infant is uncertain, for example, does not yet know what he should do.

MF (BF):   *to move around for fun*

The infant moves about with no special orientation but simply for the fun of moving about. There are no indications of uncertainty, but of enjoyment of the gross motor activity.

2.2.5. Additional rules for coding. The infant can be oriented to more than one object during a sequence when these actions do not last more than 3 sec. Each action is then consecutively noted in the sequence, for example, OO 4/LA/OO 3/OO 1.

Different actions with the same object or the parent are noted one after another, for example, OO 2/5 or OM 2/4. The different actions are considered a subroutine to the entire sequence because the point of orientation is the same.

The actions of looking, touching, and handling an object (1, 3, and 4) are implied in the action manipulation (OO 5) and need not be coded sequentially. In contrast, locomotion is not implied in the other actions and therefore must be coded separately. Only when a subroutine is very long must it be coded separately. This manner of coding is used to differentiate whether the child has handled many objects or whether he has only performed several actions with the same object.

All actions are coded in the following fashion:

1.   OM (0–4): orientations toward the mother[5]
2.   OO (0–5): orientations toward objects
3.   SO M ⎫
     GO M ⎪
     TO M ⎬ orientations toward the mother with an object
     HO M ⎭
4.   LA ⎫
     WA ⎬ no special orientation
     MF ⎭

2.3. Sequences: definitions of beginnings and ends

There are three ways in which a sequence can begin. First, the child begins a new action, as defined in § 2.2. This new action must last longer than 3 sec to qualify as a new sequence. When the action is shorter than 3 sec, the ongoing sequence itself is not interrupted; the new, short action is noted within the on-going sequence.

Second, a new sequence can start when an ongoing action leads to a new consequence. This is a case where the new sequence is not defined by the action. There is a new sequence because there is another consequence. When a consequence changes for less than 3 sec, there are two rules. Either the short change of consequence only interrupts an ongoing sequence or, if the consequence before the short change was different from the following consequence, the changed consequence becomes the beginning of the next sequence.

Finally, a new sequence begins when the action and consequence simultaneously change for longer than 3 sec. An exception to the rules for the beginning of a sequence occurs when the action of the child – even when it is longer than 3 sec – is clearly recognizable as a component of an ongoing sequence. The result of this action belongs to the activity of the child. For example, a child plays with a doll, interrupts this action to get a bottle, and then continues to play with the doll by "feeding" it with the bottle. Or when the infant goes to pick up a toy to give to the parent, this action, even when longer than 3 sec, is considered part of the entire action of giving a toy to the parent.

In summary, a new sequence begins when the infant changes orientation or when a new action is shown, when the form of interaction or social consequence has changed, or when action and consequence change together. The new sequence must last at least 3 sec.

2.4. Consequences

Consequences are defined by dyadic interactive behaviors and grouped into five categories. The categories describe the interaction as it occurs in behavioral sequences.

2.4.1. Category 1: direct communication.
Direct communication between parent and child occurs through looking or speaking. There is a direct exchange between the two. Although an object can be present, the object plays no role in the communication. The direct signals from one are answered by the partner in a reciprocal manner.

Direct communication also occurs when the partners play social games, for example, tickling, playing peekaboo, or bouncing and riding on the parent's knee. The two are primarily involved with one another; they communicate directly through their play.

2.4.2. Category 2: joint or alternate play with an object.
The parent and child do something together with an object. The object is the center of their commu-

nication. Alternate play is also considered doing something together. The parent and child alternately play with the same object, and the stopping by one is a signal for the other to continue. This creates contingent behavior. The interest of the parent and child is focused on the object, and their playing together occurs via the object.

2.4.3. Category 3: joint attention structure on an object or event without joint action. The attention of the parent and child is focused on the same object, and this attention is indicated by observable and/or audible occurrences. The partners communicate about the object, but no joint activity is observed. The object is the focus of their interest, attention, and communication.

The parent's interest may be shown by his or her comment about the child's toy or by changes in the parent's gestures or facial expression. When the two manipulate the same object but do not play together, the sequence is assigned to this category. In this case the behavioral contingency present in Category 2 is absent.

2.4.4. Category 4: actions that lead to no recognizable reaction (attempted signaling with no resulting social interaction or unsuccessful approaches). An action of the child is labeled an unsuccessful initiative if it characteristically elicits a response as seen in the first three categories but remains unattended by the mother. Examples of such approaches are looking around, walking around, orienting toward the mother, or showing something to her.

The mother does not react to a potential invitation or opportunity to participate. Nothing in the mother's behavior can be recognized by the observer as contingently connecting to the infant's activity.

Certain unanswered approaches by the mother are also included in this category. When she appeals directly to the infant through calling, body contact, or showing or wanting to give an object, this is considered an unsuccessful approach by the mother.

2.4.5. Category 5: Independent activity by parent and infant (parallel attention structure). Category 5 includes two situations. In the first, the mother and the infant are focused on a different object or look in different directions. They take no obvious notice of what the other is doing. In the second, the mother observes the infant playing without participating in the play or without showing any active interest. This is coded M^0 (or F^0 for the father). Each of these situations can be the beginning of a new sequence, as determined by the consequence of a behavioral sequence.

2.4.6. Mothers (MI) or fathers (FI) as initiators. In uncertain or difficult instances, the appropriate category for a sequence can be determined by eliminating unlikely categorizations. This means asking oneself which categories the sequence could *not* be placed in.

In order to decrease the conflict in deciding about the placement of a sequence in the correct category, one should remember that the interaction of contingent behavior between the partners in Categories 1, 2, and 3 is absent in Categories 4 and 5. For a consequence to qualify for Category 1, 2, or 3, a contingent reaction by the partner must be recognizable through the partner's facial expression, gestures, vocalizations, or a combination of these. For additional observations and other notes, another column is provided in our coding sheet. For example, it may be important to know what object is being used or to explain the placement of an unusual case into a category.

Certain actions are assigned to distinct categories. Giving and accepting are placed in Category 2. Showing something to a child and helping the child are placed in Category 3. When it is clear that the parent is the initiator of a sequence, this is noted in the additional column as MI or FI. Otherwise, the infant is defined as the initiator of the sequence.

In our coding sheets, there is one column for each of the categories listed above. Actions (§ 2.2) and expressive behavior (§ 2.5) are listed in the appropriate column for any given sequence.

2.5. Expressive behavior within sequences

When the infant moves about freely, it is not always possible to identify each expression of the face and the gestures. The infant's vocalizations, however, are more easily identified. The predominant expressive behavior in each sequence is therefore noted. Analysis of expressive behavior aims to assess the infant's interest, enjoyment, mood, and general participation as compared with the infant's withdrawal, uncertainty, lack of interest, lack of participation, and reduced expression. Because vocalization is such an important means of communication, it is also important to understand how the infant's vocalization is related to the type of interaction between mother and child. And, concerning the primary question, information about expressive behavior may provide insights into the process of reestablishing contact by avoidant (A) infants.

2.5.1. Gestures

S (S): *self-manipulation*

This gesture is most often a combination of an infant's uncertainty and embarrassment. The infant manipulates his own body or clothes or manipulates his body with an object. The infant may so react, for example, when the parent offers a new toy and when the infant is unsure. The infant may bend his head, tug at his fingers, and laugh in an embarrassed way. Other self-manipulations include putting fingers or a pacifier in the mouth, pulling at clothes or hair, or slowly twisting the body or head.

SM (BS): *stereotypic movement*

Stereotypic movement is characterized by rhythmic, slow, repetitive, monotonous motion. There is an impression of listlessness, not feeling well, or uncertainty and a lack of expression of interest or enjoyment. Stereotypic swinging, rocking, letting an object dangle, bending it back and forth, or turning it up and down are examples of stereotypic movements.

ERM (FRB): *enjoyable, rhythmical movement*

This movement accompanies the infant's enjoyment in playing with a toy or playing with the parent. Active, pleasurable swinging, waving, shaking, and bouncing are examples. The enjoyment is also expressed in the face and through vocalizing. ERM is to be differentiated from moving around for fun (MF, § 2.2.4).

ARM (ARB): *active, rhythmical movement*

This movement is fast and rhythmical, just as enjoyable, rhythmical movement is, but excitement plays a larger part than enjoyment. Delight is not expressed. The infant's fast arm movements, handling, shaking, and pounding accompany his excitement and concentration.

TM (AB): *tense lack of movement*

The infant remains in a particular position for a short time. The muscles of the face and the body are tense. The infant is for the moment taut or strained as a result of surprise, uncertainty, interest, or fear.

IH (UH): *indecisive handling*

The difference between superficial and concentrated play is partially distinguished in simple handling (OO 4) versus manipulation (OO 5). Uncertainty and indecisiveness often accompany superficial play, and these feelings can be seen in the infant's undetermined gestures. The infant often changes toys and moves somewhat indecisively. There is no interest in playing.

2.5.2. Facial expression. The free arrangement of the individuals involved in the Strange Situation cannot be confined for the purpose of continuous recordings of facial expression. Therefore, only the predominant facial expression is coded here. Many difficulties are involved in scoring facial expression from videotapes of infants who move around freely. Even photographs judged by blind raters may be influenced by the context. Izard's (1979) Maximally Discriminative Facial Movement Coding System (Max) has been rather helpful, particularly in determining any given infant's neutral face, which consists of smooth forehead, brows in resting position, eyes normally open, and mouth closed and relaxed. For a number of facial gestalts we were able to establish satisfactory reliability by making confident use of Ekman and Friesen's (1975), Izard's (1979), and Gaensbauer's (1982, 1980) helpful descriptions, as well as Oster's (1978) fine work.

In Episodes 5 and 8 of the Strange Situation we most often find the following facial expressions: interest, joy, neutral (very often), insecure, and insecure–questioning (brows slightly raised, corners of the mouth drawn downward, and sometimes more clearly raised archlike brows, the rest of the face being un-moved), mixed feelings, and conflict. Several feelings are present at the same time or in brief succession, for example, an expression of the mouth between smiling and laughing, mouth movements (e.g., trembling), slight muscle activity of the cheeks, instability of the looking response, and so on. Discontentment is also very frequent. It is indicated by lowered brows and furrowing of inner parts of the nasal bridge. Rarely, anger, seldom fear, rarely sadness, and sometimes skeptical distrust are expressed, the last by brows slightly raised, lips pressed together with slightly thickened cheeks, upper lips slightly over lower lips, and a cry face.

N (N): *neutral* (normal, expressionless, relaxed)

The neutral face shows no muscle tension. It is not possible to recognize a positive or negative feeling. Such a face occurs in situations where one would actually expect a change from a neutral expression but the neutral face remains. It is difficult to recognize the neutral face and easy to confuse the neutral face with the "hypothetical interest" face. Each child has an individual neutral facial expression, depending on the form of the head, cheeks, mouth, and other facial parts. One should be sure that the child shows no flexing of the muscles in the face. In Izard's Max system, the neutral face is described by $\left(\begin{smallmatrix} 0 \\ 0 \\ 0 \end{smallmatrix}\right)$.

E (F): *enjoyment, joy* (friendly, delighted, interested, excited, laughing, amused, beaming)

The infant's positive mood shows in his face, primarily through the position of the mouth. The corners of the mouth are pulled upward according to the intensity. The mouth is opened or closed. The eyes become smaller from laugh lines or larger from shining. The mouth span for the positive mood of enjoyment is large. Different intensities of enjoyment are not distinguished; only whether there is an expression of enjoyment is coded. Izard codes joy $\left(\begin{smallmatrix} 29 \\ 0 \\ 52 \end{smallmatrix}\right)$.

INT (INT):   *interest–concentration* (interested, attentive, goal-oriented, explorative, questioning, concentrated, serious, testing, exerting)

An infant's interest can be shown by two different facial expressions: an interested, open face and a tense, concentrated face. The interested face is characterized by a neutral or slightly open or hanging mouth. Depending on the intensity of the interest, the brow region is raised in a normal shape. The eyes become larger. Additional tension in the face is recognizable. Gaensbauer's (unpublished manuscript) affect ratings for interest served as a good training instrument.

U (Uns):   *uncertainty* (uncertain, indecisive, questioning, unsure)

The child is in a situation in which he does not know what to do or how to react. This can lead eventually to confusion. The corners of the mouth are clearly turned downward. In this position, the mouth can either be closed or slightly open. The brows are in a neutral position or slightly or clearly arched. The impression is of a questioning, unsure face. The child seems to ask "What shall I do now?" "What are you doing there?" Uncertainty can be reliably coded.

D (U):   *dissatisfaction* (dissatisfied, having misgivings, reluctant, unfriendly, serious, glum, inactive, reproachful)

The mouth is normal in appearance, somewhat tense or pulled downward. The brows are drawn in toward the nose. The nose is slightly turned up. A negative feeling is clearly recognizable. The infant would like to express, "I don't want to," "What have you done there?" or "I don't feel well."

S (S):   *skepticism, distrust* (skeptical, critical, distrustful)

The infant is confronted with a situation he does not completely trust. In no way does he appear to be uncertain. The upper lip hangs slightly over the bottom lip, the cheeks appear to be slightly inflated, and the chin is somewhat wrinkled. The infant forms a snout or presses the lips together. The mouth is widened from side to side and somewhat pulled together in a downward configuration. Small creases in the chin and cheek area appear. The brows are slightly questioningly arched or shifted quite high above the eyes, or they are pulled slightly in toward the nose. The nose can be pulled slightly upward.

F (A):   *fear*

The mouth appears rather widened and hangs down slightly. The brows are drawn inward and upward. There are wrinkles in the forehead. The deciding factor of the brows is in the eye region. The mouth can remain in a neutral position. It is described in Izard's Affex (Izard & Dougherty, 1980, pp. 15–65) and coded in the Max system $\left(\begin{smallmatrix} 24 \\ 0 \\ 24 \end{smallmatrix}\right)$.

G (T): *grief–sadness* (sad, troubled, worried, fearful, whining)

The face in this category covers a wide spectrum, from the beginnings of sadness to the beginnings of crying. This also includes a mood of sadness that does not increase in intensity. The mouth is drawn downward, and the corners hang or are distorted. The brows are drawn inward and upward together or raised quite high above the eyes. Slight wrinkles in the forehead are possible. Eventually the cheeks become somewhat inflated.

ME (GG): *mixed emotions*

An emotion such as fear or dissatisfaction is seldom expressed with total clarity. Hiatt, Campos, and Emde (1979) found that emotions, especially negative feelings, are more often expressed in blends. So this category indicates negative emotion and the expression of more than one emotion in the face – for example, fear combined with uncertainty or dissatisfaction combined with sadness.

2.5.3. Vocalizations

V (Bgl): *commenting while playing*

Sounds that accompany an infant's actions are often short and unrelated to one another. The sounds emphasize the actions of the infant and often indicate the infant's interest in playing. The sounds cover a large spectrum of vocalizing and may overlap with more specific vocalizations. The category can be considered a catchall for sounds that cannot be placed in any other category.

All short, one-syllable sounds from soft to loud and from low frequency to high frequency are placed in this category. The sounds can be loud, whispered, melodic, affectionate, and so on. All tones that fall, rise even to a scream, stay at a monotone level, but are still one syllable and are not connected to one another are considered commenting sounds.

E (E): *explaining or telling sounds*

The sounds constituting this category are long, continuous, and related. They are intensive and cover a wide spectrum. They often go up and down, but they may also follow one another at the same frequency level. The deciding characteristic of telling sounds is that there is more than one syllable and that the syllables belong together and follow one another. It is as if the infant wants to explain something.

C (K): *contact sounds* (calling sounds, questioning sounds)

These are monosyllabic sounds that rise in inflection. Generally the voice is somewhat high pitched. Sometimes it is like a short call that does not rise in pitch or a questioning sound: "hum." A contact sound can be friendly or demanding.

N (Ben):   *naming objects*

The child uses a word to name a person or an object, for example, *teddy, doll, mommy,* etc. When the naming is unclear, the vocalization is recorded as a commenting sound V (Blg).

Da (da):   *"da" sound*

The child is oriented, and a "da" is clearly identifiable. Intensity and situation are variable.

S (Q):   *squealing sounds*

Squealing is a high, shrill, pressed, very intense sound. The duration of the sound is variable, from short, pressed squealing to longer-lasting squealing. These sounds vary little in pitch and intonation. They may be shouts of joy or expressions of happiness and are noted here for their particularly shrill quality.

A (AL):   *sounds of effort*

These are tight, voiceless sounds eventually joined by panting and groaning. The infant exerts himself because he would like to achieve a goal. For example, the infant pushes something heavy away and emphasizes his effort with these sounds.

P (H):   *panting*

Panting is a strong, loud rhythmic breathing.

B (Sch):   *emphasized breath*

A breath is clearly stressed. The infant inhales and intensely exhales. The exhalation is often longer than the inhalation. It can be a breath of relief or a breath resulting from especially concentrated play. It is not panting, because more rhythmic, steady sounds do not occur.

E (F):   *enjoyment, delight*

Pleasure can be shown by chuckling ("he-he-he"), laughing, gurgling while inhaling, rejoicing, shouting for joy, and so on. These are intensive sounds in a higher than normal voice range and express positive emotions.

DI (U):   *dissatisfaction*

Dissatisfaction is expressed vocally through intense, short, constricted utterances that tend to become longer. The sounds can be angry, voiced sounds ("m-m") or monosyllables that come deep from within ("m . . ."). Dissatisfied sounds can also be soft, and listless.

2.5.4. Overlapping modes of expression

C (W):   *crying*

Crying is clearly seen in the facial expression as well as in the vocalization.

P (P):   *passivity*

Passivity can be observed as either an action or a gesture. The child's passivity is often striking. The child may appear to be focused on an object or takes a long look around but does not react to suggestions offered by the parent. The child appears to be completely introverted, somewhat absent minded, and unwilling to participate. Facial expression is neutral, and the child makes no vocalizations. Passivity is noted as part of a sequence.

2.6. Application: the meaning behind the method

The method we have presented here attempts to assess the complex signals of the infant together with his attachment figures on different levels: actions, consequences, and expressions.

There are a variety of possibilities for further evaluation of the data obtained by the application of the method. The obvious question, as mentioned before, is directed toward the quality of togetherness. In addition to the criteria developed by Ainsworth, which aim essentially at the bodily availability of the attachment figure and therefore concentrate on the signal system leading to close bodily proximity, our qualitative process analysis is designed to explore alternative ways of communication.

We are convinced that the application of a method such as ours can be learned only in a steady back and forth analysis between video events and transcripts. This is because the method is based on highly differentiated perception and interrelated definitions of several different conceptualizations of a multiplex communication process (determining actions, consequences, expressions, and integrating them into sequences). Our method evolved as a result of many months of tedious work, during which we experienced the truth of the statement that "one always oscillates from the essential to the accidental, from the universal to the individual" (Carus, 1808; Grossmann, 1983a). Learning any such method for the purpose of application implies learning concepts that are not necessarily represented by simple bits of behavior on the level of pointer reading operationalism. Instead, to learn "to see more than any nurse" (K. Bühler, 1925; Grossmann, 1983a), one has to realize that knowledge from observation depends on two things that have to come together: "the context of the psychological consideration and the exactness of the observation" (K. Bühler, 1925, p. 33). It is not easy to see the relationship and consequences of the mutual social influences behind the interactions and signals on the video screen. However, the danger of not "seeing" anything meaningful is greater than the danger of seeing too much in it. The latter can eventually be corrected, whereas having no insights never leads to anything. The great lesson learned from Ainsworth's concept of sensitivity is her success in paving the way toward assessing the quality of social relationships in order to understand emotional development.

Episode 2 of the Strange Situation was used in our case to establish a kind of baseline or reference behavior before any separation had occurred. In Episode 2 the infants were in the process of becoming acquainted with the room and toys. Episode 5 is the first reunion between infant and mother after a maximum of 3 min of separation. Episode 8 is the second reunion after the second separation, again a maximum 3 min. As in Ainsworth's original study, the method centered on the infant. However, by definition of the social consequences categories, the mother's behavior in conjunction with the infant's actions was also assessed. The identification of the parent's initiatives (MI or FI), furthermore, helped us to determine the contribution of each of the two partners to a certain social consequence.

2.7. Inter- and intraobserver reliability

For the purpose of testing the reliability of the method, videotapes were randomly drawn from all the 12- and 18-month-old infants' Strange Situation recordings. The first control check concerned the time structure of the sequences (see § 2.3). Pair comparisons between any two transcripts of seven videotapes were done. The sequences were considered congruent if they corresponded with a maximal deviation of only a 1-sec difference. The total number of corresponding sequences was compared to the total number of sequences noted by the two evaluators jointly. The upper part of Table 6.1 indicates inter- and intraevaluator reliabilities. The interevaluator reliabilities ranged from 65% (Pl/Sc, Transcript 1) to 78.5% (Be/Pl, Transcript 2). The intraevaluator reliabilities ranged from 80% (Transcript 1, Sc) to 95% (Transcripts 1 and 2, Be).

The reliabilities for corresponding sequences were not satisfactory. R. Ernst (1984) analyzed another sample of 50 18-month-olds in episodes 2, 5, and 8. She subsequently trained two other raters, D. Hollrotter (in preparation) and U. Frings (in preparation). For 10 different videotapes they established higher reliabilities for corresponding sequences: Fr/Ho, 86%; Fr Ho/Er, 86%. Subse-

Table 6.1. *Inter- and intraevaluator reliabilities based on seven video transcripts*

	Interevaluators			Intraevaluators		
Agreement	Be/Pl	Pl/Sc	Be/Sc	Sc	Pl	Be
Corresponding sequences						
Transcript 1	74.5	65	70	80	93	95
Transcript 2	78.5	72	76	83	93	95
Categories	89	79	79	92	91	98
Actions	94	95	92	90	93	96
Gestures	97	94	90	100	96	100
Kind of gesture	100	100	93	100	96	100
Facial expression	86.5	90	90	98	92	98
Kind of facial expression	81	91	94	92	92	100
Vocalization	96.25	89	90	98	95	98
Kind of vocalization	91	81	81	80	94	95
Frequency of vocalization	76.5	69	81	88	93	93
Frequency of eye contact	96	98	99	92	91	100
Frequency of body contact	99	96	99	93	100	100
Average	87.3	85.2	86.2	86	93	96

Note: Numbers represent percentages.

quently, all of the videotapes rated by rater Pl were scored again, and the new data were used for comprehensive analyses of a total of 198 Strange Situations (K. E. Grossmann, R. Ernst, U. Frings, and D. Hollrotter, in preparation).

In the next step the categories, actions, and expressions were compared. If the sequences (Table 6.1) showed a systematic time lag, the categories, actions, and expressions still could be reliably coded, that is, independently computed by the conventional formula: twice the number of agreed entries divided by the total number of entries. Gestures and facial expressions were checked twice to determine whether they had been entered into the transcript at all and whether there was agreement. In addition to the checks noted above, vocalizations were controlled for frequency. Finally, the additional entries for eye contact, body contact, and parents as initiators were compared. The lower part of Table 6.1 shows the interevaluator as well as intraevaluator reliabilities for various categories. Whereas it is not especially difficult to identify actions and gestures, the comparatively high reliability percentages for facial expression and kind of facial expression are due to the fact that we restricted ourselves to the predominant facial expression within any given sequence (see § 2.5.2).

3. Results

3.1. Classification of infants according to mood, play, signaling, and self-initiated body contact

The following aspects entered into the pattern definitions:

1. Play behavior as an indicator of the infant's well-being (Main, 1973, 1977)
2. Expressive behavior as an indicator of the infant's emotions
3. Signals, for example, individual expressions, person-directed signals, inclinations toward mother (or father)
4. Body contact, initiated by the infant, along the lines of Ainsworth's ratings of proximity-seeking and contact-maintaining behaviors (Ainsworth et al., 1978)

There were four main patterns (Table 6.2). Each pattern was subdivided, depending on the preponderance of objects without the attachment person's participation or with the attachment person's participation.

3.1.1. Behavior pattern 1.
The infants' play is concentrated and coordinated; they have high spirits and vocalize cheerfully and continuously. If in addition to their many play-related expressions (e.g., commentary while playing) the infants communicate only a little to their mothers, this behavior is called Subpattern 1a. Subpattern 1b implies that the infants address their mothers through gestures, facial expressions, and vocalizations or by showing and giving objects. The mothers appear to be important to them; the infants want to include them.

3.1.2. Behavior pattern 2.
The infants show brief faces of insecurity and negative feelings, but initial difficulties in establishing a state of well-being are rapidly resolved. Thereafter the infants play well and vocalize cheerfully. Subpattern 2a means that the infants hardly address their mothers directly, whereas Subpattern 2b implies direct communication, including negative feelings.

3.1.3. Behavior pattern 3.
The infants express longer lasting difficulties in adapting to the situation. They change their mood often but manage to overcome their gloomy mood only slowly. Their level of play declines; they play only a little and not well. They seem insecure, show mixed feelings, and may remain passive and mute, with a neutral (poker) face. Recovery is slow, but eventually the infants recover. Subpattern 3a implies that the infants do not display their misery to their mothers directly, whereas in Subpattern 3b there is direct communication.

3.1.4. Behavior pattern 4.
The infants are unhappy during the entire episode; they do not overcome their negative mood. They hardly play, do not communi-

Table 6.2. *Distribution of infants according to behavior patterns*

Behavior pattern	Episode 2			Episode 5			Episode 8		
	BC	No BC	n	BC	No BC	n	BC	No BC	n
1a	—	AA BB A B	6	—	AA AA	4	—	—	0
1b	—	AAA BBB C AAA BBB AA BB 0	18	BB BB	A B	6	—	AA A	3
2a	—	AA B AA AA	7	—	AAA B AAA AA	9	B	AA AA AA	7
2b	B C	A B	4	BB BB	AAA B AA	10	BBB BBB BB	AA AA AA	14
3a	—	AA A 0	4	—	AA AA	4	—	AA A	3
3b	C A C	B C B 0	7	B C	A B 0	6	BB C B	A 0	6
4a	—	A A	2	—	A	1	—	AA AA	4
4b	—	—	0	B	C C C 0	5	A BB BB	C 0	7
Σ	4	44	48	17	28	45	20	24	44

Note: Behavior patterns were subdivided with respect to no direct communication with mothers (a) and direct communication with mothers (b) in Episodes 2, 5, and 8 of the Strange Situation (See text for a description of the groups). An infant can show one behavior pattern in Episode 2 and another one in Episode 5 and still another one in Episode 8. Within each episode infants are grouped again with respect to body contact (BC). The symbols A, B, and C refer to the classification of infants on the basis of the traditional Ainsworth criteria; 0 represents infants who could not be classified (NTC).

cate, and cry a great deal. In Subpattern 4a the infants are passive and do not show any direct communication even when their mothers try to make contact with them. In Subpattern 4b the infants show their feelings directly but seemingly do not benefit from it.

Since the general mood of an infant determines the behavior pattern he shows, with increasing stress an infant may show one behavior pattern in one episode and another pattern in another episode. Thus, the infants are not classified according to the total behavior as the Ainsworth method prescribes; rather, in our method the changes in the behavior patterns of the infants in the course of the Strange Situation (here, over Episodes 2, 5, and 8) are documented.

Table 6.2 differentiates between infants who seek proximity and bodily contact (OM 3, OM 4) or who signal clearly toward their mother and are consequently picked up (OM 1, plus crying), that is, with the mother complying (BC), and those infants who do not gain bodily contact (no BC). This, of course, is in close agreement with Ainsworth's major classification criteria (Ainsworth et al., 1978).

Table 6.2 contains symbols for each infant's attachment classification according to Ainsworth's system. Group B infants are classified as securely attached. Group A infants represent the avoidantly attached infants, and Group C infants represent the anxiously attached infants. Infants represented by 0 could not be classified (NTC).

For Episode 2 the behavior patterns of 48 infants are shown. In Episode 5 two infants could not be properly analyzed because of videographic deficiencies. For one infant the Strange Situation had to be terminated before Episode 5 ($N = 45$). Before Episode 8 the Strange Situation had to be terminated for one additional infant ($N = 44$). Those infants whose behavior resulted in termination of the Strange Situation showed Pattern 4 by definition.

There is a general decline in mood and play intensity. Statistical tests reveal significant changes between Episodes 2 and 8, but not between Episodes 2 and 5. Only three infants showed Pattern 1 in Episode 8, as compared with 24 in Episode 2. This is in line with data reported by Ainsworth et al. (1971). In Episodes 5 and 8 many infants reflected some emotional difficulties and some initial impairment of their play after the first separation. Many of them, however, managed well; that is, they showed Pattern 2. Statistical tests applied to all four patterns revealed significant changes between Episodes 2 and 8, but not between Episodes 2 and 5. If only Patterns 1 and 2 were compared, significant changes were revealed between Episodes 2 and 5 as well as between Episodes 5 and 8.

Our re-analysis also differentiated between infants who directed their signals to their mothers and those who did not. Subpattern b of each of the four major patterns in Table 6.2 represents those infants who communicated with their mothers by eye contact, vocalization, and so on. Subpattern a of each major pattern represents those infants who looked only briefly when their mothers returned after a brief separation but who then concentrated on objects and most often did not display any personal signals. In Episode 2, 29 infants showed Subpattern b (i.e., direct communication with their mothers), 27 in Episode 5, and 30 in Episode 8. No direct communication was shown by 19 infants in Episode 2, by 18 in Episode 5, and by 14 in Episode 8. No significant changes in terms of direct or indirect communication with the mothers were observed between Episodes 2 and 5; only 8 infants changed their behavior pattern from Subpattern a to Subpattern b between Episodes 2 and 8, and 2 changed from Subpattern b to a.

There was no significant correlation between mode of communication and behavior patterns according to mood and play. This precludes making any inferences of the infants' well-being in the Strange Situation from their mode of communication with their mothers.

3.2. Comparison with Ainsworth's classifications

Twenty-four infants were classified A on the basis of the original Ainsworth criteria, 16 were B, 5 were C, and 3 were 0 (i.e., unclassifiable). Since the original purpose of our method was to find out whether the infants who had shown the avoidant pattern in the Strange Situation were to be considered generally insecure, we concentrate here on comparing the avoiders (A) with the nonavoiders (B). For this purpose we neglect the ambivalent (C) and nonclassifiable (0) infants.

In terms of mood and play there were no significant differences between the Group A and Group B infants (Table 6.3, upper half). There was, however, a slightly larger proportion of Group B infants who changed from the "good mood" Patterns 1 and 2 to the "poor mood" Patterns 3 and 4, as compared with the Group A infants.

In terms of directed signaling, however, a new picture emerged (Table 6.3). Twelve of 16 Group B infants, but only 10 of 24 Group A infants, showed direct communication in Episode 2. In Episode 5, 13 of 14 Group B infants, but only

Table 6.3. *Distribution of Group A and B infants according to mood and play patterns and mode of signaling*

Group	Episode 2		Episode 5		Episode 8	
	Good mood and play	Poor mood and play	Good mood and play	Poor mood and play	Good mood and play	Poor mood and play
A	18	6	18	6	15	9
B	14	2	11	3	9	7
	Episode 2		Episode 5		Episode 8	
	Signaling not direct	Signaling direct	Signaling not direct	Signaling direct	Signaling not direct	Signaling direct
A	14	10	17	7	13	11
B	4	12	1	13	1	15

7 of 24 Group A infants, communicated directly. And in Episode 8, 15 of 16 Group B infants did so, versus 11 of 24 Group A infants. Again, this confirms the notion that under stress all Group B infants are oriented toward the mother. For the Group B infants, however, it is not only "close bodily proximity" in the narrow view of the attachment concept that seems to be important here (the Group A infants, it should be recalled, do not establish close bodily proximity). Instead, this demonstrates the emergence of a communication system that allows for a free exchange of emotions by establishing a meaningful rapport on the basis of involvement and togetherness. This mutual control (K. Bühler, 1927/1965) is well developed by infants classified B. Many infants classified A, however, show a similar pattern of direct communication, although they do not combine it with close bodily contact. This was true for 11 of 24 Group A infants in Episode 8.

No Group B infants stayed away from the mother when their mood was poor. In contrast, the Group A infants tended not to emit person-directed signals (Table 6.3). Seven of 9 Group A infants who were in poor emotional condition did not get involved with their mothers at all in Episode 8, but 9 of 15 did when they were still cheerful.[6] In general, infants classified B communicated their gloominess directly to their mothers; many Group A infants did not. When the Group A infants felt well, some were able to communicate, although not as many communicated as the Group B infants did (12 of 24 in Episode 5, but only 6 of 25 in Episode 8). Nine Group A infants were still in good spirits in Episode 8 and maintained personal contact throughout; that is, they played intensely and in a coordinated manner, expressed no signs of distress, and vocalized or looked at their mothers often. For them the Strange Situation did not seem an unusual or highly stressful situation. The most conspicuous result, however, confirming Ainsworth's notions, was that infants who were not well off ceased to communicate with their mothers.

3.3. Sequences and social consequences

We next explored the interdependence of the infants' actions and the social consequences. There were typical behavioral patterns: Some infants acted independently. Their mothers observed them occasionally or did something else. Other mother–infant pairs were mainly in Category 3 (i.e., joint attention structure; see § 2.4.3). Their mothers participated in, commentated, and encouraged their infants' play behavior. They also responded to their infants' signals. A third pattern, shown only by a few infants, consisted of continuous change between independent activity (Category 5; § 2.4.5) and joint attention structure (§ 2.4.3).

Pattern I, then, was termed "leaning toward independence": Infants and mothers showed a parallel attention structure (Category 5), or the infants were watched by their mothers without any observable communicative participation. There were

Table 6.4. *Number of infants in Patterns I–III*

Pattern	Episode 2	Episode 5	Episode 8
I	33 (68)	18 (40)	8 (18)
II	7 (14)	5 (11)	7 (15)
III	8 (16)	22 (48)	29 (65)

Note: Numbers in parentheses are percentages. See text for a description of Patterns I–III.

also cases of "unwanted" independence. These infants often signaled in their mothers' direction or looked around (LA), but the mothers did not respond. These unsuccessful approaches (§ 2.4.4) were rare, however, and occurred most often in Episode 2.

In Pattern II the infants (a minority) played independently as well as in joint attention structure with their mothers. In Episodes 5 and 8 (after brief separation) the infants briefly communicated directly, but then they alternated continuously between Categories 3 and $5/M^0$ (§ 2.4.5). The mothers let their infants play alone, but they made it clear that they were "with them."

In Pattern III the infants predominantly established a joint attention structure with their mothers. Other categories (direct communication, joint attention structure, unsuccessful approaches, and parallel attention structure) rarely occurred.

Across the three episodes the patterns changed impressively (Table 6.4). Independence was shown by only 8 infants in Episode 8, as compared with 33 in Episode 2. Pattern III, predominance of joint attention structure, was shown by 29 infants in Episode 8, as compared with only 8 in Episode 2. This, again, is in line with the results of Ainsworth et al. (1971), which demonstrated the increasing stress exerted by the Strange Situation procedure. The number of infants whose behavior corresponded to Pattern II did not vary greatly across episodes. Eleven infants changed from Pattern I to Pattern III in Episode 5, and 21 changed from Pattern I to Pattern III in Episode 8. Only one infant changed from Pattern III in Episode 2 to Pattern 1 in Episode 8. The patterns reported here were independent of the Ainsworth classifications A, B, C (or 0). The Group A and B infants, however, interacted differently with their mothers before and after separation. More infants classified B changed to pattern III sooner (in Episode 5) than infants classified A: 54% of the Bs, as compared with 25% As. In Episode 8, 62% of the As, but 83% of the Bs, showed Pattern III. These differences are statistically significant.

We then turned to the question of whether infants' actions were related to social consequences. Of course, this was not taken to be a causal relationship. The purpose of the social consequences aspect of our method was to assess the

Table 6.5. *Distribution of infants according to Patterns I–III*

Behavior pattern	Episode 2				Episode 5				Episode 8			
	I	II	III	n	I	II	III	n	I	II	III	n
1a	A BB / B	A	A	6	A / A	—	A / A	4	—	—	—	0
1b	AA BB / AA BB / 0 BB	A B / A B	A C / A	18	A / A	B / B	BB	6	A	A	—	3
2a	AA B / AA / A	A	—	7	AA / AA / AA	B A / A	A	9	A / A / A	A / A	—	7
2b	B / B	—	C A	4	A / A	B A / A	A BB / A BB	10	A B	B	B AA BB / AA BB / AA BB	14
3a	A / A / A	—	—	4	A / A	—	A / A	4	A / A	—	A / A / A	3
3b	A B C / B 0	—	C / C	7	B	0 / 0	A B C / C C / 0 C	6	A B C / B	B / 0	A B C / B	6
4a	A	—	A	2	—	—	A	1	—	—	AA / AA	4
4b	—	—	—	0	—	—	B C C / 0 C	5	—	—	A BB C / BB / 0	7
Σ	33	7	8	48	18	5	22	45	8	7	29	44

Note: See text for an explanation of Patterns I–III.

results of different communication styles in dyads classified as securely or as avoidantly attached. The evaluations presented here are based on the hypothesis that there is a connection between the history of a dyad and the range of social consequences observed. There is no conceivable way to keep the mothers' behavior constant. The history of the two members of the dyad would defy any such attempt (Stolberg, 1981).

Table 6.5 summarizes our results. Body contact was omitted because it is part of the identification of the A and B patterns of Ainsworth. Statistical analysis of the data summarized in the table yielded the following results:

1. More infants with poor mood/play (Patterns 1 and 2 vs. 3 and 4) exhibited – in Episode 8 – Pattern III, predominant joint attention structure, and more infants with cheerful mood showed – in Episode 8 – Pattern I, independence.
2. More infants who communicated directly with their mothers (Subpattern b) showed – in Episode 5 – Pattern III, predominant attention structure, and more infants who showed expressive behavior predominantly while playing with toys showed – in Episode 5 – Pattern I, independence. In Episode 2 most infants showed Pattern I, and in Episode 8 most infants showed Pattern III (Table 6.5).
3. Mood, expression, and behavior patterns were significantly affected by the Strange Situation in Episode 8. Most infants showed Pattern III (predominant attention structure) by then and communicated directly with their mothers (Subpattern b). Infants classified C had, as expected, poor mood, direct communication, but only joint attention structure as a social consequence.
4. Infants classified A or B showed independence (Pattern I) if they were in a cheerful mood; joint attention structure (Pattern III) was related to cheerful as well as poor mood. Infants alternated between independence and joint attention structure (Pattern II) only if they were cheerful (Patterns 1 and 2 vs. 3 and 4), independently of their A or B classification. The hypothesis that security of attachment (B) was unrelated to mood/play in social consequences had to be accepted for all three episodes of the Strange Situation (Table 6.6). This statement, however, is of limited validity, since it does not pay attention to the body contact established by the Group B infants. Body contact, of course, must be taken into consideration because, on a merely empirical basis, it occupies part of the time filled by other social consequences for those infants who do not establish body contact. (The theoretical implications are discussed later.) This finding, in view of the fact that the majority of infants were classified A, is as important as the fact that these infants differed greatly from infants classified B in terms of direct communication with their mothers (see Table 6.3).

In summary, our method revealed that among the infants classified A as well as B most were cheerful, played in a lively manner, and signaled openly to their mothers in Episode 2. In Episodes 5 and 8, after brief separations, however, some infants classified A remained toy-oriented, passive, and withdrawn. The infants classified B, in contrast, continued to signal directly, particularly if their mood was poor.

The joint attention structure, achieved by infants classified A as well as B, came about for different reasons, as the following analysis revealed.

Table 6.6. *Number of Group A and B infants showing various behaviors according to their interactive behavior patterns (I, II, and III)*

	Episode 2						Episode 5						Episode 8					
	I		II		III		I		II		III		I		II		III	
Group	Good mood	Poor mood	Good mood	Poor mood	Good mood	Poor mood	Good mood	Poor mood	Good mood	Poor mood	Good mood	Poor mood	Good mood	Poor Mood	Good mood	Poor mood	Good mood	Poor mood
A	10	5	4	0	4	1	10	2	3	0	5	4	6	0	4	0	5	9
B	12	2	2	0	0	0	4	1	1	0	6	2	2	0	1	1	6	6

Note: "Good mood" denotes cheerfulness and joyful play behavior. "Poor mood" denotes gloomy mood and listless play.

3.4. Further analysis of behavior patterns of Group A infants after brief separation

In Episode 5 the mothers returned after a maximal absence of 3 min. Their infants had been with the friendly stranger. They returned again after a second brief absence of a maximum of 3 min in Episode 8. Their infants had been alone during the preceding Episode 7.

Infants classified A according to Ainsworth's criteria did not initially show direct bodily contact or even proximity-seeking behavior. In fact, they scored high on active proximity avoidance but low on contact resistance. Active proximity avoidance is difficult to recognize, because it gives the impression – for some infants at least – that they were not affected by the brief separation from their mothers. As described earlier, however, there is a noticeable impairment of their mood and play behavior, as well as changes in their mode of communication.

Proximity avoidance, nonetheless, is not typical for the entire 3 min of each of the episodes. Many infants classified A did in fact establish eye contact with their mothers immediately and displayed personal communicative gestures, mimicking, and vocalizations such as joy, interest, and negative mood. Some infants hesitated and showed avoidance for a while with the neutral face. Only a few infants kept up their passive, avoidant behaviors with no expression for the entire 3 min.

Furthermore, many mothers initiated first contacts if their infants did not show any intention of doing so themselves. As our records showed, the mothers talked to them, commented on the toys, or tried to stimulate the infants to play. Objects played an important role with both partners. After separations, with only one exception, there were always some signals between mother and infant, which resulted in direct communication, joint action, or joint attention structure.

On the basis of our method we concentrated on three aspects in order to judge the actual development of interactive events in Episodes 5 and 8 among infants classified A:

1. Who initiated the first contacts: mother (M) or infant (I)?
2. How did initiation occur (eye contact, person-directed expression, body contact initiated by mother [M] or by means of objects [O])?
3. What kind of interaction occurred during the course of Episodes 5 and 8 (independent play [IN], joint attention structure ([JA], etc.)?

Schematically this resulted in the diagram shown in Figure 6.1. In Episode 5, 10 of 22 infants initiated interaction, and 12 of 22 mothers did so. Only 4 infants and no mother presented objects. In Episode 8, only 6 of 23 infants initiated interaction, but 17 of 23 mothers did so. No infant presented objects, and only 2 mothers did so. In Episode 5, 14 of 22 infants showed some indepen-

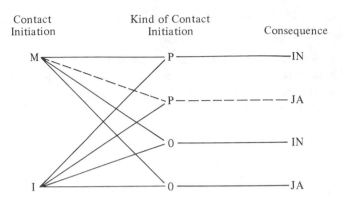

Figure 6.1. Schematic representation of the grouping of infants classified A in terms of what eventually constituted togetherness after initial avoidance of the mothers by the infants. With good mood, all possible combinations occurred (solid lines). With poor mood, however, the following combination occurred predominantly: The mother initiated contact by personally addressing her infant and establishing joint attention structure as a consequence (dashed line). M, mother; I, infant; P, person; O, object; IN, independence; JA, joint attention structure.

dent play behavior, but only 10 did so in Episode 8. Joint attention structure was predominant in Episode 8, particularly when the mothers had initiated interaction.

When the infants were in good spirits (Patterns 1 and 2), any combination shown in Figure 6.1 actually occurred. In contrast, when their mood was gloomy (Patterns 3 and 4), the sequence indicated by the dashed line in Figure 6.1 dominated. In both Episodes 5 and 8, contact was initiated by the mother (M) with calling the infant, commentaries, and occasional body contact. Joint attention structure was a consequence. This was true for 11 of 14 infants with poor mood.

3.5. Additional data

3.5.1. Intensive play. Intensive play, including goal manipulation and concentrated optomotor coordination (OO 5; see § 2.2.2) was shown by 39 of 48 infants in Episode 2, by 35 of 47 infants in Episode 5, and by 29 of 45 infants in Episode 8. The average duration of intensive play (OO 5) was 47.8 sec in Episode 2, 39.14 sec in Episode 5, and 32.42 secs in Episode 8. This is another clear indication of the distress resulting from the two separations.

There were as many Group A as Group B infants who showed intensive play. In contrast, only one infant classified C and only one infant classified 0 showed intensive play. The range for Group A and B infants was between 63% (A 1 in Episode 8) to 100% (A 2 and B 3 in both episodes). The duration of intensive play, however, was significantly shorter for infants classified B than for infants classified A. In Episode 5 infants classified A 1, A 2, B 1, and B 2 played between 70 and 78 sec intensively; those classified B 3, however, played for only 43 sec. In Episode 8 the numbers were as follows: A 1, 74.5 sec; A 2, 70.16 sec; B 2, 35.12 sec; B 3, 24.66 sec; $p \leqslant .001$.

3.5.2. Mothers' initiatives. Mothers' initiations increased significantly to an average of 3.04 in Episode 5 and 3.2 in Episode 8 as compared with 1.64 in Episode 2. The social consequences of our method were always due to the mutual interaction in a specific situation and, presumably, to the history of the relationship between mothers and infants. Mothers of infants classified C most frequently initiated a sequence: 3.4 times in Episode 2, 5.3 times in Episode 5, and 5.5 times in Episode 8. The mothers of the five infants classified B 3 seldom initiated in Episode 2 (0.5) but often initiated in Episodes 5 (5.0) and 8 (4.5), as compared with A 1 ($N = 19$: 1.47, 2.57, 3.15), A 2 ($N = 5$: 2.2, 3.4, 2.2), and B 2 ($N = 10$: 1.4, 1.9, 2.8).[7] These numbers, however, tended toward, but did not reach, statistical significance.

3.5.3. Joy and negative feelings. Expressions of enjoyment were coded from faces and voices. They were treated equally, particularly when the infants' faces were not seen but when their joyful utterances were clearly recognized. Facial expressions without vocal sounds of joy were coded separately. Of 48 infants, 23 did not show any signs of enjoyment in Episode 2, 12 showed facial expression (E), and 13 showed facial as well as vocal delight. In Episode 5, the numbers were 25, 12, and 10, respectively, and in Episode 8, 27 did not show any signs of enjoyment, 10 showed facial expression (E), and 8 showed facial as well as vocal delight. Twelve infants did not show any joy, in their faces, their voices, or their gestures.

In Episode 5 significantly more infants classified B expressed enjoyment, particularly through vocalization ($p \leqslant .05$). Infants classified A restricted their expression of joy to facial expression, but most of them did not show much of it. Only one child classified C showed some joy in Episode 2.

The average number of joyful utterances in all three episodes was 0.79 for infants classified A, 2.43 for B,[8] and 0.4 for C. The infants not classified showed 2.6 joyful utterances on the average.

3.5.4. Crying. Fourteen infants cried for some time at the beginning of Episodes 5 and 8, all 5 Group C infants cried, 7 of 16 Group B infants cried, but only 2 Group A infants cried.

3.5.5. Expression of distress. Many infants showed uncertainty (U), fear (F), skepticism (S), grief (G), and mixed emotions (ME), and they uttered dissatisfied, sometimes whining sounds (DI). These expressions increased from 10 in Episode 2 to 18 in Episode 5 and 26 in Episode 8. Twenty infants showed no sign of distress in Episode 2, but only 12 showed no sign of distress in Episode 8. Average frequencies in facial display and distress increased from 1.09 in Episode 2, to 3.2 and 2.51 in Episodes 5 and 8, respectively. Average frequencies of vocal display of distress increased from 2.5 in Episode 2 to 4.8 and 4.78 in Episodes 5 and 8, respectively. In Episode 8 infants classified B displayed more distress, facially as well as vocally, than those classified A, who restricted themselves to facial display.

The average frequency in all three episodes for dissatisfied utterances (DI) were .7 for Group A infants but 1.61 for Group B infants and an impressively high 5.92 for Group C infants.

Group B infants were generally more expressive than Group A infants of their well-being and enjoyment as well as of their distress. Group C infants did not display any signs of enjoyment, but instead showed great despair.

3.5.6. Neutral vocalizations (N). Most infants' neutral vocalizations decreased during one or both reunion episodes. Only seven showed any increase. In Episode 2 an average of 18.42 neutral vocalizations were coded, but only 11.84 in Episode 5, and 12.88 in Episode 8.

Five infants classified B 3 vocalized most in Episode 2 ($\bar{X} = 25.16$) and least in Episode 8 ($\bar{X} = 9.8$). Group B 2 infants remained constant (18.7, 17.8, 17.9). Group A 1 infants decreased from 17.84 in Episode 2 to 11.26 in Episode 8. Group A 2 infants changed somewhat in the other direction (8.8, 11.4, 13.0). Group C infants showed the most dramatic reduction: from 21.8 in Episode 2 to 6.3 in Episode 5 and 6.5 in Episode 8.

3.5.7. Delayed vocalization. Some infants were quite mute at the beginning of the reunion episodes (5 and 8). After some time, however, normal vocalization recurred. This seemed to be a part of the avoidant behavior pattern of Ainsworth's Group A. Statistical significance was obtained for Episode 5, where 14 Group A but only 3 Group B infants were silent during the first 10 sec after the mother's return. In Episode 8, however, only 5 Group A and 1 Group B infants still showed this pattern. In other words, only 5 of all 24 Group A infants did not "talk" to their mothers at all in Episode 8. Later analysis of the total sample of $N = 198$, however, revealed that Group B infants needed 18.08 sec in Episode 5 before vocalizing again, as compared with 14.59 sec for Group A infants ($p < .01$). This difference was obtained only because of one of four subsamples (Regensburg, 12 months) where the difference between B and A became significant in Episodes 5 ($p < 0.004$) and 8 ($p < 0.06$) (Frings, in preparation). Therefore, the meaning of delayed vocalization per se is not as clear as was originally assumed.

4. Outlook, evaluation, and discussion

4.1. Future directions toward understanding good quality of attachment as a developmental promoter of emotions, competence, and relationships

Originally, attachment research aimed at understanding developmental impairment as a result of insufficient mothering. The impetus came from clinical psychology, particularly from psychoanalysis. The methodology came from ethology. Conceptualizations were influenced by systems theory. New conceptualizations strive toward incorporating cognitive psychology as well. Ainsworth's empirical work has had an outstanding and justified reception in the scientific world. The Strange Situation has served as a validation procedure, aiming at the very core of the function of attachment. However, the adoption of this procedure as "the" operationalization of the concept of attachment per se implies a grave and dangerous misunderstanding. This misunderstanding is embedded in an unjustified tendency to treat instruments of search and discovery as if they were instruments of proof (Grossmann & Grossmann, 1984). The present method was an attempt to learn more about different strategies of infants who avoided their mothers after brief separations in the Strange Situation. We did not limit our method to just one (albeit utterly important) – strategy – namely, an infant's capacity to utilize his mother for emotional reassurance under stress from an unfamiliar situation and separation by seeking close bodily proximity with her.

The need for close bodily proximity to one specific person is a hypothesis derived from ideas about the phylogenetic origins of attachment. Smith (1980) has questioned the fixation to one person even in phylogenetic history. It is the use of signals that is being socialized toward cooperation and toward cultural knowledge (Grossmann, 1983b,c). Enforced independence may come about somewhat early for many infants, but it is not necessarily an indication of developmental impairment for most of them. Early demands do not automatically result in emotional disengagement, but they may do so if the balance between the resulting emotional conflicts and the mother's appropriate and prompt responses has not been properly developed.

Our analyses have provided insights into the particularities of relationships. These have been explored in a different sample in terms of empathy, relatedness, concerned attention (Main & Weston, 1981), obedience, play, and empathy. These findings will be reported soon.

The data reported here concern infants who are presently being observed and questioned and who will be tested again at 6 years of age in an ongoing longitudinal study. We have remained focused on both the "narrow" view with its emphasis on physical closeness under stress, as captured by the Strange Situation, and the "wider" view with its emphasis on the quality of the infant's overall relationship with his mother and other social resources available to the infant in general. For this the present method has provided an open and flexible basis.

4.2. Evaluation

The method has not enabled us to determine what actually dampens the direct person-to-person communication that is so conspicuous in the joint attention structure pattern (§ 2.4.3). What leads to the difficulties in direct and tension-easing communication can probably not be seen in the Strange Situation, but only in other everyday situations, which have to be analyzed from the perspectives of a wider attachment view such as implied by Ainsworth's maternal sensitivity concept (§ 1.4).

The following results will certainly influence our understanding of the quality of attachment in the German culture, where many people are not as openly expressive as in many parts of the United States:

1. Classification as Group B does not mean that an infant will have inquisitive and cheerful appearance after reunion with his mother. There was no correlation with mood and play groupings.
2. There were happy as well as unhappy infants classified both A and B, but they differed in how they expressed their feelings and how they addressed their mothers.
3. Infants classified A did not by definition establish bodily contact with their mothers (narrow view). Beyond this fact, however (wider view), some of them managed the Strange Situation rather well, and three infants did not display any indication of distress or impairment in mood and quality of play. Characteristically some of them ignored their mothers in Episodes 5 and 8, but some greeted their mothers and vocalized happily. Of course, there were also those who reacted with absolute passivity and remained expressionless after the separation, with mood and play very much depressed. Only the latter infants were close to the description of the avoidantly insecure (A) category found in Ainsworth's, Main's, Sroufe's (1984), Vaugn et al. (1979), Water's (1978), and others' publications.
4. Signaling was revealing. Distance interactions did not differentiate among the Ainsworth classifications (Ainsworth et al., 1978, pp. 99, 351–62). In our sample, analyzed by the method presented here, they did. Nearly all Group B infants were openly and directly involved in signal exchange with their mothers, particularly when they needed them badly. Group A infants were heterogeneous. When in a good mood, some remained concentrated on objects, and some engaged in direct communication. When in a poor mood, however, all Group A infants avoided direct communication. They were not well, but they did not overcome their passivity and depression. This may be the consequence of the very specific tendency of mothers to refrain from emotional involvement just when they are most urgently needed. In a play situation with our southern German sample analyzed by Escher-Gräub (1983), we found that this was par-

ticularly true for mothers whose infants had been classified A.[9] These infants may learn to close up whenever they feel left alone by a particular attachment figure. Luckily, this does not appear to be an aspect of the infant's personality at this age but an aspect of the relationship to the specific parent. We have seen many infants who were without expression toward one parent but who were happily engaged with the other parent (Grossmann et al., 1981).

5.   In general, signals directed to the mothers were dampened to a greater extent among Group A infants than among Group B infants. This was due to the passive and gloomy group of infants with the A relationship to their mothers. Other infants of this group were quite competent in their communications. Therefore, A classification in our sample seemed insufficient for an evaluation of the emotional security and stability of the infants in general. To use the term *insecurity of attachment* outside the context of the Strange Situation would be risky. Such a label would certainly be unfounded for our sample, and it has to be refuted on the basis of results generated by the method presented here.

The difference in signaling behavior among Group A infants gave support to an old assumption of ours: There were Group A infants who had managed well to keep up with their mothers' demands for independence, and there were those who suffered and tried hard to cope with their distress by avoiding any possible rejection of their emotional needs, as Main (1981) has so profoundly argued. We think that we have advanced yet another step toward understanding relationships: infants' avoidance of communication with their mothers when they need them most (see note 9). At 12 months, this is mainly, however, a matter of a relationship and not of infant personality (Grossmann et al., 1985). And, luckily, at this age there often are other partners available to most infants who clearly compensate for this lack of direct communication in particular dyads. For the purpose of further analyses the present method has been adapted to the analysis of an open-play situation, as well as to structured and unstructured family situations with 6-year-old children.

4.3. Discussion

The present method was developed to gain some deeper understanding of infants' response to repeated separation from their mothers in Ainsworth's Strange Situation. The Strange Situation was developed by Ainsworth as a standardized observational procedure to validate extensive home observations (Ainsworth & Wittig, 1969) in which she found differences in the way mothers responded to their infants' communications during the first year. Particularly, differences in tenderness as expressed by loving bodily proximity were impressive. These differences corresponded closely with the infants' behavior in the Strange Situation. Infants of sensitive mothers showed their affection and need for tender closeness directly, and they let the mother know immediately and directly when they were ill at ease emotionally. The infants' behavior patterns were even more impressive when they were compared with observations reported by Spitz (1945) and Bowlby (1969). Infants who had been separated for lengthier periods of time from their mothers first showed the pattern of despair, as the Group C infants did, and then, when the mothers had returned after several days or weeks, actively avoided.

However convincing this was for the original Ainsworth sample, it needed further validation. After all, the Strange Situation concentrated on a narrow view of attachment, whereas the whole concept, of which the Strange Situation was but one validating procedure, aimed toward understanding the social (Ainsworth & Bell, 1974), emotional (Main, 1981), and relational consequences of the early quality of attachment relationship. In this regard it would be unwise to constrict the rich theoretical and productively heuristic potentialities of the attachment concept by misinterpreting the Strange Situation classifications as the only measure of quality of relationship. In the meantime, evidence for a culture-specific pattern reflected by the Strange Situation classifications has accumulated (Bretherton & Waters, 1985).

In the present context, we have to limit ourselves to answering the question as to how our method can widen the perspectives of the multiplex interactional and relational events taking place in the Strange Situation (Hinde, 1981).

First, the method has generated much more information than is presented here. It is not biased toward any particular event but can be readily adjusted to any question under investigation. Our specific interest was in how infants who avoided their mothers after brief separation reestablished contact with them. The method also represents a compromise between fairly crude and fairly fine behavior categories. It is also flexible along this dimension. Any of our categories, obviously, could be differentiated to a much greater extent and defined much more precisely. But there simply is no categorical decision about what gestalts constitute signals that, on the basis of a dyadic history, constitute different qualities of mutual influence – or its reduction. Consequently, one has to adapt one's methods to what is feasible given a certain technical quality of a film or video recording and given a certain degree of freedom of movement in a flexible and fairly open situation like the Strange Situation. And of course, there is always the problem of a reasonable balance between the degree of accuracy and the knowledge gained from one's efforts. The method took about 2 years to develop. On a more general level, we believe that Karl Bühler's ideas, which he developed some 60 years ago, have to be taken seriously in any observational methodology concerned with mutuality between people. Codable behavior (symptoms), its effects (signals), and its embedded meaning (relationship and purpose) are inseparably interwined. Our method tries to accommodate this fact.

It was our goal to develop a method that would enable us to interpret any of the three interrelated aspects in context – actions, sequences, and consequences – on the basis of infants' emotional and communicative expressions. The development of the method was initiated by our attempt to understand the fact that about two-thirds of our infants were classified on the basis of Ainsworth's criteria as insecurely attached (i.e., ambivalently [C], avoidantly [A] or nonclassifiable [0]). We thought of several explanations, such as undue identification with the scientific procedure, cultural aspects, training of infants using discipline versus compliance by mothers, mothers' own insecurity, striving for independence, and so on (see note 1). These considerations, however, were not satisfactory. Only the fact that we did not accept the Strange Situation as a valid test for the quality of attachment per se, but only as an instrument that has proved its validity under the rearing conditions documented by Ainsworth et al. (1971) encouraged us to utilize its inherent potential. Many of our infants classified A did not have mothers who were nearly as insensitive as those of infants classified A by Ainsworth (Grossmann et al., 1985). At 10 months the relationship was insignificant between maternal sensitivity and infant classification in the Strange Situation for our sample. This gave us some ideas about different influences, in line with cultural demands (Grossmann & Grossmann, 1981b). A temperamental aspect of the infants also contributed to the classifications; good orientation at newborn age significantly enhanced the likelihood of an infant being classified B at 12 months with the mother, and B at 18 months with the father. Finally, maternal sensitivity at 2 and 6 months of age, as well as the mean score at 2, 6, and 10 months, significantly correlated with Strange Situation classifications at 12 months. These facts made us very curious, and our method was designed to provide expanded explanations – not alternatives to those available in the literature.

Many of Ainsworth's observations and important conclusions have been reconfirmed here. For most of the infants there was increasing stress in the course of the Strange Situation. But about half of the infants regained their good spirits and resumed their play; three did not show impairment of mood or quality of concentrated play at all. Many infants showed the pattern expected by attachment theory in Episode 8: sadness induced by separation, tilting the balance between exploration and attachment systems toward activating attachment behavior, and subsequent improvement of emotional conflict by the secure base qualities of sensitive mothers. Many infants were not reassured despite maternal efforts and bodily contact within the 3 min of Episodes 5 and 8 of the Strange Situation, whereas others felt secure enough to play cheerfully without close contact and after only a brief greeting of their mothers upon their return. The multiplexity of such observations demands multiplex methods.

Two patterns of social consequences were found: one in which the infants communicated directly with their mothers at the beginning with the joint attention structure and thereafter changed to independent exploration and play, and one dominated by joint attention structure for the whole episode. A third pattern, alternation between joint attention structure and independent play, was shown by only a few infants. Most infants played well and independently in Episode 2 but were closer to their mothers in Episodes 5 and 8; the mothers' own initiative contributed much to this. Infants whose mood was not cheerful had mothers who came closer to them and helped to establish joint attention. Cheerful infants were more independent. In general, if an infant avoided the mother, she usually went to her infant. This facilitated but did not always result in person-to-person interaction. In contrast, Group B infants went to their mothers directly and, by definition, established close bodily proximity.

Notes

1. We actually thought of eight possible reasons, other than dyadic history in terms of sensitivity, for the distribution of insecurely versus securely attached dyads observed in our Strange Situations:

    1. Parental submission to the authority of the scientist conducting the research
    2. No body contact as a specific cultural expectation, but no rejection
    3. Lack of expectation of reassurance on the part of the infant in a situation perceived by the parents to be a play session
    4. Discipline vs. compliance as an educational goal (Grossmann & Grossmann, 1981b)
    5. The cultural perception that reenforcing the infant's dependency needs create later heavy demands on the parents by the infants, i.e., intentional ignoring without rejection (this may explain the four points listed above, particularly 2)
    6. Sensitivity on the basis of a time schedule (i.e., on the basis of a strict time schedule for various chores with a special time niche for the infant)
    7. The earlier introduction of distal signals into the relationship structure in Germany than in the United States
    8. The establishment of an extradyadic attention structure focusing on objects and external events as part of the cultural pattern to train the infants to become independent by very early insistence on self-reliance

    Most of these ideas are compatible with the fact that the north German mothers whose infants had shown the A pattern in the Strange Situation when observed with the mothers were not rejecting, but they did behave like teachers in accordance with cultural demands by selectively ignoring pleas for tender closeness and by strengthening independent play behavior.

    In Germany it is culturally acceptable for a mother to leave her baby alone for a short while or to leave the baby with others, even if she is not working. Infants should be able to tolerate separation and play by themselves. From interviews with the mothers, we found that by 10 months all except two children had been looked after by people other than the mother. Sixteen mothers had left their infant alone for a short while or while they slept; 36 mothers claimed proudly that their infants could already play alone nicely without their assistance.

2. Gestures, facial expressions, and vocalizations were developed in cooperation with Anna Schwan. Actions and consequences were developed in cooperation with Josef Plab and Jeannie Beckham. The latter also assisted in reliability control and in the translation from German into English. The help of all three is greatly acknowledged.

3. We use codes M for mothers, F for fathers, and S for strangers. Since here the application of the method is discussed only in connection with an infant–mother Strange Situation, only the M codes are listed. They can be easily changed and adapted to other interacting persons.

4. Our abbreviations are derived from German words. They are enclosed in parentheses to allow for future comparisons and retranslations. The code names have been adjusted to English.

5. In the process of developing this method, the first and third authors first developed a category for infants' actions and for infants' expressive behaviors. The definitions of the consequences were developed independently on the basis of a variety of videotapes. During this process we concentrated predominantly on the special quality of infant–mother or infant–father togetherness. We owe much to the preliminary work of Ursula Stolberg (1981). The final sequences of conse-

quences were developed by the first author and Josef Plab. Jeannie Beckham helped to integrate actions, consequences, and expressive behavior by determining criteria for defining sequences. As a third step we developed a record sheet that enabled us to evaluate the videotapes as follows: identification of an action, identification of a consequence, determination of a sequence, and assessment of the expressive behavior.

6. This finding was replicated by applying the method presented here to the Strange Situation as well as to open play sessions performed at the University of Regensburg (see note 9).
7. No infants were classified B 1 at 12 months of age in our sample.
8. One infant classified B 3 uttered 13 joyful utterances in Episode 8, which heightened the mean value considerably.
9. Forty-seven Strange Situations with fathers and 18-month-old infants were also analyzed by this method. These data will be reported soon in connection with the re-analysis of another 100 Strange Situations performed with infants at 12 months of age (40 with the mother, 10 with the father) and at 18 months of age (40 with the father, 10 with the mother). Results obtained so far indicate that Group B infants, in a play situation, tend to find parental support more often when their mood is no longer cheerful, whereas parents of Group A infants tend to interact when the infant is happily playing; these parents tend to overlook their infants' emotional conflicts (Escher-Gräub & Grossmann, 1983).

References

Ainsworth, M. D. S. *Infancy in Uganda: Infant care and the growth of love.* Baltimore: Johns Hopkins University Press, 1967.

Ainsworth, M. D. S., & Bell, S. M. Mother–infant interaction and the development of competence. In K. Connolly & J. Bruner (Eds.), *The growth of competence.* London: Academic Press, 1974.

Ainsworth, M. D. S., Bell, S. M., & Stayton, D. J. Individual differences in Strange Situation behavior of one-year-olds. In H. R. Schaffer (Ed.), *The origins of human social relations.* London: Academic Press, 1971.

Ainsworth, M. D. S., Bell, S. M., & Stayton, D. J. Infant–mother attachment and social development: "Socialization" as a product of reciprocal responsiveness to signals. In P. M. Richards (Ed.), *The integration of a child into a social world,* Cambridge University Press, 1974.

Ainsworth, M. D. S., Blehar, M. C., Waters, E., & Wall, S. *Patterns of attachment.* Hillsdale, NJ: Erlbaum, 1978.

Ainsworth, M. D. S. *Infancy in Uganda: Infant care and the growth of love.* Baltimore: Johns Hopkins University Press, 1967.

Bowlby, J. *Attachment.* London: Hogarth Press, Vol. 1: 1969; Vol. 2: 1973; Vol. 3: 1980.

Bretherton, I. Young children in stressful situations: The supporting role of attachment figures and unfamiliar caregivers. in G V. Coelho & P. I. Ahmed (Eds.), *Uprooting and development, dilemmas of coping with modernization.* New York: Plenum, 1980.

Bretherton, I., & Waters, E. (Eds.). Growing points in attachment theory and research. *Monographs of the Society for Research in Child Development,* 1985.

Bruner, J. S. Nature and uses of immaturity. *American Psychologist,* 1972, *27,* 687–708.

Bruner, J. S. Learning how to do things with words. In J. Bruner & A. Garton (Eds.), *Human growth and development.* Wolfson College Lectures 1976. Oxford: Clarendon Press, 1978.

Bühler, C. *Psychologie im Leben unserer Zeit* [Psychology in the life of our times]. Munich: Drömersche Verlagsanstalt, 1962.

Bühler, C., & Hetzer, H. *Zur Geschichte der Kinderpsychologie* [History of child psychology]. Beiträge zur Problemgeschichte der Psychologie, Festschrift zu Karl Bühlers 50. Geburtstag. Jena: Fischer, 1929.

Bühler, K. *Abriss der geistigen Entwicklung des Kindes* [An outline of the mental development of the infant (2nd ed.). Leipzig: Quelle & Meyer], 1925.

Bühler, K. *Die geistige Entwicklung des Kindes* (6th ed.). Jena: Fischer, 1930.

Büher, K. *Die Drise der Psychologie* [The crisis of psychology] (3rd ed.). Stuttgart: Fischer, 1965. (Original work published 1927.)

Bühler, K. *Die Krise der Psychologie* [The crisis of psychology] (3rd ed.). Stuttgart: Fischer, 1965. (Original work published 1927.)

Carus, F. A. *Psychologie*. Leipzig: Barth & Kummer, 2. Band, 1808.

Ekman, P., & Friesen, W. *Unmasking the face: A guide to recognize emotions from facial cues.* Englewood Cliffs, NJ: Prentice-Hall, 1975.

Emde, R. N., & Gaensbauer, T. Some emerging models of emotion in human infancy. In K. Immelmann, G. W. Barlow, L. Petrinovich, & M. Main (Eds.), *Behavioral development* (The Bielefeld Interdisciplinary Project), Cambridge University Press, 1981.

Escher-Gräub, D., & Grossmann, K. E. Bindungsunsicherheit Zweiten Lebensjahr: *Die Regensburger Querschnittuntesuchung* [Insecure attachment in the second year of life: The Regensburg cross sectional study]. Unpublished manuscript. University of Regensburg, 1983.

Ernst, R. *Emotionaler Ausdruck 18 Monate alter Kinder und dessen Wirkung auf die Bindungsfigur vor und nach kurzfristiger Trennung* [Emotional expression in 18-month-old infants and its effect on the attachment figure before and after brief separation]. Diplom-thesis, Universität Regensburg, 1984.

Gaensbauer, T. Regulation of emotional expression in infants from two contrasting caretaking environments. *Journal of American Academy of Child Psychiatry, 1982, 21,* 163–71.

Gaensbauer, T. *General outline for affect ratings*. Unpublished manuscript, 1980.

Grossmann, K. E. (Ed.). Entwicklung der Lernfähigkeit. Munich: Kindler, 1977.

Grossmann, K. E. Die Entwicklung von Beziehungsmustern in der frühen Kindheit [The development of relationship patterns in early childhood]. In G. Lüer (Ed.), *Bericht über den 33. Kongress der Deutschen Gesellschaft für Psychologie in Mainz, 1982*. Göttingen: Hogrefe, 1983a.

Grossmann, K. E. Vergleichende Entwicklungspsychologie [Comparative developmental psychology]. In R. Silbereisen & L. Montada (Eds.), *Entwicklungspsychologie*. Munich: Urban & Schwarzenberg, 1983b.

Grossmann, K. E. Bindungsgefühl [Feeling of attachment]. In H. A. Euler & H. Mandl (Eds.), *Emotionspsychologie*. Munich: Urban & Schwarzenberg, 1983c.

Grossmann, K. E., & Grossmann, K. The mother–child relationship. *German Journal of Psychology, 1981a, 5* (3), 231–52.

Grossmann, K. E., & Grossmann, K. Parent–infant attachment relationships in Bielefeld: A research note. In K. Immelmann, G. W. Barlow, L. Petrinovich, & M. Main (Eds.), *Behavioral development*. Cambridge University Press, 1981b.

Grossmann, K. E., & Grossmann, K. Discovery and proof in attachment research. *The Behavioral and Brain Sciences, 1984, 7*(1), 154–5.

Grossmann, K. E., Grossmann, K., Huber, F., & Wartner, U. German children's behavior towards their mothers at 12 months and their fathers at 18 months in Ainsworth's Strange Situation. *International Journal of Behavioral Development, 1981, 4,* 157–81.

Grossmann, K., Grossmann, K. E., Spangler, G., Suess, G., & Unzner, L. Maternal sensitivity and newborns' orientation responses as related to quality of attachment in northern Germany. I. Bretherton & E. Waters (Eds.), Growing points in attachment theory and research. *Monographs of the Society for Research in Child Development,* 1985.

Harlow, H. *Learning to love*. San Francisco: Albion, 1971.

Hiatt, S. W., Campos, I. I., & Emde, R. N. Facial patterning and infant emotional expression: Happiness, surprise, and fear. *Child Development, 1979, 50,* 1020–35.

Hinde, R. A. *Towards understanding relationships*. London: Academic Press, 1979.

Hinde, R. A. Attachment: Some conceptual and biological issues. In C. M. Parkes & J. Stevenson-Hinde (Eds.), *The place of attachment in human behavior*. New York: Basic Books, 1981.

Izard, C. E. The Maximally Discriminative Facial Movement Coding System. Newark: University of Delaware, Instructional Resources Center, 1979.

Izard, C. E., & Dougherty, L. M. *A system for identifying affect expressions by holistic judgements (Affex)*. Newark: University of Delaware, Instructional Resources Center, 1980.

Mackay, D. M. Formal analysis of communicative processes. In R. A. Hinde (Ed.), *Non-verbal communication* pp 3–25. Cambridge University Press, 1972.

Main, M. *Exploration, play and cognitive functioning as related to child–mother attachment*. PhD Dissertation, Johns Hopkins University, 1973.

Main, M. Sicherheit und Wissen [Security and knowledge]. In K. E. Grossmann (Ed.), *Entwicklung der Lernfähigkeit* pp 47–95. Munich: Kindler, 1977.

Main, M. Avoidance in the service of attachment: A working paper. In K. Immelmann, G. W. Barlow, L. Petrinovich, & M. Main (Eds.), *Behavioral development*, pp. 651–93. Cambridge University Press, 1981.

Main, M., Tomasini, L., & Tolan, W. Differences among mothers of infants judged to differ in insecurity. *Developmental Psychology*, 1979, *15*, 472–3.

Main, M., & Weston, D. The quality of the toddlers' relationship to mother and to father: Related to conflict behavior and the readiness to establish new relationships. *Child Development*, 1981, *52*, 932–40.

Oster, H. Facial expression and affect development. In M. Lewis & L. A. Rosenblum (Eds.), *The development of affect*. New York: Plenum, 1978.

Porter, R. H., & Laney, M. D. Attachment theory and the concept of inclusive fitness. *Merrill–Palmer Quarterly*, 1980, *26*, 35–51.

Portmann, A. *Zoologie und das neue Bild vom Menschen* [Zoology and the new perspective of man]. Hamburg: Rowohlt, 1956.

Smith, P. K. Shared care of young children: Alternative models to monotropism. *Merrill-Palmer Quarterly*, 1980, *26*, 371–89.

Spitz, R. A. Hospitalism: An inquiry into the genesis of psychiatric conditions in early childhood (I). *Psychoanalytic Study of the Child, 53*, 1945.

Sroufe, A. L. Infant caregiver attachment and patterns of adaptation in preschool: The roots of maladaptation and competence. In M. Perlmutter (Ed.), *Minnesota Symposium in Child Psychology*, Vol. 16, 1984.

Stolberg, U. *Kontaktaufnahme 18 Monate alter Kinder zu ihren Vätern in der Fremden Situation nach Ainsworth* [Contact initiation of 18 month old infants with their fathers in Ainsworth's Strange Situation]. Diplom thesis, University of Regensburg, 1981.

Tinbergen, E., & Tinbergen, N. Early childhood autism: An ethological approach. *Fortschritte der Verhaltensforschung* (Vol. 10). Berlin: Parey Verlag, 1972.

Vaughn, B., Egeland, B., & Sroufe, L. A. Individual differences in infant–mother attachment at 12 and 18 months: Stability and change in families under stress. *Child Development*, 1979, *50*, 971–5.

Waters, E. The reliability and stability of individual differences in infant–mother attachment. *Child Development*, 1978, *49*, 483–94.

7 Infant temperament: theory, tradition, critique, and new assessments

Marc H. Bornstein, Jane M. Gaughran, and Peter Homel

Introduction

Despite much recent progress in defining and measuring temperament in infancy, the concept of temperament remains imperfectly understood, and its significance as a psychological construct is not completely certain. The value of any construct, including temperament, lies in its capacity to explain phenomena, to generate hypotheses, to predict outcomes, and to relate meaningfully to other key constructs. To meet these criteria we believe that investigators must first describe the origins of temperamental differences, elucidate mechanisms by which temperament operates, and distinguish temperament from other constructs. Insofar as progress has been limited on these fronts, the construct of temperament lacks rigor and, thus, purpose.

In this chapter we survey research on infant temperament from theoretical, from methodological, and from our own practical vantages. We first discuss some central theoretical concerns regarding the construct of temperament. Specifically, we consider the origins of individual temperamental differences in infancy. An emerging model that depicts temperamental differences as regulated in part by genetic endowment but also responsive to environmental inputs is described, and relevant theory and research are discussed. We next present a critical overview of principal contemporary measures of temperament with recommendations for improvement in this domain. Finally, we report some preliminary research that directly addresses these methodological issues, and we conclude by offering proposals for future study.

Preparation of this chapter was supported by a Research Career Development Award (K04 HD00521) from the National Institute of Child Health and Human Development, by a Guggenheim Foundation Fellowship, and by an Invited Professorship to the Laboratoire de Psychologie Expérimentale, Paris, to M. H. B. We thank A. Kuchuk, I. Seguí, C. Sobin, B. Smith, T. Strauman, and M. Tress for comments and assistance. Request reprints from Marc H. Bornstein, Infancy Studies Program, Department of Psychology, New York University, 6 Washington Place, Room 1065, New York, New York 10003.

172

Toward defining temperament in infancy: theoretical foundations

No single definition of temperament has gained universal adherence, but most researchers would agree that temperament includes individual behavioral differences in affective expressiveness, motor activity, and stimulus sensitivity. Temperament was traditionally defined in terms of component behaviors, usually organized into dimensions. The more recent focus on specific response characteristics, such as duration, frequency, and intensity, has proven useful from methodological and theoretical standpoints (e.g., Campos, Barrett, Lamb, Goldsmith, & Stenberg, 1983; Derryberry & Rothbart, 1984). This focus affords ease and precision in the measurement of temperament; more importantly, it allows for a conceptualization of temperamental differences that extends beyond the behavioral level to the physiological and experiential (see Derryberry & Rothbart, 1984).

A considerable effort has been made to explicate the origins of temperamental differences, with some success. Temperament has long been understood to be a constitutionally based source of variance in personality functioning, but the search for constitutional determinants has been arduous and not always fruitful. Some researchers have looked to adverse prenatal and perinatal antecedents of temperamentlike variation. For example, recent investigations of clinical samples suggest that severe postnatal illness has some (apparently slight) influence on temperament (e.g., Bakeman & Brown, 1980; Field, Dempsey, & Shuman, 1981). Similarly, there is growing evidence that teratogens, such as alcohol, caffeine, and nicotine, as well as obstetrical medication affect behaviors that are conceptually akin to temperament. Behavioral variation ascribable to these sources is found after birth and sometimes considerably later (e.g., Brackbill, 1979; Jacobson, Fein, Jacobson, Schwartz, & Dowler, 1984). We question the advisability of this focus on aberrant physiological or environmental conditions as a means of investigating the origins of temperamental differences. As early as 1978, Carey and McDevitt warned against confusing normal temperamental variation with behaviors that reflect physiological dysfunction, as has been done with so-called difficult temperament and minimal brain dysfunction. In this spirit, we contend that temperament is best defined – and investigated – as a normal phenomenon. Documenting relations between abnormal circumstances of birth and temperamental outcome has potential clinical relevance but does little to clarify the nature of temperamental differences in the general population. It would be more advantageous first to study constitutional and environmental sources of normal variation. However, without a clear understanding of the construct of temperament, it is difficult to posit what these sources of variation are. This may be why, as Buss and Plomin (1984) note, relatively little attention has been paid to the question of nonpathological sources of normal variation in infant temperament.

Behavioral genetics explicitly accounts for sources of normal variation in temperament; as a result, the model of temperament emerging from this perspective possesses unusual clarity. In essence, this model posits that the individual genotype in part governs temperamental differences in the organism's spontaneous activity and responsivity to various aspects of the environment; the environment affects the individual but not determinatively (Scarr & Kidd, 1983; Scarr & McCartney, 1983; see also Buss & Plomin, 1984; Goldsmith, 1983; Matheny, 1983; Wilson, 1983, 1984). In this view, individuals "prompted" by their unique genetic endowments selectively experience and shape the environments they encounter. The process of acting on the environment, termed "evocative" and "active" genotype–environment effects or correlations (Buss & Plomin, 1984; Fuller, 1984; Plomin, deFries, & Loehlin, 1977; Scarr & McCartney, 1983), is multifaceted; individuals can evoke specific responses from the environment in which they find themselves, or they can seek out those environs that best fit their predilections and talents.

The emphasis on an interaction between endowment and environment is akin to the transactional perspective proposed by Sameroff and Chandler (1975; see also Lerner & Lerner, 1983; Thomas & Chess, 1977). However, an advance of behavior geneticists over traditional temperament theorists would seem to be that the geneticists attempt to specify the origins of this transactional process, in that the individual genotype is hypothesized to provide the anlage from which temperamental differences emerge.

Some investigators take issue with evocative and active models; Wachs and Gandour (1983), for example, present data that indicate to them that environments are not shaped by individual differences, but rather are experienced differently. Nevertheless, their "organismic specificity" hypothesis can be interpreted as being consonant in part with the genetic model. They note that the environment is often regarded as working uniform effects on individuals, whereas in actuality individual reactivity may determine how comparable environments are experienced. Thus, their view is consistent, though not explicitly allied with, a genetic model insofar as they emphasize that individual differences mediate experience.

Approaches to validating a genetic model empirically have come through two sources: One is twin research, and the other is cross-cultural research. Standard twin methodology has frequently been employed to study the heritability of temperamental differences, since this technique provides a powerful means of measuring the effects of genotype as opposed to prenatal and postnatal environments. Direct estimates of the magnitude of genetic influences can be made by established correctional procedures, but these are problematic on two counts. First, as Goldsmith (1983) notes, correlational procedures lack the rigor and potential for hypothesis testing that more complex model-fitting techniques offer. Second, whereas heritability estimates yielded by these procedures have been regarded as preferable to simple comparisons of *MZ* and *DZ* concordance levels, the concept of heritability itself is questionable in this context. It appears that the magnitude of heritability estimates for various temperamental variables differs little from those obtained for other personality variables (Goldsmith, 1985b), so that heritability loses its meaning as criterial for temperament. Moreover, Goldsmith points out that heritability and genetic influences are not synonymous: "Heritability [is not] a crucial definitional issue for temperament in part because . . . some dimensions may be genetically influenced but not heritable" (p. 1). Still, estimations of genetic and environmental influences tend to be expressed in terms of differential *MZ–DZ* concordance rates or heritability estimates of the temperamental variable in question. The practical and conceptual limits of these expressions should be kept in mind in approaching the twin literature.

The presence of "moderate" genetic influence on temperamental variation is increasingly well documented (Goldsmith, 1985b). Several investigators have found evidence of differential concordance rates or heritability estimates for different dimensions of temperament based on data derived from parent questionnaires that possess a reasonable degree of psychometric adequacy. Goldsmith and Campos (1982), for example, have found that *MZ* correlations were significantly greater than *DZ* correlations for Rothbart's (1981) Infant Behavior Questionnaire dimensions of activity level and distress to limitations. In this study, *DZ* correlations were not lower than would be predicted by a genetic model, a problem that has emerged in other studies using parent report measures. Heritability estimates for activity level and fear were moderate, .36 and .40; for distress to limitations, the estimate was a sizable .77. In contrast, the estimates of genetic influence were negligible for dimensions of smiling and laughter, undisturbed persistence, and soothability.

Like Goldsmith and Campos (1982), Plomin and Rowe (1979) found evidence for differential heritability of social behaviors that were indexed during structured home observations. Of all the social behaviors sampled, only that which indexed infants' reactions to a novel observer yielded a moderate heritability estimate (approximately .45). Differences in infant responses to the mother appeared to be mediated, not by genotypic, but by environmental factors – in particular, individual-specific environmental factors. Again, this finding is consistent with a growing consensus in the literature that nonshared environmental sources of variation may represent more significant influences on development than shared environmental influences (Goldsmith, 1983; Rowe & Plomin, 1981; see also Wilson & Matheny, 1983). Modifications of the Bayley Infant Behavior

Record (IBR) have also proved useful in investigating the heritability of temperamental differences. For example, Goldsmith and Gottesman (1981) found that a factor they labeled activity level yielded a heritability estimate of .44.

Matheny (1980, 1983) investigated *MZ/DZ* differences longitudinally from 6 to 24 months using his modifications of the IBR. Findings approximated those of similar studies; significant differences between *MZ* and *DZ* twin pairs obtained for factors of task orientation, test affect–extroversion, and activity. However, he did not observe significant differences at every age; such differences emerged after 12 or 18 months. More compelling are Matheny's longitudinal analyses of patterns of age-to-age change in factor scores for *MZ* and *DZ* twins. First, Matheny found that longitudinal correlations of factor scores at 6, 12, 18, and 24 months were variable and moderate at best, suggesting that substantial age changes in profiles may be typical in infancy. However, he found striking differences between the *MZ* and *DZ* groups in terms of the overall consistency in patterns of change. That is, *MZ* twin pairs evidenced a significantly higher degree of synchrony in their patterns of change across timme than did *DZ* twin pairs. Specifically, *MZ* concordances for age-to-age changes ranged from .27 to .53, whereas *DZ* concordance levels extended from .06 to .21. These data require replication and elaboration, but are significant in two ways: First, they introduce a promising unit of analysis – differential profiles of age-to-age change for *MZ* and *DZ* twins – and, second, they illustrate that apparent behavioral instability may reflect complex genetic processes. We shall return to this point later as we discuss the issue of continuity and change in infant temperament.

Goldsmith and Rieser-Danner (1984) presented concordance estimates for their laboratory measures of a composite dimension, negative versus positive affect on visual cliff. Again, consistent with a genetic model, *MZ* correlations averaged .56, whereas *DZ* correlations averaged .38. Overall, then, twin data lend some support to a genetic model of temperamental variation.

Assessments of infant temperament based on traditional maternal questionnaires or interviews (e.g., Matheny, Wilson, Dolan, & Krantz, 1981; Torgersen & Kringlen, 1978) also offer evidence of higher *MZ* concordance but are compromised by psychometric deficiencies and questions of validity (see below). In particular, the use of parent reports poses specific problems for twin research. For example, the literature suggests that parents tend at times to inflate the concordance of *MZ* twins and to overdifferentiate *DZ* twins (Buss & Plomin, 1984, discuss these "assimilation and contrast effects").

Cross-cultural studies of neonatal behavioral differences lend further credence to a constitutional if not explicitly genetic model, since such neonatal differences are most readily attributable to endogenous rather than exogenous origins (Bornstein, 1980; Freedman, 1974). At first glance this cross-cultural strategy might appear inappropriate, insofar as cultural differences among infants are often attributed to differential child-rearing practices (e.g., Ainsworth, 1967; deVries & Sameroff, 1984; deVries & Super, 1978; Super, 1976). Moreover, as Scarr and McCartney (1983) indicate, genetic and environmental influences on the developing child are wholly confounded. Yet neither environmental determinism nor interactionism can fully account for temperamental differences that are evidenced in the first days of life, when the infant's contact with the environment is minimal (Plomin et al., 1977). Evidence for prenatal origins of temperamental variation across ethnic or racial groups is sparse (cf. Chisolm, 1983) and problematic, since nonpathological variation in prenatal environments could reflect genetic differences among mothers from different ethnic groups. As a consequence, cross-cultural data regarding newborn behavioral differences are most easily accommodated by a genetic hypothesis. In this perspective (see Freedman, 1974; Smith & Freedman, 1983), the contributions of cultural practice to temperamental variation are not discounted, but culture itself is understood to be in part a product of the unique genetic disposition of the group.

Most cross-cultural studies of temperamentlike variation among neonates have employed Brazelton's (1973) Neonatal Behavioral Assessment Scale (NBAS). This measure was not explicitly devised to index temperament, however, and there are considerable psychometric problems associated with using it as a temperament measure, particularly if NBAS scores are used to predict a criterion (Campos et al., 1983; Kaye, 1978; Sameroff, Krafchuk & Bakow, 1978). Still, cross-cultural data generated by the NBAS merit consideration because the NBAS has been found to be sensitive to ethnic differences in temperamentlike behaviors among neonates. Freedman (1974) discusses several such ethnic differences. For example, he found that Chinese-American and Japanese-American neonates are less perturbable, less labile in terms of state, better able to soothe themselves, and quicker to habituate than their European-American counterparts (see also Callaghan, 1981). Keefer, Tronick, Dixon, and Brazelton (1982) compared Gusii (Kenyan) and European-American neonates on the NBAS. Gusii neonates were more labile in state and irritable, and they demonstrated an enhanced capacity for self-soothing through hand-to-mouth behaviors. With a larger sample, Keefer et al. found other significant group differences: Gusii neonates habituate more rapidly to tactile stimulation, whereas American newborns orient better and habituate more quickly to visual and auditory stimuli. Like Freedman, Keefer et al. attributed their findings of neonatal group differences in part to genetic differences between Gusii and American samples, since a sole emphasis on postnatal experience cannot account for differences evidenced so early in life.

We reiterate, however, that scores obtained on the NBAS must be interpreted with some caution. DeVries and Super (1978), for example, found evidence of significant differences among various African ethnic groups on specific NBAS items. As would be predicted by a genetic model, some of these differences emerged irrespective of the place of examination, that is, in the home as well as in the hospital. However, they also found that, for certain NBAS items, examination in a home or hospital context – and not ethnic affiliation – differentiated among neonates. Moreover, their data suggest some modest degree of interaction between ethnic affiliation and locale of NBAS examination, although the authors acknowledge that age variation may account for some of the apparent differences attributable to context. Taken in sum, these data support a genetic model insofar as some neonatal group differences were found irrespective of context. Still, the possibility that certain NBAS items may better index contextual than ethnic differences compromises those studies that do not explicitly account for contextual sources of variation. Studies that fail to control for contextual differences among groups provide at best a weak confirmation of genetic hypotheses. A more rigorous test should include multiple assessments of the same neonates at hospital and at home within a sufficiently brief period to rule out age effects. This strategy enables the researcher to determine whether the pattern of cross-cultural differences among groups of neonates obtained in relatively homogeneous hospital settings is maintained despite environmental variation and experimental noise.

Data derived from older infant samples are difficult to interpret; in most ethnological traditions, cross-cultural differences in late infancy are understood to reflect divergent cultural practice. Yet striking parallels between older infant and neonatal studies suggest that genetic factors must be included in an adequate model of cross-cultural variation in later infancy. In a longitudinal comparison of Chinese-American and European-American infants from birth to 5 months, Kuchner (1980) found that Chinese-American infants are more passive, less prone to state changes, and better self-regulated in contrast to more active, labile European-American infants. Similarly, Caudill and Weinstein (1969), studying infants between 3 months and 1 year, presented a picture of highly active, vocal European-American infants in contrast to more motorically placid, self-quieting, and subdued Japanese.

In an attempt to investigate the sources of these apparent behavioral differences, both Kuchner (1980) and Caudill and Weinstein (1969) indexed mother–infant interaction. They found that Asian-American mothers are not as interactive with their infants, gearing their ministrations toward soothing rather than stimulation – in direct contrast to European-American mothers. As such, these data suggest that temperamental differences among older infants may be fostered by caretaking practices. Consider, however, Kuchner's argument that the less labile, active, and alert Chinese-American infant may engender and maintain the low-key interactive style observed in Chinese mothers during the first 5 months of the infant's life. This perspective is congruent with Scarr and McCartney's

(1983) discussion of "evocative" genotype–environment effects wherein the biological endowment of infants evokes certain responses from their environment.

In passing, we note that there are other cross-cultural studies of temperament in infancy but that they offer little additional clarification. Typically, researchers have used versions of the Carey Infant Temperament Questionnaire that have been widely criticized for their questionable metric properties (see below) and because evidence indicates that such questionnaires may tap maternal variables as much as infant temperament (Sameroff, Seifer, & Elias, 1982; Vaughn, Taraldson, Crichton, & Egeland, 1981). For example, maternal ratings of Chinese-American infants provide a picture of noncompliant, intense, negative, arrhythmic, and unadaptable babies (Hsu, Soong, Stigler, Hong, & Liang, 1981; Smith & Freedman, 1983) – in marked contrast to the quickly habituating, passive, tractable, and self-regulating infants described in behavioral observations (Caudill & Weinstein, 1969; Kuchner, 1980; Smith & Freedman, 1983). Smith and Freedman (1983) hold that this disparity reflects Chinese-American mothers' sensitivity to negative affect and to expressions of resistance or autonomy in their babies. Studies that employ both maternal and objective measures are called for, so that method-specific sources of error can be identified and patterns of divergence among mothers and observers can be indexed.

Behavior genetics and cross-cultural findings have been useful in elucidating the origins of temperamental variation. However, they do not address other important questions, such as the developmental course of temperamental differences over time and context. It has been traditional to conceive of temperament as continuous over time (e.g., Buss & Plomin, 1975; Campos et al., 1983; Thomas & Chess, 1977) and thus to gear investigations toward assessing stability. This is not to say that researchers expect overt expressions of temperament to be invariant over time; manifestations of temperamental proclivities are appropriately thought to reflect children's rapidly changing faculties and skills as well as changing environmental demands (Campos et al., 1983; Lerner & Lerner, 1983; Lerner, Palermo, Spiro, Nesselroade, 1982; Sameroff & Chandler, 1975). In fact, Chess (1979; Thomas & Chess, 1977; see also Rothbart & Derryberry, 1981) emphasized the developmental plasticity of temperament. Still, stability of items or dimensions has been viewed as essential to predictive validity for the construct of temperament.

Indeed, this expectation of stability has been seen as a necessary corollary to some genetic models of temperamental variation (e.g., Buss & Plomin, 1984). Thus, even modest age-to-age correlations have been treated as evidence of longitudinal stability. It has become increasingly clear, however, that age-to-age correlations obtained for items, dimensions, or factors of temperament are variable and may be low in the first years of life. This apparent instability has typically been attributed to measurement error or to environmental flux. Some researchers have, however, begun to ascribe the variable course of reported temperamental differences to the possible discontinuous action of genes over time (Matheny, 1980, 1983; Plomin, 1983; Scarr & McCartney, 1983; Wilson, 1983, 1984). Recognizing that gene action itself may be discontinuous, researchers like Wilson (1978, 1983, 1984) have argued that patterns of developmental "acceleration" and "lag" should be more synchronous in more genetically similar organisms. Wilson's work on physical growth and mental development and Matheny's (1983) investigations in the temperament domain support this hypothesis. The model of temperament we describe here admits of a longitudinal course that is fluctuant and complex in the earliest years, as befits characteristics that are regulated in part by an "on again, off again" gene program (Plomin, 1983). Most likely, dimensions of temperament are differentially stable over time; certain ones may show considerable longitudinal stability, whereas others will fluctuate.

Finally, implicit in a constitutional model is the concept of behavioral disposition: That is, differences reflecting within-person characteristics should be relatively constant across situations (e.g., Campos et al., 1983). Of course, all dimensions of temperament will not be equally responsive to environmental influences. Rather, following our temporal expectations we predict that different dimensions of temperament will evince greater and lesser degrees of sensitivity and susceptibility to environmental contexts (see also Goldsmith & Campos, 1982).

Overview and critique of the principal measures of infant temperament

Considering the widespread recognition that infants differ in characteristic modes of affective expresseness, motor activity, and stimulus sensitivity, there is still relatively little consensus as to how such characteristics of temperament are to be measured. Since several literature reviews have appeared recently (e.g., Campos et al., 1983; Hubert, Wachs, Peters-Martin, & Gandour, 1982; Rothbart & Derryberry, 1981), our intention here is not to treat extant studies exhaustively; rather, we focus on the prominent issues in the measurement of temperament.

The acknowledged wellspring of interest and research on the topic of infant temperament is Thomas, Chess, Birch, Hertzig, and Korn's (1963) New York Longitudinal Study (NYLS). Their initial endeavors engendered many further explorations, notably those of Carey (e.g., 1970; Carey & McDevitt, 1978a), Rothbart (e.g., 1981; Rothbart & Derryberry, 1981), and Bates (e.g., Bates, Freeland, & Lounsbury, 1979; see also Lounsbury & Bates, 1982). From extensive parent interviews, Thomas and Chess (1977, pp. 21–22) derived nine dimensions of temperament, including activity level, rhythmicity (regularity), approach or withdrawal, adaptability, intensity of reaction, attention span and persistence, distractability, quality of mood, and threshold of responsiveness. On the basis of three distinct patterns of dimension scores, they then characterized infants in their sample as difficult, easy, or slow-to-warm-up.

From the original Thomas and Chess parent data, Carey (1970) developed the Infant Temperament Questionnaire (ITQ), later refined by Carey and McDevitt (1978b). The ITQ is a parent report questionnaire that rates infants along each of the nine Thomas and Chess dimensions and also allows for a summary characterization of infants as easy, slow-to-warm-up, difficult, intermediate low, and intermediate high. Bates (e.g., Bates et al., 1979) developed a second parent report measure, the Infant Characteristics Questionnaire (ICQ). Factor analysis of items in the ICQ yields four main dimensions of temperament, including fussiness–difficult, unadaptable, dull, and unpredictable, among which only the first has proved to be psychometrically adequate (see below). Finally, Rothbart (e.g., 1981; Rothbart & Derryberry, 1981) developed a third parent report measure, the Infant Behavior.Questionnaire (IBQ), also applicable during the first year of life. The six dimensions of the IBQ are activity level, soothability, fear (distress and latency to approach intense or novel stimuli), distress to limitations (anger/frustration), smiling and laughter, and duration of orienting. Rothbart's work is informed by perceptual–cognitive, neurophysiological, genetic, interactional, and adult temperament perspectives as well as by the traditional Thomas & Chess approach to infant temperament research. As such, Rothbart's work has the advantage of having a broad conceptual base (Derryberry & Rothbart, 1984; Posner & Rothbart, 1980; Rothbart & Derryberry, 1981; Rothbart & Posner, 1984). This orientation is useful, especially when the validity of a construct is still in question, since converging evidence from a variety of theoretically relevant sources fortifies a psychological construct.

Researchers working within behavior genetics have at times made use of parent report measures such as the Rothbart IBQ (e.g., Goldsmith & Campos, 1982) or some adaptation of the NYLS methodology described above. Matheny, Wilson, and Nuss (1984), for example, used the Toddler Temperament Questionnaire (Fullard, McDevitt, & Carey, 1984), which like the Carey ITQ indexes temperament along the nine dimensions first discussed by Thomas and Chess.

More recently attention in temperament research has been directed toward laboratory-based observational measures consisting of structured vignettes. This method greatly facilitates reliable data collection, in contrast to less structured observations of free play (see Wilson & Matheny, 1983), and it avoids the potential contamination of parent bias. Matheny (1983; see also Matheny, 1980) developed a laboratory-based assessment measure from the Bayley IBR from which he obtained three principal components labeled test extroversion, activity level, and task orientation. These bear a conceptual similarity to some a priori dimensions discussed above.

Despite this surge of interest in infant temperament, the psychometric adequacy of many instruments appears uncertain. In approaching the question of psychometric adequacy, we consider two fundamental issues: first, reliability in available measures of infant temperament and, second, validity.

Reliability

Three main methodological shortfalls with respect to reliability in infant temperament can be identified in past research. The first concerns the test–retest reliability of infant temperament measures, the second concerns inter-rater reliability, and the third concerns the internal consistency and orthogonality of dimensions in temperament.

First, the issue of *test–retest,* or *short-term, reliability* of temperament assessment instruments or of specific dimensions of temperament has been insufficiently addressed. Evidence of test–retest reliability is basic for validating the construct of infant temperament. Some reports do not include estimates of test–retest or short-term reliability of the dimensions (e.g., Pederson, Zaslow, Cain, Anderson, & Thomas, 1976; Rothbart, 1981). Sometimes test–retest estimates based on observer data are provided, but corresponding estimates are not provided for maternal reports, which are themselves used for the assessment of infant temperament (e.g., Bates et al., 1979). In other instances, estimates of test–retest reliability have been made over long temporal intervals or with small samples, so that it is unclear whether low reliability estimates reflect measurement error or actual developmental change (e.g., Carey & McDevitt, 1978b, as cited in Hubert et al., 1982; Persson-Blennow & McNeil, 1982).

Inattention to the issue of short-term reliability is inconsistent with traditional formulations of temperament as a construct that, though mutable through maturation and experience, is believed to evidence some continuity over time (e.g., Buss & Plomin, 1975, 1984; Campos et al., 1983; Lerner et al., 1982; Matheny et al., 1984). This is why the question of the test–retest reliability of temperament measures requires resolution. The stability or instability of within-child characteristics cannot be delineated until the two issues – reliability of measure and stability of behavior – are fully differentiated. Many researchers have attempted to document extended stability of temperament (e.g., Carey & McDevitt, 1978a; Rothbart & Derryberry, 1981; Thomas & Chess, 1977). We argue that such investigations will be indeterminate until the test–retest reliability of instruments and component dimensions is established.

Second, we turn to the issue of *inter-rater reliability* of temperament measures. Reliability estimates of observer assessments are typically high (e.g., Bates et al., 1979; Thomas & Chess, 1977). In practice, however, these observer estimates have been made from measures other than those given to mothers, who provide the actual data base for temperament assessments. Instead, reliabilities have been derived from observers' reports, which were necessarily incomplete because observation sessions were too limited to index all of the behaviors included in the maternal questionnaires. Many investigators are not able to corroborate maternal reports of temperament at all. Some do not address this question (e.g., Carey & McDevitt, 1978b), whereas others attempt to demonstrate reliability by correlating maternal assessments with father and/or caretaker assessments (e.g., Field & Greenberg, 1982; Pederson et al., 1976; Rothbart, 1981). Such estimates are disappointingly low, even when the caretakers who are recruited are in all-day employ with the children (as in Field & Greenberg, 1982). For example, Rothbart's (1981) relatively high IBQ "household reliability" values range from .45 to .69. More typically, researchers cite parent–observer convergence estimates in the .30 to .40 range.

The third methodological problem concerns the reliability of specific dimensions of temperament, that is, whether these dimensions are both *internally consistent* and *orthogonal* to one another. As pointed out by Nunnally (1978) and Allen and Yen (1979), deficiencies in either the internal consistency or orthogonality of dimensions of an assessment instrument will affect the reliability of the instrument as a whole. Of course, orthogonality among dimensions need not be absolute; some modest degree of overlap among dimensions is acceptable if anticipated by theory. A high degree of overlap among dimensions, however, indicates that the dimensions are redundant and requires their reformulation, irrespective of prior theoretical rationale.

Internal consistency estimates for the dimensions of some infant temperament instruments are quite variable (Bates et al., 1979; Carey & McDevitt, 1978b), and occasionally they are unacceptably low, according to the conventionally employed criterion of .70 to .80. Rothbart (1981) is particularly attentive to issues of internal consistency and orthogonality. In addition to relatively high coefficient alpha values, the average item–dimension correlations for each of her six dimensions (ranging from .41 to .61) provide further evidence of homogeneity within given dimensions. Moreover, due to her efforts to reduce "conceptual overlap," intercorrelations among the six IBQ dimensions are low, ranging from .00 to .36. Some of these intercorrelations are significant, however, and suggest that Rothbart's dimensions, though internally consistent, may not index completely different kinds of information. These dimensions bear distinct and face-valid labels, but it is possible that the labels mask an underlying unity. In fact, Rothbart (1984) has discussed collapsing internally consistent but nonorthogonal dimensions into "composites."

Matheny's (1980, 1983) three principal components of test extroversion, activity level, and task orientation have the advantage of relative psychometric adequacy. All factors have loadings of .60 or better, which suggests an acceptable degree of internal consistency. Moreover, these principal components have been replicated in an independent study (van der Muelen & Smrkovsky, 1982, as cited in Matheny, 1983). In addition, single factors have been extracted in previous, unrelated studies of the IBR that bear a close resemblance to the three factors described by Matheny (see Freedman, 1965, as cited in Matheny, 1983; Goldsmith & Gottesman, 1981).

In general, however, the need for orthogonality seems to be insufficiently appreciated (cf. Goldsmith & Rieser-Danner, 1984). This inattention compromises infant temperament research because redundancy of dimensions inflates measurement error. The problem becomes most acute if dimensions are used to describe individual differences, as in profile analysis (Allen & Yen, 1979) or for purposes of prediction (Cohen & Cohen, 1983).

A simple strategy for assessing the relative orthogonality of theoretically or empirically derived dimensions would be to compare the results of orthogonal and oblique factor analyses to ensure that the former's methodological constraints are not masking substantial overlap among dimensions. Another complementary technique would involve editing or refining single items that load highly on more than one factor. And, of course, confirmatory analyses on new samples provide the best evidence of consistency and orthogonality among dimensions.

The apparent difficulty of developing internally consistent, independent dimensions calls into question the prevalent approach to measurement construction in the temperament domain. Most attempts to define and operationalize temperament have been based on the delineation of multiple dimensions. Unfortunately, the validity of this approach has yet to be established. It is possible that, despite extensive validity studies and efforts to enhance discriminability among dimensions, relatively few dimensions of temperament will be empirically validated. It may be that two or three central dimensions will subsume the current larger array of six or nine. If fewer dimensions emerge as psychometrically sound, and particularly if these dimensions give evidence of validity (via clear-cut individual and group differences, predictive utility, etc.), investigators will be compelled to relinquish the prevailing multiple-dimension perspective. Consideration of underlying unity among dimensions, reformulation, empirical testing, and factor analyses are necessary to yield dimensions of temperament whose independent validity can be established.

Before we leave the issue of reliability, a final observation regarding current statistical procedures may prove useful. Despite its currency in the temperament domain, the Pearson product–moment correlation (r) is not the most apposite measure to assess inter-rater reliability. The Pearson correlation indexes whether two sets of scores are related to one another by measuring the extent to which pairs of scores across the two data sets show the same distance relative to each of their respective means. To that extent, the Pearson correlation does not take into account differences between the means in each of the two data sets and, accordingly, differences in absolute value between members of each pair. Such differences can, however, be taken into account by using the intraclass correlation (ICC), which indexes the extent to which the pairs of scores across data sets agree in absolute value. Haggard (1958), Shrout and Fleiss (1979), and Lahey, Downey, and Saal (1983) stress that when equivalence between sets of scores is essential, as in situations involving inter-rater reliability, the intraclass correlation should be used in preference to the Pearson product–moment correlation.

Validity

At the outset of their studies of infant temperament, Thomas et al. (1963) proposed that mothers, by virtue of extensive contact with their babies, would serve as a rich source of information about babies and would provide the best assessments of infant temperament. There are obvious economic advantages to this method of data collection as well. Many researchers have made the assumption that maternal reports are inherently valid, that is, are accurate reflections of the construct of temperament in infants, and have often sought to establish the convergent validity of maternal reports of temperament by indexing the extent to which maternal reports agree with other assessments of temperament, typically father, caretaker, or observer ratings.

Unfortunately, attempts to corroborate maternal reports with those of other observers have tended to show relatively little evidence of convergent validity. Mother–father and mother–caretaker correlations are quite variable but generally are low (e.g., Bates et al., 1979; Field & Greenberg, 1982; Rothbart, 1981). Similarly, mother–observer correlations have ranged from nearly zero to "significant but modest" values (Bates et al., 1979; Lounsbury & Bates, 1982; Rothbart & Derryberry, 1981; Sameroff et al., 1982). Overall, the data are inconclusive and raise serious questions about the validity of maternal report measures. These findings are consistent with general investigations of parent–observer convergence made outside the temperament domain. Parents' reports of childhood behaviors or even their own child-rearing practices have frequently been found to be less than accurate; Lytton's (1971) comprehensive review of studies of the convergence between maternal and objective assessments cites correlations of only .30 to .40.

The fact that investigators have been willing to report "low but significant" correlations as evidence of the validity of their measures undermines attempts to establish validity. In focusing solely on the issue of statistical significance, it is easy to overlook the fact that the proportion of variance accounted for by a significant correlation may be so small as to be of little practical value, for example, for predictive purposes or as a means of concurrent validation.

Furthermore, nonsignificant correlations are suspect. Most work described in the temperament literature has relied on small samples, making it unclear whether the nonsignificant correlations obtained show some lack of relation between the variables involved or are a function of inadequate statistical power. Techniques such as power analysis (Cohen, 1977) are available to facilitate a priori assessments of the potential magnitude of the correlation between two variables. These assessments then allow a determination of the appropriate sample size for testing the statistical significance of relations in question.

In the face of low mother–observer convergence estimates, a number of researchers have proposed that maternal ratings of infants reflect characteristics of the mother as much as or more than those of the infant. Several maternal variables have been investigated in this connection, including employment status (Pederson et al., 1976), extroversion, achievement orientation, and primiparity (Bates et al., 1979), psychological status as measured by mental test batteries (Vaughn et al., 1981), and socioeconomic status, anxiety level, mental health status, and race (Sameroff et al., 1982). Some of these variables have been found to exhibit stronger relationships to maternal assessments of infant temperament than have objective measures of infant behavior. In one study, for example, Bates et al. (1979) compared the contribution of infant behaviors to maternal ratings of fussy–difficult against the contribution of maternal personality and demographic variables to maternal ratings of fussy–difficult. They found that maternal variables predicted maternal ratings better than did objectively observed infant behaviors. Similarly, Vaughn et al. (1981) found significant associations between maternal variables and maternal temperament ratings, whereas correlations between infant or maternal behavior with maternal ratings of temperament failed to reach significance. In a third study, Sameroff et al. (1982) compared maternal ratings of 4-month-olds on Carey's ITQ, first with laboratory and home observations of babies' temperaments and then with maternal variables such as anxiety level and socioeconomic status. Multiple regression analyses established that, for this study, maternal variables were better predictors of temperament score variance than were child variables. Maternal variables tended to remain significant when child variables were partialed out, but the reverse was not true.

Apart from studies of mother– (or parent–) observer agreement, other means of assessing the validity of parental report measures have been employed, but only infrequently and with relatively little positive outcome. A few studies give evidence of associations between items in parent temperament ratings and concurrently measured target variables, such as aberrant levels of dopamine-β-

hydroxylase (Rapoport, Pandoni, Renfield, Lake, & Ziegler, 1977) or amount of, rated aversiveness of, and acoustic properties of infant crying (Lounsbury & Bates, 1982). However, we have suggested that the strategy of corroborating a wide range of temperamental differences through clinical or abnormal concurrent variables reveals little about temperament as a normal phenomenon. Moreover, the correlations discussed in these studies, though statistically significant, are again relatively small. It is interesting that the results of these two very different studies are consistent in one respect: Only those items that indexed fussiness or negative affect bore significant relationships to psychophysiological target variables.

In summary, these data suggest that parents do not function as accurate reporters of infant temperament; rather, parental or maternal perceptions of temperament are colored by life circumstances, psychological functioning, and expectations regarding the baby. In this spirit, Sameroff et al. (1982, p. 172) propose that "in the face of labile infant behaviors on a changing developmental trajectory, the parents' responses to the questionnaire items must reflect . . . their attributions rather than . . . [the] infant's behavior."

However, given the limitations and flaws of contemporary measures and assessment strategies, firm conclusions regarding the contribution of attributional dispositions of parents seem premature. It is possible, first, that the instruments used by observers to corroborate maternal reports inadequately index infant temperament. Some observations appear to have been quite brief or limited in terms of the behaviors measured (e.g., Vaughn et al., 1981). Some observational measures possess psychometric problems, such as low internal consistencies (e.g., Sameroff et al., 1982). In fact, in discussing the low parent–observer convergence obtained in their study, Rothbart and Derryberry (1981) explicitly pointed to possible limitations of their observational measures of infant temperament. Even those investigators disposed to focus on the effects of maternal bias do not rule out observer measurement failure as a possible source of poor mother–observer convergence (e.g., Sameroff et al., 1982; Vaughn et al., 1981).

Second, it is possible that the assessment task typically required of mothers may be conducive to unreliability. Nearly all maternal report measures rely on single assessments that are global in that mothers are asked to condense their wealth of experience into statements about their babies' average or typical behavior. Even when mothers are asked to review and report behaviors occurring within a 1-week interval, as with Rothbart's IBQ, the dual tasks of retrospection and summarization can be expected to engender a certain amount of measurement error.

Third, irrespective of the merits and problems associated with independent observations and maternal reports, it is clear that the two kinds of measures differ considerably. Maternal reports are typically made once; observer scores are often derived from data obtained on two or more occasions. Mothers' reports call on recollections of the past week or longer, whereas observers rate the infant on the basis of what they see and code during specific fixed periods (see also St. James-Roberts & Wolke, 1984a). Finally, as Hubert et al. (1982) point out, it has never been certain that mothers (or fathers) and observers define behaviors similarly or whether they employ the same criteria when rating behaviors.

Thus, the strategy of comparing global maternal questionnaires with more focused and delimited observer measures seems inappropriate; the convergent validity of parent reports cannot be properly evaluated by comparing sets of observations obtained by different methods and with different demands. In this context, findings regarding poor parent–observer convergence may speak as much to measurement failure as to parent bias. It is informative in this context, there-fore, to consider the results of an observational technique used by Cummings, Zahn-Waxler, and Radke-Yarrow (1981). These investigators trained mothers to observe and report the reactions of 1- to 2.5-year-olds to emotional expressions of family members, and they found that mothers' reports closely agreed with those of observers. It is significant that mother and observer ratings in this study were comparable when specific behaviors were observed and the time reference was the same for the two raters.

It should be recognized, of course, that a resolution of current methodological concerns should not produce mothers who approach the rating task as observers do. It is probable – and desirable – that both kinds of measures, even if func-tionally equivalent, will validly index different kinds of perceptions or beliefs about infant temperament. There is growing interest in more subjective and eval-uative aspects of parental temperament ratings. Bates (1983) has emphasized the value of exploring parents' "social perception" of difficult temperament, in ad-dition to the infant temperament construct itself, and St. James-Roberts and Wolke (1984b) have argued that maternal perceptions are a necessary component of the infant temperament system. This perspective is appealing on two counts. First, we think it highly unlikely that complex behavioral phenomena such as temper-ament can be adequately represented from a single vantage. Second, in certain contexts the objective assessment of infant temperament may be less useful or predictive than its perception in the parental eye. That is, some developmental phenomena will be best understood by sampling the attitudes and beliefs that surround the growing child. We suggest, therefore, that maternal and observer perspectives be compared by means of a methodology that is time-limited and focused. In that way, similarities and differences between maternal and observer perceptions – derived from observations of the same behaviors – can be com-pared, and their implications for the child contrasted.

Empirical work: a new measure and experimental design to study temperament in infancy

Our approach to the assessment of temperament in infants has been designed with several purposes in mind. (a) Initially, we hypothesized that five dimensions would be salient at 5 months of age. We wished to establish the psychometric adequacy of a new home-based observation measure of these dimensions in order to construct reliable profiles of individuals and of groups of infants. (b) We wished to assess whether ratings of temperament made by observers and by mothers remained stable over a 2-week period (short-term reliability). (c) We wished to index the reliability and convergent validity of maternal reports of infant temperament by comparing observer and maternal ratings on the basis of the same structured, time-limited observation sessions in the home. In so doing, we hoped to tap the potential source of information mothers represent in a way that would control for measurement error as much as possible. (d) We wished to compare mothers' responses on a parent report questionnaire used in the traditional way with mothers' and observers' ratings based on structured observation sessions of infants to determine whether and how mothers' initial perceptions differ from observer ratings and whether mothers' participation in such observations would appreciably affect ratings of their own infants. To accomplish these goals, we devised a new temperament assessment instrument, improvised a new design to study temperament in infancy, and conducted preliminary studies applying the instrument to the design.

Measures

In devising a home-based instrument to assess temperament in the first year of life, we initially selected 62 items, which represent approximately one and one-half the number we anticipated necessary for a final measure (Allen & Yen, 1979). We then assessed infant temperament with three separate but interrelated instruments built on the same 62 items: a Maternal Perception Questionnaire (MPQ), an observer form of a Baby Temperament Questionnaire (BTQ-O), and a mother form of a Baby Temperament Questionnaire (BTQ-M). In the MPQ, all items are framed as general statements. An example is "When playing a face-to-face game like peek-a-boo with my baby, he/she usually: laughs and vocalizes . . . has no reaction." This questionnaire is intended to be an analog of the usual task presented to mothers in temperament studies, namely, to rate their infants' "global," "average," or "typical" behaviors on a single instrument. The BTQ-O focuses on the same items as they occur in the course of a 2-hour observation session. The BTQ-M frames the same items so as to obtain the mother's observations about her infant's behavior during this same 2-hour observation period.

Infant behaviors are observed in a combination of structured vignettes and periods of free play that sample a wide array of experiences. The order of vignettes and free play periods is invariant. As others have noted (e.g., Matheny et al., 1984; Wilson & Matheny, 1983), structured vignettes facilitate reliable data collection and provide a standardized context in which individual differences can clearly emerge. Complementary free-play periods allow for individual differences in spontaneous behavior; we index behavioral items simply and reliably through frequency counts. Our vignettes include structured face-to-face interactions and object play, during which behaviors are rated along continua described below.

Our 62 items comprise five a priori dimensions of temperament:

1. *Positive affect:* The baby's positive affect as well as the mother's perceptions of the baby's positive affect in everyday situations (e.g., during play with the mother, while exploring a toy), judged on a 6-category scale (*no reaction* to *laughs and vocalizes*) or measured by the frequency of smiles, vocalizations, and types of affective responses babies display to social and nonsocial stimuli. This dimension has 14 items.

2. *Negative affect:* The baby's negative affect as well as the mother's perceptions of the baby's negative affect in everyday experiences (e.g., when hungry, when the mother leaves, when a toy is removed), judged on a 6-category scale (from *no reaction* to *screams*) or indexed by the frequency of crying or fussing. This dimension has 11 items.

3. *Persistence:* The duration of the baby's visual attentiveness to social games and nonsocial attention-getting stimuli, and maternal perceptions of infant visual attentiveness. This dimension has 6 items.

4. *Motor responsivity:* The baby's tendency to react motorically and the quality of motoric reactions to social and nonsocial stimuli, indexed by the frequency of targeted behaviors such as reaching for, banging, or mouthing an object and judged on a 6-category scale (*body not moving, limbs relaxed* to *attempts to sit, stand, or crawl*). Our emphasis is on the quality of purposeful motor reactions, in contrast to diffuse motor activity. This dimension has 19 items.

5. *Soothability:* The effectiveness and frequency of different soothing styles (e.g., rocking, singing), observed and recorded through frequency counts. Soothability is considered whenever distress emerges (e.g., soiled diapers, hunger, seeking attention). This dimension has 12 items.

After initial data collection, the internal consistency of these five dimensions is assessed in two ways, and orthogonality is assessed in one way. First, item analysis is performed to determine the extent to which individual items correlate with a total dimension score, that is, the extent to which an item is related to all the other items in the dimension considered as a group. Items that correlate significantly (after their own contribution to the overall dimension score is controlled) are retained; those that do not are discarded. Second, coefficient alpha measures the internal consistency of a given dimension and is based on the extent to which all of the items making up the dimension are intercorrelated. By extension, coefficient alpha serves as a measure of the reliability of the dimension. The usual criterion for acceptability of obtained coefficient alphas is approximately .70 to .80; those dimensions that fail to meet this criterion are either reformulated or eliminated with caution, since dropping items from a dimension may attenuate coefficient alpha (Nunnally, 1978). Finally, correlations among the dimensions are also examined, since lack of orthogonality indicates that dimensions are composed of overlapping or redundant items. Apart from the problems that lack of orthogonality raises with regard to the conceptual integrity of dimensions, redundancy is also a source of increased measurement error for the instrument as a whole. This is especially pertinent if dimensions are to be used to form profiles (Conger & Lipshitz, 1973).

Design

Our general experimental design follows three main phases (Figure 7.1). First, the mother is sent the MPQ and asked to complete and return it 7 days before a series of home observations. Second, 1 week after the mother completes the MPQ, the first of three home observations of the infant begins. Home observations last 2 hours and are spaced on the average about 5 days apart. Two assessments of the infant's temperament are made during each home visit: A trained observer completes the BTQ-O during the home visit, and the mother responds to the BTQ-M immediately after the observation session ends. Third, about 1 week after the final home visit, the mother again completes the MPQ as well as a demographic questionnaire about her age, education, socioeconomic status, obstetric history, and so on.

An example study

In order to begin to address the questions framed by our original goals, we conducted a small-scale preliminary study on a sample of a dozen 5-month-old infants. The results discussed here were performed on a subset of 39 of our original

	─────DAYS─────	
1	8, 13, 18	25
MPQ Initial	BTQ-Mother Visits 1, 2, 3	MPQ Final
	Visits 1, 2, 3 BTQ-Observer	

Figure 7.1. Design of the observer and maternal assessment series.

62 items; a number of the original items were eliminated because we found that certain behaviors occurred too infrequently or because too little variance was associated with a given item.

Our main results concerned the short-term reliability of infant temperament, the reliability of maternal reports, mothers' knowledge of their infants before participating, and the effects of mothers' participation in the observation series on their perceptions. The results were as follows. First, the short-term reliability of observer ratings was assessed by obtaining correlations among observer reports made during the three home visits. Correlations among corresponding maternal reports offer an estimate of the short-term reliability of maternal ratings as well. These data indicate that temperament in 5-month-old infants as indexed by our preliminary measure is moderately stable over a 2-week period. The average intraclass correlation between pairs of visits on all items was .51 for observers (range, .28 to .65) and .77 for mothers (range, .55 to .88). However, the use of a finely differentiated array of items reveals a richly textured picture: Inspection of the range of standardized item alphas for this measure confirms our hypothesis that individual items are differentially stable (range, .00 to .95). The question raised by these data is, Which items or dimensions of temperament are reliably observed *and* evidence stability and which are reliably observed but evidence instability over time?

Second, the reliability of maternal reports for the home observations was indexed by correlating mother and observer values on all items. This analysis provided mother–observer convergence estimates for the instrument as a whole. A high level of agreement obtained. Mother–observer correlations on all items across the three home visits averaged .85 (see Figure 7.2, which also provides Pearson *r*'s for comparison). Although we do not advocate the exclusive use of maternal reports, these data indicate clearly that maternal ratings obtained within a structured context can be reliable. The results tend to confirm our conclusion that past findings of poor mother–observer convergence might reflect in part methodological problems as well as more formal differences in maternal and observer perceptions.

Third, we addressed the interrelated questions of how well mothers knew their infants before participating in the observation sessions and how mothers' participation in such observations affected their perceptions. We estimated mothers' prior knowledge by correlating their initial, preparticipation ratings with the average of observer reports across the three home visits. Mothers' preparticipation knowledge of their infants as measured by our instrument was low, with a mean ICC of .31 (Figure 7.2). (The degree of association between mothers' reports made before participation and the average of mothers' reports obtained during the home visits was higher, with a mean ICC of .76.) Apparently, mothers' global perceptions do not so well match their babies' behaviors as rated by our

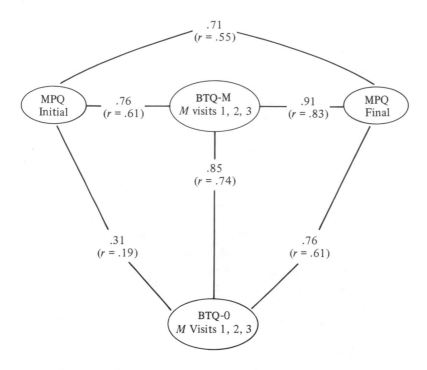

Figure 7.2. Intraclass correlations among observer ratings and maternal reports (Pearson product–moment correlations in parentheses).

observers. Therefore, as we believed, mothers' averaging over months may have introduced disagreement. Or some material perceptions may originate outside mother–infant interaction. As reviewed earlier, socioeconomic status, stress, and personality could be influential factors.

The effect of participation on maternal perception was indexed, first, by correlating mothers' final, postparticipation ratings with the average of observer estimates across the three home visits and, second, by correlating maternal ratings made before and after the home visit series. The level of convergence between maternal reports made after the home visit series and the average of observer ratings during home visits was .76 (Figure 7.2). Convergence between postparticipation maternal reports and the average of maternal reports obtained during the home visits was also high; the mean ICC was .91 (Figure 7.2). Thus, mothers' final, postparticipation reports bore a considerably stronger relationship to ratings made by the observer (and to reports made by the mothers themselves during the home visits) than did their preparticipation ratings. (The intraclass correlation between initial and final maternal reports was quite high nevertheless, with a mean ICC of .71.) Overall, then, the data in this preliminary study seem to indicate that there is some modest stability in mothers' perceptions of their infants' temperaments but that maternal perceptions can be somewhat refined through participation in formal observations. Significance testing via Fisher's z transformation (Kraemer, 1980) indicated that the difference between the ICC of mothers' preparticipation reports and the average of observer ratings (.31) against the ICC of mothers' postparticipation reports and the average of observer ratings (.76), although strong, was not significant. It is quite probable, however, that with a sufficient sample size the magnitude of such a difference would indeed reach statistical significance.

Thus, we can cautiously state, first, that participating in structured home visits is valuable when mothers are confronted with relatively complex rating tasks and, second, that maternal report is amenable to training (see also Cummings et al., 1981). Possibly we will find that some items or dimensions of temperament give clear evidence of training effects, whereas others remain relatively untouched by mothers' experiences in formal observations.

Recently, we reassessed relations among observer ratings and maternal reports with an expanded sample of 21 infants. The overall pattern of results depicted in Figure 1 remained intact, although the magnitude of correlations decreased in some instances.

In order to investigate the dimensional structure underlying the behaviors we measured, we performed factor analyses on that subset of items demonstrating the strongest psychometric properties. A two-factor confirmatory model was tested. We predicted that all behaviors pertaining to positive affect would load strongly and positively on the first factor, whereas fussing/crying behaviors would load moderately and negatively on this same factor. (This does not suggest that we regard positive and negative affect as extreme ends of a bipolar dimension. We made this prediction as a temporary expedient to accommodate these limited data.) We also predicted that specified items pertaining to spontaneous object-seeking motor behaviors, such as mouthing or reaching, would load on the second factor together with items indexing spontaneous vocalizations. We expected a moderate degree of correlation between this factor and the positive affect factor. Our two-factor model called for an oblique solution on theoretical grounds; we chose to employ an oblique Procrustes method to test our specific hypotheses. Three factor analyses were performed in total, one for each visit; thus, factor analyses based on the first and second visits served as replications of the factor structure derived from the first visit. We also tested the tenability of our hypotheses with an exploratory method to guard against the possibility that obtained factor structures were method specific. For this reason, we performed principal factor analyses with varimax rotation on the data from the first visit as well.

Overall, these analyses revealed a basic factor structure that is fairly consistent across visits and methods of analysis. Two factors emerged, and we tentatively labeled them Affective Expressiveness and Motor Activity. The first consists of items that index the frequency of smiles toward social and nonsocial objects; as expected, the negative affect item loads negatively on this factor. The second factor is of equivalent interest because it suggests linkages between purposeful, exploratory motor behaviors and vocalizing. Our present efforts are directed toward a full-scale standardization of the MPQ–BTQ complex that assays all three dimensions of temperament.

Summary and conclusions

In this chapter, we observed that temperament is typically understood as behavioral differences in affective expressiveness, motor activity, and stimulus sensitivity. These dimensions are probably constitutionally endowed and mutable through experience. We presented arguments that genetic rather than prenatal or perinatal differences represent a significant source of variation in temperament in normal populations. Behavior genetic and cross-cultural studies that corroborate this model were discussed. We then offered an extended critique of temperament measures and, finally, we presented an instrument, a design, and data representing our initial efforts toward a working assessment of infant temperament in short-term and, potentially, longitudinal contexts.

A better understanding of the development of temperament – that is, whether and how individuals change over time and context – will serve definite theoretical and clinical utility. Researchers will be in a position to delineate interactions among temperamental dispositions and environmental variables with greater precision when it is known how dimensions respond to the vicissitudes of maturation and experience. Possibly some longitudinal fluctuations will be found to be systematically related to key environmental variables, such as maternal stress, physical conditions in the home, or cultural differences among families. These fluctuations may also be related to other salient aspects of child development, such as attachment behavior and peer competence.

At this juncture, with so little known about temperament as a developmental phenomenon, child clinicians can neither evaluate nor predict what temperamental differences will mean in the family or in other social contexts. Clinicians need age-appropriate norms regarding the stability of temperamental attributes and ranges of possible outcomes; it is axiomatic that a solid understanding of normal development is the foundation of decision making in clinical work with children.

It is also becoming clear that the temperament construct will gain greater theoretical and empirical meaning only when its associations with other psychological constructs, such as cognition (Campos et al., 1983; Peters-Martin & Wachs, 1984; Wachs & Gandour, 1983) or attachment (Sroufe, 1979, 1985) can be established. Cronbach and Meehl (1955) have termed this broader context a "nomological network." Psychological constructs do not exist in isolation, but operate in relation to other independent constructs to form a mutually influential system. It is not sufficient simply to demonstrate that relations exist among diverse constructs or to assert that these relations are theoretically tenable. The nomological network expresses the organizing principles that underlie and give meaning to a web of relations. When temperament finds an integral rather than ancillary role in theories of child development, its significance as a construct will be certain.

References

Ainsworth, M. (1967). *Infancy in Uganda*. Baltimore, MD: Johns Hopkins University Press.
Allen, M. J., & Yen, W. M. (1979). *Introduction to measurement theory*. Monterey, CA: Brooks/Cole.
Bakeman, R., & Brown, J. V. (1980). Early interaction: Consequences for social and mental development at three years. *Child Development, 51,* 437–47.
Bates, J. E. (1983). Issues in the assessment of difficult temperament: A reply to Thomas, Chess, and Korn. *Merrill–Palmer Quarterly, 29,* 89–97.
Bates, J. E., Freeland, C. A., & Lounsbury, M. L. (1979). Measurement of infant difficultness. *Child Development, 50,* 794–803.
Bornstein, M. H. (1980). Cross-cultural developmental psychology. In M. H. Bornstein (Ed.), *Comparative methods in psychology* (pp. 231–81). Hillsdale, NJ: Erlbaum.
Brackbill, Y. (1979). Obstetrical medication and infant behavior. In J. D. Osofsky (Ed.), *Handbook of infant development* (pp. 76–125). New York: Wiley.
Brazelton, T. B. (1973). *Neonatal behavioral assessment scale* (Clinics in Developmental Medicine, No. 50). Philadelphia: Lippincott.
Buss, A. H., & Plomin, R. (1975). *A temperament theory of personality*. New York: Wiley.
Buss, A. H., & Plomin, R. (1984). *Temperament: Early developing personality traits*. Hillsdale, NJ: Erlbaum.
Callaghan, J. W. (1981). A comparison of Anglo, Hopi, and Navajo mothers and infants. In T. M. Field, A. M. Sostek, P. Vietze, & P. H. Leiderman (Eds.), *Culture and early interactions* (pp. 115–31). Hillsdale, NJ: Erlbaum.
Campos, J. J., Barrett, K. C., Lamb, M. E., Goldsmith, H. H., & Stenberg, C. (1983). Socioemotional development. In P. H. Mussen (Ed.), *Handbook of child psychology* (Vol. 2, 4th ed., pp. 783–915). New York: Wiley.
Carey, W. B. (1970). A simplified method for measuring infant temperament. *Journal of Pediatrics, 77,* 188–94.
Carey, W. B., & McDevitt, S. C. (1978a). Revision of the Infant Temperament Questionnaire. *Pediatrics, 61,* 735–9.
Carey, W. B., & McDevitt, S. C. (1978b). Stability and change in individual temperamental diagnoses from infancy to early childhood. *Journal of the American Academy of Child Psychiatry, 17,* 331–7.
Caudill, W., & Weinstein, H. (1969). Maternal care and infant behavior in Japan and America. *Psychiatry, 32,* 12–43.
Chess, S. (1979). Developmental theory revisited. *Canadian Journal of Psychiatry, 24,* 101–12.
Chisholm, J. S. (1983). *Navajo infancy: An ethological study of child development*. New York: Aldine.

Cohen, J. (1977). *Statistical power analysis for the behavioral sciences.* New York: Academic Press.

Cohen, J., & Cohen, P. (1983). *Applied multiple regression/correlation analysis for the behavioral sciences.* Hillsdale, NJ: Erlbaum.

Conger, A. J., & Lipshitz, R. (1973). Measure of reliability for profiles and test batteries. *Psychometrika, 38,* 411–27.

Cronbach, L. J., & Meehl, P. E. (1955). Construct validity in psychological tests. *Psychological Bulletin, 52,* 281–302.

Cummings, E. M., Zahn-Waxler, C., & Radke-Yarrow, M. (1981). Young children's responses to expressions of anger and affection by others in the family. *Child Development, 52,* 1274–82.

Derryberry, D., & Rothbart, M. K. (1984). Emotion, attention, and temperament. In C. E. Izard, J. Kagan, & R. B. Zajonc (Eds.), *Emotions, cognition, and behavior* (pp. 132–66). Cambridge University Press.

deVries, M. W., & Sameroff, A. J. (1984). Culture and temperament: Influences on infant temperament in three East African societies. *American Journal of Orthopsychiatry, 54,* 83–96.

deVries, M. W., & Super, C. M. (1978). Contextual influences in the Neonatal Behavioral Assessment Scale and implications for its cross-cultural use. *Monographs of the Society for Research in Child Development, 43* (5–6, Serial No. 177).

Field, T. M., Dempsey, J. R., & Shuman, H. H. (1981). Developmental follow-up of pre- and postterm infants. In S. L. Freidman & M. Sigman (Eds.), *Preterm birth and psychological development* (pp. 299–327). New York: Academic Press.

Field, T. M., & Greenberg, R. (1982). Temperamental ratings by parents and teachers of infants, toddlers, and preschool children. *Child Development, 53,* 160–3.

Freedman, D. G. (1974). *Human infancy: An evolutionary perspective.* New York: Wiley.

Fullard, W., McDevitt, S. C., & Carey, W. B. (1984). *Toddler temperament scale.* Unpublished manuscript, Temple University, Philadelphia.

Fuller, J. C. (1984). Psychology and genetics. In M. H. Bornstein (Ed.), *Psychology and its allied disciplines* (Vol. 3, pp. 65–107). Hillsdale, NJ: Erlbaum.

Goldsmith, H. H. (1983). Genetic influences on personality from infancy to childhood. *Child Development, 54,* 331–5.

Goldsmith, H. H. (May 1985a). *Theories of temperament.* Conversation hour at the Society for Research in Child Development, Toronto.

Goldsmith, H. H. (July 1985b). *Heritability: An inappropriate criterion for temperament and heritability of individual differences in emotional expression.* Paper presented at the Workshop on Temperament and Development. Leiden, The Netherlands.

Goldsmith, H. H., & Campos, J. J. (1982). Toward a theory of infant temperament. In R. N. Emde & R. J. Harmon (Eds.), *The development of attachment and affiliative systems* (pp. 161–93). New York: Plenum.

Goldsmith, H. H., & Gottesman, I. I. (1981). Origin of variation in behavioral style: A longitudinal study of temperament in young twins. *Child Development, 52,* 91–103.

Goldsmith, H. H., & Rieser-Danner, L. A. (April 1984). *The measurement of temperament in developmental context.* Paper presented at the Fourth International Conference on Infancy Studies, New York.

Haggard, E. (1958). *Intraclass correlation and the analysis of variance.* New York: Dryden.

Hsu, C., Soong, W., Stigler, J. W., Hong, C., & Liang, C. (1981). The temperamental characteristics of Chinese babies. *Child Development, 52,* 1337–40.

Hubert, N. C., Wachs, T. D., Peters-Martin, P., & Gandour, M. J. (1982). The study of early temperament: Measurement and conceptual ideas. *Child Development, 53,* 571–600.

Jacobson, S. W., Fein, G. G., Jacobson, J. L., Schwartz, P. M., & Dowler, J. K. (1984). Neonatal correlates of prenatal exposure to smoking, caffeine and alcohol. *Infant Behavior and Development, 7,* 253–65.

Kaye, K. (1978). Discrimination among normal infants by multivariate analysis of Brazelton scores:

Lumping and smoothing. *Monographs for the Society for Research in Child Development, 43*(5–6, Serial No. 177).

Keefer, C. H., Tronick, E., Dixon, J., & Brazelton, T. B. (1982). Specific differences in motor performance between Gusii and American newborns and a modification of the Neonatal Behavioral Assessment Scale. *Child Development, 53,* 754–9.

Kraemer, H. C. (1980). Extension of Feldt's approach to testing homogeneity of coefficients of reliability. *Psychometrika, 46,* 41–5.

Kuchner, J. F. R. (1980). *Chinese-American and European-American: A cross-cultural study of infant and mothers.* Unpublished doctoral dissertation, University of Chicago.

Lahey, M. A., Downey, R. G., & Saal, F. E. (1983). Intraclass correlations: There's more than meets the eye. *Psychological Bulletin, 93,* 586–95.

Lerner, R. M., & Lerner, J. V. (1983). Temperament–intelligence reciprocities in early childhood: A contextual model. In M. Lewis (Ed.), *Origins of intelligence.* New York: Plenum.

Lerner, R. M., Palermo, M., Spiro, A., & Nesselroade, J. R. (1982). Assessing the dimensions of temperamental individuality across the life span: The dimensions of temperament survey (DOTS). *Child Development, 53,* 149–59.

Lounsbury, M. L., & Bates, J. E. (1982). The cries of infants and different levels of perceived temperamental difficultness: Acoustic properties and effects on listeners. *Child Development, 53,* 677–86.

Lytton, H. (1971). Observation studies of parent–child interaction: A methodological review. *Child Development, 42,* 651–84.

Matheny, A. P. (1980). Bayley's Infant Behavior Record: Behavioral components and twin analyses. *Child Development, 51,* 1157–67.

Matheny, A. P. (1983). A longitudinal twin study of stability of components from Bayley's Infant Behavior Record. *Child Development, 84,* 356–60.

Matheny, A. P., Wilson, R. S., Dolan, A. B., & Krantz, J. Z. (1981). Behavioral contrasts in twinships: Stability and patterns of differences in childhood. *Child Development, 52,* 579–88.

Matheny, A. P., Wilson, R. S., & Nuss, S. M. (1984). Toddler temperament: Stability across settings and over ages. *Child Development, 55,* 1200–11.

Nunnally, J. (1978). *Psychometric theory.* New York: McGraw-Hill.

Pederson, F. A., Zaslow, M., Cain, R., Anderson, B. J., & Thomas, M. (1976). *A methodology for assessing parental perception of baby temperament.* Paper presented at the Southeastern Conference on Human Development.

Persson-Blennow, I., & McNeil, T. F. (1982). New data on test–retest reliability for three temperament scales. *Journal of Child Psychology and Psychiatry, 23,* 181–3.

Peters-Martin, P., & Wachs, T. D. (1984). A longitudinal study of temperament and its correlates in the first 12 months. *Infant Behavior and Development, 7,* 285–98.

Plomin, R. (1983). Developmental behavioral genetics. *Child Development, 54,* 253–9.

Plomin, R., DeFries, J. G., & Loehlin, J. G. (1977). Genotype–environment interaction and correlation in the analysis of human behavior. *Psychological Bulletin, 84,* 309–22.

Plomin, R., & Rowe, D. C. (1979). Genetic and environmental etiology of social behavior in infancy. *Developmental Psychology, 15,* 62–72.

Posner, M. I., & Rothbart, M. K. (1980). The development of attentional mechanisms. In J. Flowers (Ed.), *Nebraska symposium on motivation.* Lincoln: University of Nebraska Press.

Rapoport, J. L., Pandoni, C., Renfield, M., Lake, G. R., & Ziegler, M. G. (1977). Newborn dopamine-beta-hydroxylase, minor physical anomalies, and infant temperament. *American Journal of Psychiatry, 134,* 676–9.

Rothbart, M. K. (1981). Measurement of temperament in infancy. *Child Development, 52,* 569–78.

Rothbart, M. K. (April 1984). *Temperament and the development of behavioral inhibition.* Paper presented at the Fourth International Conference on Infant Studies, New York.

Rothbart, M. K., & Derryberry, P. (1981). Development of individual differences in temperament.

In M. E. Lamb & A. Brown (Eds.), *Advances in developmental psychology* (pp. 37–86). Hillsdale, NJ: Erlbaum.

Rothbart, M. K., & Posner, M. I. (1984). *Temperament and the development of self regulation.* Unpublished manuscript, University of Oregon, Eugene.

Rowe, D. C., & Plomin, R. (1981). The importance of nonshared (E_1) environmental influences on behavioral development. *Developmental Psychology, 17,* 517–31.

St. James-Roberts, I., & Wolke, P. (1984a). Comparison of mothers' with trained observers' reports of neonatal behavioral style. *Infant Behavior and Development, 7,* 299–310.

St. James-Roberts, I., & Wolke, P. (April 1984b). *Towards a systems theory of infant temperament.* Paper presented at the Fourth International Conference on Infant Studies, New York.

Sameroff, A., & Chandler, M. J. (1975). Reproductive risk and the continuum of caretaking casualty. In F. D. Horowitz (Ed.), *Review of child development research* (Vol. 4, pp. 187–244). Chicago: University of Chicago Press.

Sameroff, A. J., Krafchuk, E. E., & Bakow, H. A. (1978). Issues in grouping items from the Neonatal Behavioral Assessment Scale. *Monographs of the Society for Research in Child Development, 43*(5–6, Serial No. 177).

Sameroff, A., Seifer, R., & Elias, P. (1982). Sociocultural variability in infant temperament ratings. *Child Development, 53,* 164–73.

Scarr, S., & Kidd, K. K. (1983). Developmental behavior genetics. In P. H. Mussen (Ed.), *Handbook of child psychology* (Vol. 2, pp. 346–420). New York: Wiley.

Scarr, S., & McCartney, K. (1983). How people make their own environments: A theory of genotype–environment effects. *Child Development, 54,* 424–35.

Shrout, P. E., & Fleiss, J. L. (1979). Intraclass correlations: Uses in assessing rater reliability. *Psychological Bulletin, 86,* 420–8.

Smith, S., & Freedman, D. G. (1983). *Mother–toddler interaction and maternal perception of child temperament in two ethnic groups: Chinese-American and European-American.* Unpublished manuscript, University of Chicago.

Sroufe, L. A. (1979). Socioemotional development. In J. D. Osofsky (Ed.), *Handbook of infant development* (pp. 462–516). New York: Wiley.

Sroufe, L. A. (1985). Attachment classification from the perspective of infant–caregiver relationships and infant temperament. *Child Development, 56,* 1–14.

Super, C. (1976). Environmental effects on motor development: The case of "African infant precocity." *Developmental Medicine and Child Neurology, 18,* 561–7.

Thomas, A., & Chess, S. (1977). *Temperament and development.* New York: Brunner-Mazel.

Thomas, A., Chess, S., Birch, H., Hertzig, M., & Korn, S. (1963). *Behavioral individuality in childhood.* New York: New York University Press.

Torgersen, A. M., & Kringlen, E. (1978). Genetic aspects of temperamental differences in infants. *Journal of the American Academy of Child Psychiatry, 17,* 433–44.

Vaughn, B., Taraldson, B., Crichton, L., & Egeland, B. (1981). The assessment of infant temperament: A critique of the Carey Infant Temperament Questionnaire. *Infant Behavior and Development, 4,* 1–17.

Wachs, T. D., & Gandour, M. J. (1983). Temperament, environment, and six-month cognitive–intellectual development: A test of the organismic specificity hypothesis. *International Journal of Behavior Development, 6,* 135–52.

Wilson, R. S. (1978). Synchronies in mental development: An epigenetic perspective. *Science, 202,* 939–48.

Wilson, R. S. (1983). The Louisville twin study: Developmental synchronies in behavior. *Child Development, 54,* 298–316.

Wilson, R. S. (1984). Twins and chronogenetics: Correlated pathways of development. *Acta Geneticae Medicae et Gemellologiae: Twin Research, 33,* 149–57.

Wilson, R. S., & Matheny, A. P. (1983). Assessment of temperament in infant twins. *Developmental Psychology, 19,* 172–83.

Part V

The conceptualization of emotion

8 Concepts of emotion in developmental psychology

Merry Bullock and James A. Russell

The concepts of anger, fear, happiness, sadness, and the like are not technical concepts. They are everyday folk concepts regularly employed by everyone. Nevertheless, they play two important roles in the psychology of emotion.

One role of an emotion concept is that of a phenomenon to be investigated. The psychologist is interested in the nature of the concepts underlying the use of such everyday words as *angry, afraid, happy,* and *sad.* For example, a child might say of someone that "he looks sad today." To understand the child's concept of sad, a psychologist might ask the child to make a facial expression that is sad, to tell a sad story, or to pick out the sad person in a photograph. The psychologist's job in examples such as this is to understand the processes involved in the development and use of the concepts children employ in their everyday affairs.

The second role of an emotion concept is that of a scientific construct in theories about behaviors and states. Everyday emotion concepts provide scientists with a ready-made descriptive taxonomy for emotional states, a convenient means of parsing an aspect of psychological reality. Izard (1977), for example, believes that there is a distinct class of psychological events, called emotions, and that there are a small number of basic emotions, which he describes by words that would have been familiar to Chaucer: fear, anger, disgust, and the like. Tomkins (1962–3) and Ekman (1972) similarly place a list of everyday emotion concepts at the core of their theories of emotion. In designing studies on emotion, psychologists employ everyday concepts in framing their hypotheses. As a consequence, emotion concepts play a role in the assumptions made, the questions asked, and the answers offered.

Which of these two roles the psychologist has in mind should determine the

Work in this chapter was completed when M. Bullock was assistant professor at the University of British Columbia. Preparation of the chapter was supported by a grant to the authors from the Social Sciences and Humanities Research Council (410-83-0054). We thank E. McCririck, who aided immeasurably in the preparation of the manuscript, and K. Wesson, who constructed the figures.

use and measurement of an emotion concept. In this chapter, we discuss emotion concepts in each of these roles in developmental psychology. We begin by discussing the nature of concepts of emotion as they exist in everyday vocabulary. This discussion draws on current cognitive and psycholinguistic research with adult speakers in an attempt to advance a set of hypotheses that will guide our later discussion. We then turn to the nature of the child's concepts of emotion. Needless to say, it would be foolish to assume that what a child understands by a term such as *anger* is just what an adult understands. We explore how our hypotheses on the nature of emotion concepts in general can help us understand how children acquire and use emotion concepts. We argue that, indeed, what a preschool child means by *fear* or *anger* is systematically different from what an adult would mean, and we offer some ideas on the development of emotion concepts. Finally, we turn to the second role of emotion concepts, their use in the psychological study of children's actual emotion states. Whereas our concern with concepts in the first sections is *descriptive,* the concern in the last section is *prescriptive:* We are principally concerned with how psychologists use everyday concepts as theoretical constructs in the study of children's emotional states as they unfold developmentally. Our theme is that this use is heuristic but problematic.

The nature of adults' concepts of emotion

As speakers of English, we all know what such words as *emotion, anger, fear, happiness,* and *sadness* mean – that is, until asked to give a definition. Then, it seems, no one is sure. Problems of definition are routinely discussed by writers on emotion and have sometimes been blamed for much of the confusion and wrangling in the writings of emotion theorists. The problem may lie not in the events referred to by these words but in an inappropriate notion of how natural concepts can be defined. For many years, natural language concepts about everyday events were not distinguished from logically defined concepts, or ''proper sets.'' Although rarely stated, it was probably assumed that such everyday concepts as vehicle, furniture, fear, and emotion could be defined in the same way that proper sets are: by one or more individually necessary and jointly sufficient features. This classical view of concepts has appealed to most scholars, at least as far back as Aristotle. And, of course, some concepts can be defined in this way: Dollar bill, even number, corporation, and triangle can be given precise definitions and can therefore be thought of as proper sets. But, as various writers now argue, many everyday concepts cannot be so defined.

Skepticism over the classical view arose in philosophical writings. William James (1902/1929) was the first writer we know of to argue that some concepts cannot be given precise definitions. Langer (1942/1980) made a similar point, but it was Wittgenstein's (1953) analysis of the concept of a game that drew widespread attention to the difficulties of the classical view. There is no one feature that is shared by all games and that could therefore serve as a defining feature for the concept of game. Rather, any game has some features in common with most other games. One game thus resembles other games in much the same way that one member of a family resembles the others. Following Wittgenstein, writers in various disciplines have identified natural language concepts that appear to lack defining features and whose boundaries are therefore "fuzzy" (Labov, 1973; Lakoff, 1973; Mervis & Rosch, 1981; Rosch, 1973; Zadeh, 1965).

Prototypes and fuzzy borders

It is not yet clear how everyday concepts can be best characterized (Jones, 1982; Mervis & Rosch, 1981; Osherson & Smith, 1982; Smith & Medin, 1981), or even if one characterization will apply to all (Armstrong, Gleitman, & Gleitman, 1983). In psychology, Eleanor Rosch (1973, 1975, 1977) rekindled an interest in the nature of concepts by articulating one alternative to the classical view, an alternative known as prototype theory. Rosch began by noting that many natural concepts form a hierarchy of inclusion. For example, the set *fruit, apple, MacIntosh apple* illustrates a hierarchy with superordinate (most inclusive), middle, and subordinate (least inclusive) levels. The superordinate concept includes an indefinite number of categories at the next lower level. Fruit, for example, clearly includes apples, oranges, and pears, but coconuts, olives, and tomatoes are not so clear. Fruit is organized around its clearest examples, which are referred to as prototypes. Other instances vary in their degree of resemblance to the prototypes, with prototypes shading gradually into nonprototypes, and nonprototypes shading gradually into nonmembers. Graded membership thus creates an internal structure of a concept.

Figure 8.1 shows an inclusion hierarchy for the concept emotion. *Emotion* is at the topmost, or superordinate, level. The middle level is represented by such terms as *fear, love,* and *anger.* Of course, in addition to these would be less prototypical emotions such as *pride, envy,* and *lust,* all at the same, middle level. The number is indeterminate because there is no sharp boundary distinguishing emotions from nonemotions. Many of the middle-level categories may also be divisible, forming a subordinate level.

In a recent series of studies, the feasibility of this line of thinking (Russell, 1980b) was explored empirically (Fehr & Russell, 1984; Fehr, Russell, & Ward, 1982; Russell & Bullock, in press). As hypothesized, the concept of emotion was found to have an internal structure: Happiness, love, anger, fear, awe, respect, envy, and other middle-level categories could be reliably ordered from better to poorer examples of emotion. In turn, the goodness-of-example (or pro-

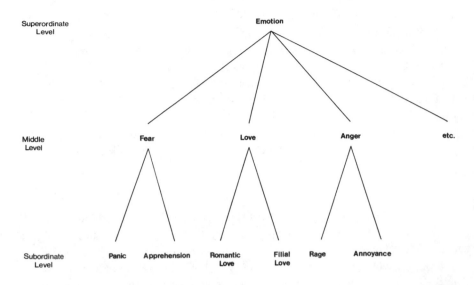

Figure 8.1. A portion of an inclusion hierarchy for emotions.

totypicality) rating for each emotion was found to predict how readily it comes to mind when subjects are asked to list emotions, how likely it is to be labeled as an emotion when asked what sort of thing it is, how readily it can be substituted for the word *emotion* in sentences without their sounding unnatural, the degree to which it resembles other middle-level emotion categories in terms of shared features, and the speed with which subjects can verify that it is indeed a type of emotion. In short, converging sources of evidence showed that the concept of emotion has an internal structure and that the internal structure predicts various indices of the cognitive processing of emotion concepts. Moreover, the border separating emotions from nonemotions is fuzzy rather than clear-cut.

Middle-level emotion categories (anger, fear, sadness, etc.) also show signs of internal structure and fuzzy borders. In a series of studies, we examined how adults categorize the message conveyed by emotional facial expressions (Russell & Bullock, in press). As predicted by prototype theory, facial expressions varied in their degree of exemplariness. Some expressions were prototypical examples, others were intermediate examples, and still others were very poor examples. There were also borderline cases in which subjects could not decide whether particular facial expressions were or were not members of a particular category.

That categories of emotion consist not only of their prototypical cases but of intermediate and borderline cases seems to explain a further and too often overlooked property of emotion categories: the large degree to which they overlap in their extension. Overlap of categories is illustrated in Figure 8.2. Along the abscissa are ordered 14 different facial expressions of emotion, labeled A through

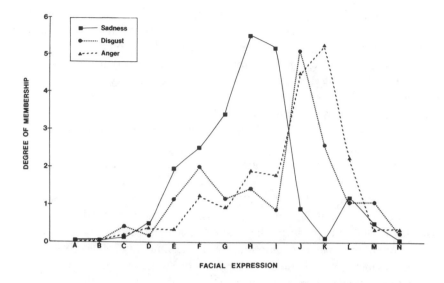

Figure 8.2. Overlap of emotion categories. Letters refer to facial expressions of emotion, the modal labels for which are as follows: A, excitement; B, happiness; C, happiness; D, calmness; E, calmness; F, sleepiness; G, sleepiness; H, sadness; I, sadness; J, disgust; K, anger; L, fear; M, surprise; N, surprise.

N, most of which were taken from the photographs of Ekman (1976). Mean ratings on the degree of membership are given on the ordinate for three categories: sadness, disgust, and anger. Although the peaks differ (and correspond to Ekman's, 1976, prototypical expressions for these three categories), all three categories are at least somewhat applicable to many of the same expressions.

Dimensions and intercategory structure of emotion

Dimensional accounts of emotion are those that emphasize continua such as pleasantness–unpleasantness along which all emotional states vary. Structural accounts are those that emphasize interrelationships among emotions. Talk about dimensions or structures is often thought of as contrasting with, or at least somewhat dissonant with, talk about categories of emotions. In our view, there is no dissonance. Consideration of categories, once their fuzzy boundaries and overlapping nature are seen, leads directly to the notion of intercategory structure, for structure represents the way in which categories overlap. And structure, in turn, leads directly to dimensions.

An interest in intercategory structure arose when Woodworth (1938) examined the "errors" subjects made when categorizing facial expressions of emotions. (Of course, if the view of emotion categories we are advocating is correct, these

were not errors, but manifestations of overlapping categories with fuzzy borders.) Woodworth found that "errors" were systematic: Subjects who did not
choose the correct category for a particular facial expression nonetheless chose
among a limited set of categories. From the systematic overlap of emotion categories, Woodworth derived a simple model of intercategory structure: a linear
ordering. Woodworth's student, Schlosberg, noticed that the two ends of Woodworth's continuum were also occasionally confused for one another. Schlosberg
(1952) therefore tied the two ends together, forming his well-known circular
structural model of emotion.

The relationship between intercategory structure and the fuzziness of categories can be demonstrated more directly. Taking the 14 facial expressions used in
the Russell and Bullock (in press) study, we derived a measure of the similarity
between each of all possible pairs of expressions. A pairwise similarity matrix is
just what is needed to produce, via a multidimensional scaling procedure, a representation of the structure of emotions. Pairwise similarity had been used in this
way many times, but this time our measure of similarity was derived entirely
from ratings of each expression's degree of membership in emotion categories.
Specifically, the similarity between two facial expressions was defined as the
correlation between their degrees of membership in 14 emotion categories. The

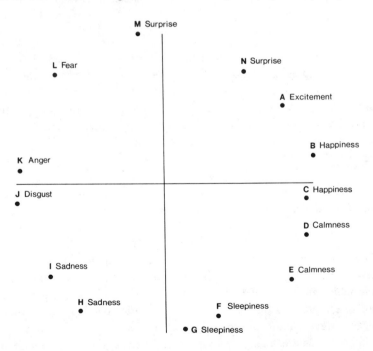

Figure 8.3. Circular order of emotion and facial expressions.

structure that resulted (Figure 8.3) placed emotions in a particular circular order in a two-dimensional space. That order corresponds remarkably closely to the circular ordering of emotions obtained by other methods (Russell, 1980a), including scaling of self-report data from both adults and children (Russell & Ridgeway, 1983) and semantic similarity ratings from Chinese, Japanese, Gujarati, and Croation speakers (Russell, 1983).

Intercategory structures, in turn, lead directly to dimensions. Schlosberg's circular order of emotions revealed two underlying dimensions, which he initially interpreted as pleasure–displeasure and attention–rejection. Later research favored degree of arousal as the interpretation of the second dimension (Abelson & Sermat, 1962; Russell & Bullock, 1985). Did the structure of emotional facial expressions derived from our measures of prototypicality reveal the same pleasure and arousal dimensions? Confirming what is clear from inspection of Figure 8.3, values on the horizontal dimension of Figure 8.3 correlate .93 with ratings of how much pleasure is expressed by the face. Values on the vertical dimension correlate .82 with ratings of degree of arousal shown in the face.

In short, far from being in competition, categories, structures, and dimensions are interrelated aspects of the human conceptual network used to understand emotion. With hindsight, this should not be surprising. Those who have thought and written about emotion have, since ancient times, expressed their ideas in terms of lists of categories, of more general dimensions of emotion, and of relations among categories. However, as we argue next, dimensions, categories, and their interrelationships far from exhaust the contents of that network.

Emotion scripts

All human beings, and probably many of our nonhuman relatives, encounter emotional states almost every day. Emotions are no small element of the social world surrounding each person. Much like the scientist interested in emotion, each person must understand how to detect emotions, how to distinguish different emotions, what brings emotions about, what settings emotions occur in, what the temporal sequence of emotion reactions can be, and what the consequences of emotions typically are. Taking the lead from Heider (1958) and Kelly (1955), we might benefit from the metaphor of person as scientist. Let us say, very loosely, that each person develops a taxonomy and theory for emotion. Categories, dimensions, and structure are metaphors with which to describe the taxonomic function of our mental processing of emotion. But clearly there is more than taxonomy to our understanding of emotion. We can describe other aspects of the folk ''theory.''

Consider what comes to mind when you hear the word *fear*. You may imagine some scenario like the following. A danger suddenly appears. You gasp and stare at it. Your jaw drops, your heart pounds, your hands tremble. You try to figure out what to do, but thoughts race through your mind and you feel overwhelmed with panic. You turn and flee.

The folk theory includes knowledge that emotions occur over time, follow particular sequences, and occur in particular settings. In other words, the folk theory includes a *script* (Abelson, 1981) in which events unfold in order. The script contains prototypical causes, appraisals of the situations, physiological reactions, feelings, facial expressions, actions, and consequences.

Identification of an actual sequence of events as fear involves its implicit comparison with the script. The sequence of events narrated above might never have actually occurred in just that way. Fear may be said to exist even if the events listed occurred in a different order, or if some were altered or absent altogether. For example, you might stand and face the danger rather than flee. You might hide or inhibit some of the physiological or behavioral signs of fear. You might bluff, by ignoring the danger. You might not even believe the situation is dangerous, as in the case of phobics who readily admit that their debilitating fear is unfounded. Of course, if enough events in the sequence are absent or altered or out of order, we are unlikely to call it fear. But the border is fuzzy, and there exist cases in which so few of these events occur that one is unsure whether *fear* is the right term. The notion of script can thus be seen to extend to episodes the notion of prototype.

The nature of children's concepts of emotion

In the preceding section, we presupposed a distinction between emotion concepts and emotion events. To say that the everyday word *fear* is understood by means of a script is to say nothing about actual instances of fear. We did not mean that fear is an act rather than real, nor did we mean that fear is a reflexlike fixed pattern of action. In turning to children's concepts of emotion, we must emphasize the distinction between emotion concepts and emotion events.

Psychologists disagree on the nature of emotion events. One position is that emotions can be divided naturally into coherent units, each a distinct, recognizable bundle of particular behaviors, expressive signs, patterns of physiological activity, and subjective experience. It is usually assumed that these coherent units correspond to basic emotion terms of the English language. Another position is that there are no natural units of emotion. Rather than forming coherent bundles, any pattern of behavior, expressive signs, physiological activity, and subjective experience is as likely to occur as any other. Other positions can be defined between these extremes, but the point here is that, whatever the reality of emotion events may be, the child must still organize, categorize, and interpret that reality. Whether or not emotion reality consists of discrete units does not tell us how the child conceptualizes emotion. If emotion reality is discrete, the child may not know this; if reality is not discrete, the child may impose discrete categories on it.

Research on children's interpretation of emotional states has typically presupposed just the opposite. This research has generally not been thought of as being concerned with the development of *concepts,* but with how children come to "recognize" different emotions "accurately." Accuracy is taken to be conformity with an adult standard, which is usually defined as the way that adults divide emotions into a set of discrete units. Although accuracy scores can tell us some things, they may not tell the whole story.

We prefer to think in terms of the nature of the child's concepts and to ask how such concepts develop. Useful information can come from an analysis of what children do, accurately or not, when they are asked to label, categorize, or discriminate among emotions. From our perspective, the important question is whether their responses are systematic. It is when children's interpretations are systematic that we can begin to specify the bases of those interpretations – their emotion concepts – and the ways in which such concepts develop.

Children's interpretation of emotions has been addressed in a number of ways. Children have been asked to match emotional expressions with situations, to label emotional expressions, to produce emotional expressions for a given label, and to state which emotions arise in different situations. For example, investigators have asked when children come to identify such "basic" emotions as anger, fear, sadness, and happiness, and what cues they use to do so. The sources of information provided as cues include faces, emotion words, situations, or some combination of these (Borke, 1971; Felleman et al., 1983; Field & Walden, 1982; Gates, 1923; Gitter, Mostofsky, & Quincy, 1971; Gnepp, Klayman, & Trabasso, 1982; Guthrie & Smouse, 1981; Izard, 1971; Odom & Lemond, 1972; Reichenbach & Masters, 1983).

The most consistent finding from such tasks is that children's accuracy improves with age. Preschoolers typically perform at close to chance levels on most tasks. The youngest school-age children perform at levels above chance but so far from adult accuracy that it is unclear how their responses are best interpreted. Older school-age children and teen-agers are progressively more accurate, and it eventually becomes reasonable to conclude that their concepts are equivalent to those of adults.

A second conclusion is that children's accuracy varies with the emotion presented (Borke, 1971; Felleman et al., 1983; Gitter et al., 1971; Guthrie & Smouse, 1981). The general result is that happiness is identified, differentiated, and labeled more consistently than other emotion states such as fear, anger, surprise, sadness, and pain. For example, Felleman et al. (1983) asked 5-year-olds to label photographs of facially expressed happiness, anger, and sadness. Children were most accurate at labeling happy expressions (89 to 91% correct), moderately accurate at labeling sadness (63% correct), and less accurate at labeling anger (52 to 58%). (Accuracy was defined as a match between the child's label and that provided by adults to the same expression.) Felleman et al. noted that any such result must be viewed in the context of children's emotion vocabulary: The label *happy* may have been more likely to be used and thus more likely to be overgeneralized.

Another technique is to ask children to produce facial expressions of particular emotions. Children are given a word, a facial expression to imitate, or a situation (Odom & Lemond, 1972; Field & Walden, 1982; Felleman et al., 1983). Again, preschoolers are not very good at this sort of task when accuracy is defined as producing an expression that can reliably be labeled by adult raters. There is a suggestion (Hesse & Cichetti, 1982) that young children are best at imitating facial expressions that they can label. However, because voluntary production or imitation requires special skills for which there are, even in adults, large individual differences, this technique cannot play a definitive role in assessing children's concepts.

Although most of the responses of young children are classified as "errors," there are few reports of any analyses of the pattern of these responses. This neglect is unfortunate because those investigators who have examined errors have reported a consistent pattern: Children do not err randomly (e.g., Borke, 1971; Felleman et al., 1983; Reichenbach & Masters, 1983). They tend to err by confusing emotions that are similar, according to the structural model (Figure 8.3) presented earlier. For example, children are likely to confuse anger and sadness, anger and fear, and the like. As noted above, they are most accurate at imitating or labeling happiness; this emotion is usually the only positive one included and thus, according to the structural model, maximally distinct from the other, less pleasant emotions.

In the remainder of this section, we summarize several studies from our own laboratory. In these studies we have not focused on accuracy, but rather on three other central issues: (a) What is the nature of children's emotion concepts? Are they organized around prototypes? Are they the same as adults' concepts? Or is there a change with development in the range and breadth of the content? (b) Is the emotion domain structured for children? That is, do children see emotions as varying in similarity in a systematic way? (c) What is the basis for the formation of categories and intercategory structure? We have collected information on children's interpretation of one aspect of emotions: facial expressions. Although a full account of a child's understanding of emotion clearly requires evidence concerning a number of aspects of emotion, we began with facial expressions because they are one clear medium of emotional communication available to all seeing children. We focused on a particular age group – preschoolers – because the preschool years are the period when children are least "accurate," when they come to acquire a lexicon of emotion words, and when they refer to internal states such as emotion as potential causes of behavior.

Matching faces with words

To ascertain the referents for child's emotion concepts, we designed three tasks in which children were asked to match photographs of emotion expressions with emotion words. Across the tasks we used a core set of photographs and words, which we shall describe here. Additional words and photographs were synonyms or alternate examples of the ones to be discussed here (for full results see Bullock & Russell, 1984; 1985; Russell & Bullock, 1985; 1986).

The facial expressions we used were portrayed in black and white photographs of female actresses (Figure 8.4). Six of the nine are from Ekman's (1976) *Pictures of Facial Affect*. The remaining three are from our own set, which were pretested and consistently labeled as the intended emotion by adults. Nevertheless, neither Ekman's labels nor our own play any role in our experiments with children. We therefore use Labels A through I, which correspond to their order according to our circular structural model of emotion (Figure 8.3).

The words covered a range intended as referents for the faces. They included *happy, excited, surprised, afraid* (or *scared*), *angry* (or *mad*), *disgusted, sad, sleepy,* and *calm* (or *relaxed*).

Task 1: choosing from an array. We presented the following task to 114 children between 3 and 5 years of age (Bullock & Russell, 1984). Each child was presented with 10 facial expressions, spread in a random array (the 9 in Figure 8.4 plus a neutral expression). An experimenter asked the child to survey the pho-

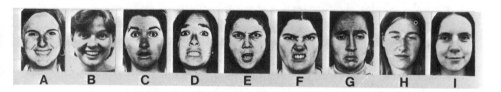

Figure 8.4. Nine facial expressions ordered according to a structural model. Photographs A, C, D, E, F, and G are taken from P. Ekman (1976), *Pictures of Facial Affect* (Palo Alto, CA: Consulting Psychologists Press, Inc.) and are reproduced here with permission. Investigators interested in using these photographs should obtain original prints from Consulting Psychologists Press rather than attempt to reproduce them from what is shown here. Reproduction inevitably further degrades the image and could introduce errors in any experimental procedure. Results obtained with degraded images would be difficult to interpret or to compare with results obtained with the original photographs. Photographs B, H, and I show actors asked by the authors to pose excitement, sleepiness, and calmness, respectively.

Table 8.1. *Proportion of "errors" that were of the two faces adjacent to the "correct" choice*

	Age		
Category	3 years	4 years	5 years
Happy	*89*	*88*	*60*
Excited	32	33	*63*
Surprised	36	*43*	*71*
Afraid	*55*	*64*	*79*
Scared	*63*	70	*56*
Angry	*75*	*90*	*94*
Mad	*90*	*90*	*89*
Disgusted	*40*	22	*32*
Sad	14	14	25
Calm	24	*42*	*46*

Note: Data are expressed as percentages. The proportion expected by chance is 22%. Italics indicate a result significantly different from chance (alpha = .05).

tographs and to make three choices without replacement for each emotion word. Before each choice the experimenter asked, "Which person is [emotion word]?" The words substituted are given in Table 8.1.

When scored for accuracy, the children's choices were consistent with previous findings in the literature. Examination of their "errors" was much more revealing. Our first finding was that even 3-year-olds were systematic in their choices. By "systematic" we mean that their "errors" were predictable from our structural model. Table 8.1 shows the proportion of "errors" that resulted because the first choice was the one expression to either side (according to our structural model) of the "correct" expression for that word (e.g., errors were E or G if the correct choice was F). Although there is evidence for random error with some words (*excited, surprised, sad,* and *calm*), many more of the errors were as predicted than would occur by chance. A quantitative analysis of the data in Table 8.1 confirmed this interpretation. We combined responses from all the trials and asked what proportion of errors were as predicted: 54.7% of the 5-year-olds' errors, 43.3% of the 4-year-olds' errors, and 40.1% of the 3-year-olds' errors were as predicted. Each of these results was significantly different from the 22.2% expected by chance responding ($p < .001$ for each age group). Preschoolers were systematic in their selection of facial expressions as referents for emotion words even when they did not select the modal adult choice.

To examine the entire pattern of children's choices, we constructed histograms of their first choices for each of the test words. To illustrate, Figure 8.5 presents

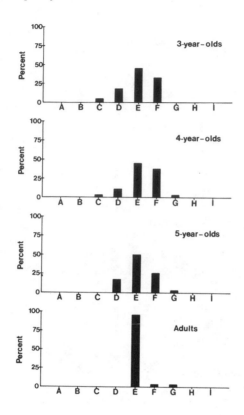

Figure 8.5. Choices for the word *mad*, Task 1.

the results for children's first choices for the word *mad*. Photographs are ordered on the abcissa in terms of their placement in the circular model. The modal response was Face E (Ekman's prototypical expression of anger) for each age group. As already indicated, children were most likely to "err" by choosing faces close to E. There was thus a focal point, the expression most likely to be chosen, with the probability of a choice decreasing with distance from the focal point. In terms of the faces we used, this means that those children who did not pick the focal expression E tended to choose Ekman's prototypical fear (D) or disgust (F) picture. This result illustrates how the circular model reveals the breadth and systematic nature of emotion categories. The general pattern illustrated for *mad* was repeated for the other words.

We also found ways in which emotion categories change with age. For most of the words, the category narrowed with age. This narrowing pattern is seen in Figure 8.5 with *mad* and is illustrated again with results for the word *afraid* in

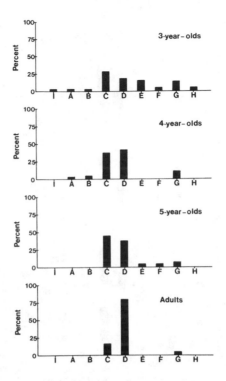

Figure 8.6. Choices for the word *afraid*, Task 1.

Figure 8.6. The range around the focal point (in this case, Face D, Ekman's prototypical expression of fear) appears to sharpen with age – or broaden as we look at each younger group. On their first choice, adults tended to agree in selecting Face D, with only a few selecting C (Ekman's surprised expression). Five-year-olds selected D and C about equally often, as did 4-year-olds. Thus, their focal point was broader than for adults. Three-year-olds had an even broader focal point for *afraid*, encompassing Faces C, D, and E. The range around a focal point for the test words *scared, miserable, disgusted,* and *happy* showed a similar change with age.

Several categories also showed a shift in focal point. The results for *surprised* (Figure 8.7) illustrate a shift. For adults, the focal point for *surprised* was C (Ekman's prototypical expression of surprise), with some choices falling to the two adjacent faces, B and D (the "afraid" expression on the unpleasant side and the "excited" expression on the pleasant side). For 5-year-olds, the focal point shifted to B (the "excited" expression), with C in a tie for second place with A (the "Happy" expression). For 4- and 3-year-olds, the focal point remained B, but A was now a more frequent choice than C ("surprised" expression). Indeed,

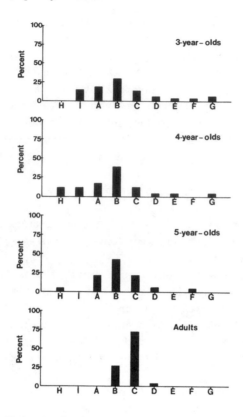

Figure 8.7. Choices for the word *surprised,* Task 1.

the adult modal choice, C, was no more likely to be chosen than was Face I (the "calm" expression). Thus, the meaning of the word *surprised* for 3- and 4-year olds was something closer to *excited* or even *happy* than the adult meaning for *surprised*. The terms *sleepy, excited,* and *relaxed* also displayed shifts in focal point.

To summarize, given an array of facial expressions, children as young as 3 categorize them in a meaningful way, although their categories are not equivalent to adults'. Children's categories are broader and, in a few instances, shifted relative to adults'.

Task 2: forced choice. Task 1, it might be argued, may have required attentional or scanning abilities (e.g., Vurpillot, 1976) beyond those of our younger children. We therefore repeated the same general procedure with a simpler task. We asked children to select a facial expression as a referent for a word, but their choice was between only two expressions, one of which was always the prototypical expression for the category named. This simpler procedure allowed us to include a group of younger subjects, 2-year-olds, and to obtain more precise data on children's categories.

We presented the following task to 240 children, aged 2 to 5 years, and 30 adults for comparison purposes (Bullock & Russell, 1985). In a given trial the subject was shown two photographs and asked, "Which person is [target label]?" The labels substituted were the same as in the previous study. For each word, we paired the target facial expression (prototypical for that category) with each of the eight other photographs of Figure 8.4. We labeled the pair according to distance between the target and alternative photo. In a Step 1 pair, the alternative photograph was adjacent to the target, according to the circular model. In Steps 2, 3, and 4, the target was paired with expressions progressively more distant. Since a photograph can be thought of as being farther from the target in either a clockwise or a counterclockwise direction, there were two test pairs for each step.

As predicted, errors were most frequent when the alternative was an adjacent expression (one step away). The likelihood of an error then decreased at each additional step. The one exception to this pattern occurred for 3-year-olds, with a reversal between Steps 3 and 4. Quantitative analyses of these data confirmed that both the main effects of Age [$F(4,580) = 92.7$, $p < .001$] and Step [$F(3,580) = 17.97$, $p < .001$] were significant and that their interaction was not. Separate analyses showed that distance from the target was a significant factor for every age group but the 3-year-olds.

As in the first study, we constructed histograms showing the proportion of subjects who chose each expression as a referent for each word. The patterns we had identified in the first study were apparent in these histograms as well. There was a focal point, with most "errors" at adjacent faces (one step removed) and the probability of choice declining to either side. The pattern of category narrowing with age was replicated for the words *mad, disgusted, sad, scared,* and *excited.* As in the first study, we also noted a shift in focal point for the words *surprised* and *excited.*

In this second study we were able to assess developmental changes in more detail than in the first study. For many of the words tested, the 2-year-olds, although responding above chance levels, could not be said to have a clear focal point at all. Rather, they seemed to treat a range of expressions as relatively equivalent. The responses of the older groups, though, showed a focal point emerging. We shall illustrate this pattern with histograms for *mad* shown in Figure 8.8. Two-year-olds were about equally likely to select Face D as E and Face F as E when paired together. The broad range of choices for 2-year-olds is narrowed somewhat for the 3-year-olds, who show a clear focal point at Face E, consistent with 4-year-olds, 5-year-olds, and adults.

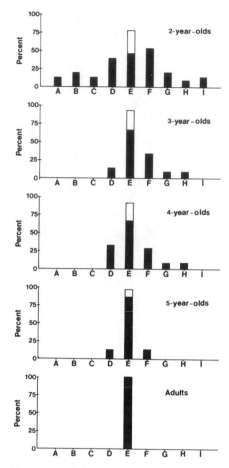

Figure 8.8. Choices for the word *mad*, Task 2.

Task 3: the boundaries of emotion categories. In the two studies discussed so far, the child was asked to find the *best* representative for a category. In the next study, the child was asked to select all the members of the category. One prediction from our model is that each emotion category may apply to a range of expressions, and any one expression may belong to more than one category. That is, different categories overlap one another. For adults, this idea is represented by findings such as those in Figure 8.2, where degree of membership ratings indicated that, although there are prototypical expressions for each term, other expressions are applicable as well. If, as we have suggested, children's emotion concepts are broader than those of adults, we would expect them to include even more expressions within the border and hence to overlap categories even more.

Table 8.2. *Percentage of subjects agreeing that an expression is a member of a category*

	Facial expression								
	A	B	C	D	E	F	G	H	I
Three-year-olds									
Happy	*92*	*100*	17	0	0	8	8	*67*	*92*
Excited	*58*	*67*	25	17	17	17	8	25	*42*
Surprised	*67*	*67*	*33*	17	8	8	8	*42*	*50*
Scared	8	0	*50*	*50*	25	17	8	0	8
Mad	0	0	17	*42*	*92*	*75*	25	0	0
Disgusted	17	8	25	*50*	*58*	*67*	*33*	25	25
Sad	0	0	25	*42*	17	25	*67*	0	0
Sleepy	*33*	25	*33*	25	*33*	*33*	*50*	*42*	*42*
Calm	*42*	25	*42*	8	17	25	*42*	*83*	*75*
Four-year-olds									
Happy	*92*	*92*	8	0	0	0	0	17	*67*
Excited	*50*	*83*	*33*	0	8	0	0	0	8
Surprised	*50*	*67*	*42*	8	0	0	8	17	25
Scared	0	0	25	*57*	17	0	8	0	0
Mad	0	0	8	17	*92*	*92*	8	0	0
Disgusted	0	0	*42*	*33*	*42*	*42*	*33*	25	8
Sad	0	0	17	17	0	0	*75*	8	0
Sleepy	0	0	8	17	8	8	*58*	*42*	8
Calm	25	*33*	17	8	0	0	17	*58*	*67*
Five-year-olds									
Happy	*92*	*92*	8	0	0	0	0	25	*75*
Excited	*58*	*75*	17	8	0	8	0	0	17
Surprised	*33*	*58*	*67*	17	0	0	0	0	17
Scared	0	0	*42*	*100*	0	0	8	0	0
Mad	0	0	0	8	*100*	*83*	0	0	0
Disgusted	0	0	25	25	*50*	*75*	8	25	17
Sad	0	0	0	0	0	0	*100*	17	0
Sleepy	0	8	0	0	0	0	*42*	*50*	17
Calm	25	0	0	0	0	0	*33*	*83*	*83*

Note: Percentages of 33% or greater are in italics to indicate range and overlap of yes endorsements.

We presented the following task to 36 children. We asked the child whether or not a particular facial expression was an example of an emotion term. "Is this person [word]?" The child responded yes or no. Because the results have not been published, we shall describe them in detail. The percentage of children responding yes for each of several test words is given in Table 8.2. The results again showed the narrowing of categories. Consider the responses for the word *mad*. The 3-year-olds endorsed both prototypical (Face E) and nonprototypical expressions as members of the category *mad*. In contrast, the 4- and 5-year-olds showed more narrow categories. Peripheral expressions included by 3-year-olds were included by fewer 4-year-olds and no 5-year-olds. A similar pattern can be seen for almost every word. On the average, a facial expression was placed into 4.0 categories by 3-year-olds, 2.5 categories by 4-year-olds, and 2.2 categories by 5-year-olds, out of the possible nine categories listed (with placement defined as endorsement by 4 or more of the 12 subjects in each age group). The category *surprised* also showed the expected shift in focal point. For 3-year-olds, the focal point comprised Faces A and B; for 4-year-olds, Face B; and for 5-year-olds and adults, Face C. *Excited* was a word for which the category focal point was shifted in the previous studies. In Table 8.2, it is evident that there is a shift with age, but a shift not so much in the focal point as in the range of applicable expressions. For some 3-year-olds *excited* includes the whole range of positive emotions. This becomes narrowed to those expressions high in arousal, both positive and negative.

Dimensions and the structure of emotion

The three studies described above indicate that children as young as 2 years impose an order on emotions, an order that is similar to but not identical to that provided by adults. The studies on categorization, however, provide only one part of the picture. We have also asked how the entire emotion domain is structured. In this work we have not focused on the structure of individual emotions, such as fear, anger, and happiness, but have examined how children perceive similarities and differences across the entire domain.

For adults, the intercategory structure of the emotion domain can be represented in terms of the circular ordering portrayed in Figure 8.3. Information for this characterization comes from multidimensional scaling procedures applied to data from tasks in which subjects are asked to indicate similarities they perceive between emotions. We have used some of the same procedures with children. The basic procedure is to ask subjects to group faces into a preordained number of "piles" – from 2 to 10. From this task we can derive a measure of similarity between pairs of expressions. This measure is the frequency with which the two expressions are grouped into the same pile, weighted in accordance with the number of piles. Multidimensional scaling procedures can then be applied to the set of pairwise similarity measures to yield a simultaneous representation of the entire set. The result of such a procedure portrays the "distance" between emotions: Closer emotions are more similar to one another; ones farther away are more different.

We collected data on preschoolers' responses to emotional facial expressions in two studies (Russell & Bullock, 1985; 1986). In each study, subjects were asked to group emotional facial expressions into specified numbers of piles. The precise procedures differed to provide tasks appropriate for the ages tested. The first study involved thirty adults and thirty-two 4- and 5-year-olds, who were shown 20 facial expressions. The second study involved seventy-eight 2-, 3-, and 4-year-olds, who were shown 10 facial expressions. The solutions for each age group are illustrated in Figures 8.9 and 8.10, respectively, where each facial expression is represented by a modal label given by adults. Despite some discrepancies, the overall similarity across ages is apparent. Children as young as 2 years structured the emotion domain in roughly the same ways as older children and adults.

What accounts for this similarity? An answer to this question requires a discussion of the hypothesized dimensions underlying such an ordering, the dimensions of pleasure and arousal. The axes of each solution in Figures 8.9 and 8.10 are clearly interpretable in terms of these two dimensions. Correlations of the multidimensional scaling coordinates with independently obtained ratings on pleasure and arousal (given by adults) support this interpretation. Pleasure ratings correlated .80 or above with scores on each horizontal dimension. Arousal ratings correlated .80 or above with scores on each vertical dimension.

Another test of the use of the pleasure and arousal dimensions is to ask if expressions prototypical of different categories will be grouped according to their values on the dimensions of pleasure and arousal. We designed two parallel tests – one for pleasure and one for arousal – which we presented to one hundred 2- to 5-year-olds (Bullock & Russell, 1985). Each test consisted of several trials. In each trial the child was shown three photographs, each of different expressions. Two were more similar to each other on the dimension tested than the third. No knowledge of emotion words was required for this task; the subject was simply asked to judge which two of the three feelings expressed were most similar. For example, in one trial on the pleasure test subjects were shown photographs of actresses portraying fear, anger, and excitement, all high arousal states. To "pass" this item the subjects had to group together the two faces expressing displeasure (fear and anger) and leave aside the one expressing pleasure (excitement). The dimensions of pleasure and arousal were used by children as young as 3 years. The 2-year-olds' performance fell at chance levels, but it was unclear during the testing whether they understood the task.

Evidence discussed so far on dimensions came from tasks without the use of emotion-descriptive words. We also found evidence for the same structure and same dimensions when we examined tasks that used emotion words. We took the data from the matching tasks (Tasks 1 to 3 described above) to derive pairwise similarity measures for facial expressions, much as had been done with adults to produce Figure 8.3. Again, the result was roughly the same (Bullock & Russell, 1984).

Figure 8.9. Multidimensional scaling solutions for 20 facial expressions.

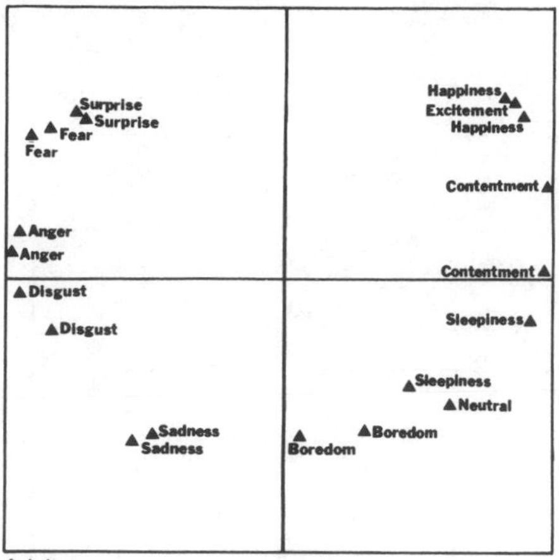

Adults

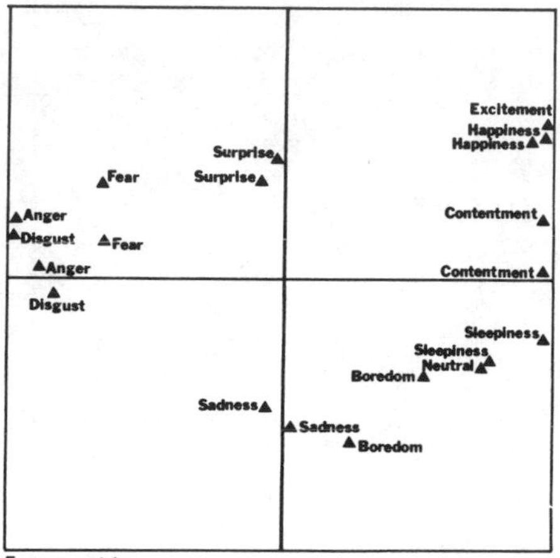

5-year-olds

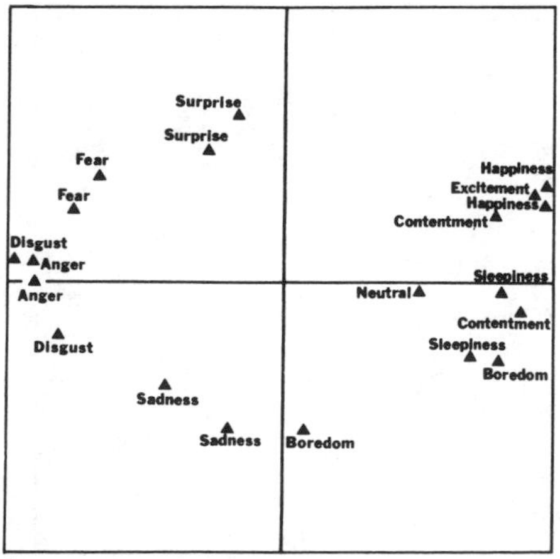

4-year-olds

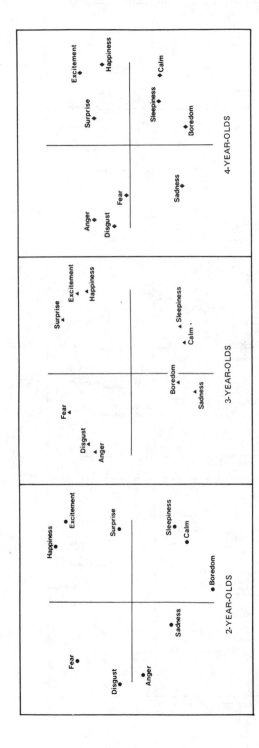

Figure 8.10. Multidimensional scaling solutions for 10 facial expressions.

Summary

The evidence we have gathered is consistent with previous findings on the accuracy of children's interpretation of emotions, although we would describe the findings differently. Improvement in accuracy corresponds to a narrowing of the category. At any given age, some categories such as happiness are used more consistently because they overlap less with other categories presented to the child. Children's "errors" are not errors but manifestations of their conceptual system.

This conceptual system exists at a very young age. Long before children are "accurate" in labeling facial expressions of emotion, they interpret those facial expressions in a meaningful way. They can categorize and judge the similarity between expressions. Their categories are broad, overlap one another, and are organized with respect to one another. Underlying this organization appear to be the dimensions of pleasure and arousal, dimensions that children can use to sort emotions adults label as distinctly different. There is a remarkable similarity in how children and adults structure the emotion domain, but the categories are not equivalent to those of adults. The major developmental changes seen in these studies is the decreasing breadth of children's categories of emotion: From age 2 on children's categories become more narrow, approaching those of adults.

Two different lines of evidence converge to reveal a systematic order underlying preschoolers' interpretation of emotional messages. One line of evidence came from tests of categories as labeled by everyday vocabulary items. The other line had little to do with language, relying on grouping of facial expressions according to perceived similarity. Because the structure seen in Figures 8.9 and 8.10 can be seen distinctly in 2-year-olds and seen in tasks that do not involve emotion labels, this structure and the dimensions that underlie it appear to represent primitive and basic processes in the interpretation of emotion. This possibility is explored in the next section.

Development of emotion concepts: a hypothesis

The ways in which infants and young children interpret emotions and the ways in which such interpretations change over development is fertile ground for exploring the hypotheses proposed about concepts of emotion. The order in which categories, dimensions, structures, and scripts emerge in the course of development can tell us about the fundamental nature of emotion concepts.

How does the child develop a conceptual scheme for emotions? Psychologists differ in their answers. One position is that there are something like innate emotion categories. Biological theories of emotion emphasize the evolutionary advantages of the communicative function of emotional facial expressions (Andrew, 1963; Darwin, 1872). Perception and interpretation of facial expressions may have evolved for the same reason (e.g., Oster, 1978). If facial expressions are thought of as releasing mechanisms, again something like emotion detectors is implied. At the opposite extreme is the position that the child must learn or construct from experience every aspect of the conceptual scheme for emotions. Perhaps the culture or language community must teach this scheme. Perhaps the child constructs it via general cognitive mechanisms. Positions can be defined that lie between these extremes, and the correct position is not known.

Here we sketch one possibility that lies midway between these extremes. We suspect that children do not possess innate emotion categories, but they do not begin as blank slates either. The child begins with general constraints on how to interpret the emotion world. What those constraints are is a matter of speculation. Little is known about the developmental course of children's conceptualization of emotion. Perhaps the division of emotions into categories occurs first, with integration into the structure represented in Figure 8.3 and the abstraction of pleasure and arousal coming later. Alternatively, structure and dimensions may represent the initial perception of emotion, with differentiation into more discrete categories occurring later. No definitive evidence favors one of these solutions, but we believe that the evidence we have reviewed in this chapter lends plausibility to the second alternative, and that is the one we shall pursue here.

The constraint we emphasize is therefore that emotional states of others are initially perceived in terms of dimensions of pleasure–displeasure and degree of arousal. A variety of events in the child's world can be given meaning in terms of emotion: subjective experiences that the child undergoes, certain words spoken by caregivers, and facial and vocal expressions of the caregivers. Our proposal is that the child initially gives meaning to each such event in terms of pleasure and arousal. A subjective experience might be felt as pleasant and aroused; the caregiver's sad demeanor appears unpleasant and unaroused. This hypothesis does not deny that very young children discriminate and even categorize different emotions. What it does is specify the basis of discrimination and categorization as pleasure and arousal dimensions, rather than adultlike categories appropriately labeled anger, fear, and the like.

If our assumption is correct, the child's initial interpretation of any emotional event can be described as global and relatively "undifferentiated." The child's developmental task, then, is to differentiate within this global interpretation to reach an adultlike taxonomy for emotional states. Consider a case of jealousy: A child watches his or her teenage brother shout and glare when his girlfriend dates another boy. Our hypothesis is that a very young child does not interpret this scene as jealousy, but perceives the brother to be in a state of displeasure and high arousal. How does the child move from the global interpretation to the particular one? Our answer, in brief, is that the child learns a script about jealousy. We would rephrase the question: How does the child acquire the emotion script labeled jealousy?

There are two general, not mutually exclusive answers to this question. The first is that the surrounding community labels some episodes as particular emotions. Parents and others interpret the young child's own emotional states as well as those of others the child may observe. Older children are exposed to stereotyped narratives about romantic love, jealousy, fear, and other emotions. And, of course, children acquire a lexicon of emotion terms. Different terms may lead a child to search for different features.

The second answer is that the features that make up an emotion script are likely to be correlated. When the child observes someone with wide-open eyes and raised eyebrows, the other is more likely than not facing some threatening situation and is likely to withdraw from that situation. When the child observes another person with glaring eyes and clenched fists, that person may be facing a threat but there is more likely to be an element of frustration and injustice in the situation. The second person is also more likely than the first to make threats and to act aggressively. Thus, two episodes initially interpreted as unpleasant and aroused can come to be differentiated into fear and anger.

With these general considerations in mind we propose the following sequence of steps.

Level 1. Infants develop the ability to perceive gestures in others and to perceive changes in the face, voice, and posture. Research on infant's abilities to discriminate facial expressions (e.g., Caron, Caron, & Meyers, 1982; La Barbera, Izard, Vietze, & Parisi, 1976; Oster, 1978) suggests that at least by the time a child is 6 to 10 months old the perceptual abilities for extracting facial features and for combining these into a pattern are in place. However, at this stage, the child may not find any meaning in these patterns.

Level 2. Infants begin to find meaning in facial expressions of emotion. Initially, the meanings infants give to facial expressions are relatively undifferentiated. They are quantitative, distinguishing emotions only in terms of pleasure–displeasure and degree of arousal. These meanings facilitate social interactions and guide infants' reactions to ambiguous events. For example, Klinnert, Campos, Sorce, Emde, & Svejda (1983) report that infants as young as 10 months use their mother's facial expression as a guide for their own behavior in what is termed "social referencing." Infants approach or withdraw from a novel toy depending on their mother's facial expression. Infants also respond to ambiguous situations such as the visual cliff or the approach of a stranger either positively or negatively depending on their mother's facial expression. It is not clear from these reports, however whether the infants distinguish anything more than negative from positive expressions.

Level 3. The child now comes to expand the meanings attached to emotions by distinguishing the situations in which they occur. Expressions that are similar in pleasure–displeasure or arousal are associated with different contexts, different outcomes, or different causes. Children begin to associate expressions with the immediate contexts in which they occur. For example, the child notes the context in which a smile or a frown occurs, notes that frowns or smiles go with certain tones of voice, notes that an unpleasant and aroused expression in the context of spilled milk is different from an unpleasant and aroused expression in the context of soiled diapers or a cut finger. The child learns to associate pairs of elements. These two-element combinations are the basis for emotion scripts, although at this point they are not organized into a temporal sequence. The language of emotion becomes important at this level because the child now has some basis for distinguishing different emotion words according to the situations in which they occur.

Level 4.   From observing combinations of emotional expressions, situations, and words, the child now comes to construct emotion scripts. This involves two related processes. One is that the child associates multiple elements together. The second is that the child begins to combine the elements into temporal and causal sequences. From observing particular patterns at various times, the child begins to form generalized scripts. Labels supplied by the culture stimulate the child to differentiate among events previously treated as if they were alike. (In Chapter 9, Stein and Jewett detail a similar view on how the child comes to differentiate fear, anger, and sadness.)

The developmental sequence just outlined is, of course, oversimplified and very general. For one thing, emotion concepts develop beyond the generalized scripts suggested in Level 4. Our everyday concepts of emotion are a varied lot. Some specify little more than combinations of pleasure and arousal: Upset is displeasure and high arousal, and excitement is pleasure and high arousal. Other concepts involve a more elaborate script, including more information about the surrounding events. To be afraid is not only to feel upset, but to face a threat of future harm and to be motivated to escape that threat. Still other concepts presuppose even more: Jealousy implies certain interpersonal relationships; guilt and shame imply rules to be violated. A distinction between guilt and shame presupposes a further differentiation on the basis of internal versus external causes of the displeasure at having violated a rule.

Just as preschoolers may treat the terms *anger* and *disgust* as though they had the same meaning, some adults may treat *guilt* and *shame* as though they had the same meaning. Experts, in turn, can propose even finer distinctions. The differentiation of emotions according to their scripts does not, in our view, lead to a fixed set of emotion types. Thus, there is no end point in the developing taxonomy of emotion concepts.

The psychology of emotional events

In this section, we turn to the study of emotion events, the phenomena behind the word *emotion*. The psychological study of emotion events flounders over seemingly intractable conceptual problems. Should everyday concepts of *emotion, anger, fear,* and the rest be used as scientific constructs, and if so how can these concepts be defined? Is behavior an adequate operational definition of emotion? If not, what would be? If an infant smiles, it is legitimate to infer that the infant is happy? When does emotion first occur in a person's life? How many emotions are there? Psychologists have yet to settle such questions and, more important, have yet to agree on how such questions might be settled.

Although everyday folk concepts need not be used by scientists to analyze emotion events, psychological theorizing about emotion relies heavily on everyday concepts and everyday thought. Notice that in the preceding paragraph it was almost impossible to write about events without assuming the categories implied by such English words as *emotion*. Analysis of everyday concepts may clarify some implicit assumptions psychologists make when everyday concepts are part of the questions asked and the theories proposed. It may also help separate genuine empirical issues from questions that are semantic, arbitrary, or impossible to answer. It may also be useful in another, more positive way: The analysis can offer hypotheses and suggestions about the nature of emotion events. One way to evaluate the perspective advocated in this chapter is to examine the answers it suggests to the sorts of questions raised above. In this section, we therefore very briefly discuss implications of our view of emotion concepts on these issues.

Writers on emotion commonly distinguish three aspects of emotion. One aspect is *emotional behavior*. Included here are such physical activities as expressive actions (via the face, vocalization, or body movements) and instrumental behaviors (such as flight and aggression). The second aspect is *emotional physiological change*. Included here are physiological indices of various sorts. The third aspect is *emotional experience*. By this, we mean affective interpretations and evaluations of external events plus subjective feelings of emotions. We perceive events as threatening, pleasant, likable, valuable, disgusting, and so on; and we feel happy, sad, angry, or whatever.

The first half of the twentieth century witnessed arguments about which of these is really emotion: subjective emotional experience, emotional behavior, or physiological activation. Modern emotion theorists have come to the realization that emotion is not any one of these events. Debate has given way to the notion that emotion is composed of all of these. But where does that leave the concept of the "emotion"? It is a mistake to say that the emotion is another event in

addition to physiological change, behavior, and subjective experience. To say
so would be to commit the category mistake made famous when Ryle (1949/1963)
pointed it out. To think of emotion as another event along with behavior, physiological change, and subjective experience is to make the same sort of error as
thinking of the university as another thing in addition to the faculties, schools,
colleges, and administration that form the university.

If emotion is not another such event, what is it? Our discussion of emotions
as scripts suggests a possible hypothesis. An emotion is *composed of* these three
events, including the *pattern* among them. The sequence of events and the causal
links between events must be approximately right for something to count as a
particular emotion. The statement that emotion is a pattern is consistent with
conclusions reached by most modern emotion theorists. In Volume I, Schwartz
(1982) describes emotion as just such an emergent pattern composed of subpro-
cesses (also see in Volume I Izard's review of other similar views). Nevertheless,
the conceptual and methodological implications of this statement have not been
fully explored. We shall sketch one approach to the study of emotion that takes
this idea as its major premise.

Which patterns are emotions and which are not? From our perspective, a quest
for a classical definition of the concept of emotion is futile. It is impossible to
state precisely which events are and which are not emotions. Membership in
middle-level categories like anger and fear is likewise a matter of degree rather
than all or none and is determined by resemblance to the prototypical pattern
rather than by possession of defining attributes. Rarely do actual instances match
the prototypical script in every detail, and there is no clear boundary between
sufficient and insufficient resemblance. In short, the first implication of our perspective is that, when everyday concepts are used as scientific constructs, excep-
tions and borderline cases are endemic in matters of definition.

Operational definitions are equally problematic. Standard practice is to use
expressive behaviors, verbal self-report, instrumental behaviors, and psychophysiological indices as interchangeable operational definitions of such constructs as
emotion, fear, stress, and anger. From our perspective, this practice is suspect:
Each operation is relevant to only one of the three aspects of emotion distinguished above. If each emotion is a pattern, no one feature of which is defining,
and if different emotions overlap, then no *single* operation will suffice to capture
a particular emotion. This conclusion is consistent with the recommendations on
measurement offered by Izard (1982) in Volume I, recommendations based on
practical efforts to measure emotion rather than analysis of everyday concepts.
Taking fear as his example, Izard (p. 9) wrote:

We can set up a hierarchical table of data sets that go from least to most convincing with
respect to their contribution to the identification of a specific emotion.
a. Escape-avoidant behavior (child fleeing) (Br), alone

b. Vocal expression or scream (V-ex), alone
c. Facial expression (F-ex), alone
d. Br + V-ex
e. Br + F-ex
f. Vex + F-ex
g. Br + V-er + F-ex

That a, b, or c alone is least convincing is to speak against operational definitions as commonly understood. That Br + V-ex + F-ex is the most convincing sign of fear is to say that the case in which the child's state most closely resembles the fear script is the best example of a fear event. Of course, it is not only the presence or absence of a feature that contributes to resemblance to the script. Each feature has a prototypical value, and actual features vary in the extent to which they resemble that prototype. For example, if the facial expression (F-ex) Izard mentions were the prototypical fear expression, it would contribute most. If it were a milder version of the fear face, a neutral face, a blend of fear and disgust elements, or the prototypical expression of another emotion, then it would contribute less and less. We would also add that the pattern that constitutes each emotion includes events not mentioned by Izard: aspects of the situation, the person's appraisal of the situation, and the subjective experience of emotion.

The impossibility that a single operational definition will capture such concepts as emotion, anger, and fear suggests a two-step research strategy. In the first step, the everyday concepts of emotion are set aside and each of the three aspects of emotion is studied separately. Within each such domain, operational definitions are not only possible but clear-cut and used regularly. During this first step, we set aside any questions concerning which one of these is really the emotion and emphasize that each aspect is a legitimate domain worthy of scientific interest. Then, in the second step, patterns among these three processes are studied, and reliable patterns are identified and labeled. If one such pattern turns out to coincide with the pattern identified by the everyday term *anger,* then the everyday category of anger will have been empirically found to be a useful scientific construct. If new patterns are discovered, we shall have a new and empirically justified taxonomy for emotions. The idea is to move back and forth between parts and the wholes so that (a) the description of the whole (the pattern that is emotion) is the best description, and (b) the variables descriptive of the parts maximize our understanding of the patterns. Everyday categories such as anger are hypotheses to be validated rather than unquestioned assumptions.

Emotional behavior, physiological activation, and subjective feelings are undoubtedly interrelated. In the everyday manner of thinking, all three are assumed to be aspects of one event, the emotion. Hence, the everyday way of thinking leads us to infer one from the other and to assume that all three co-occur. Rather than pursue that well-worn line of thinking, we are suggesting an alternative theoretical tack: We assume the three domains to be at least conceptually separable from one another and take the relationship among them to be an empirical question. This approach does not deny the possibility that the three domains always co-vary, but it does allow the possibility that they do not – a possibility that should be maintained, especially in the study of the development of emotion.

This simple theoretical tack puts traditional questions in the psychology of emotion in a new light. Our approach suggests that the development of emotional behavior, emotional physiological activation, and subjective emotional experience need not follow the same lines. The development of emotional behavior may turn out to be mainly a maturational process. Certain forms of emotional behavior can be seen shortly after birth. For example, full-term and premature neonates show all the facial action patterns (with possibly one exception) that are distinguishable in adults as parts of emotional expressions (Oster, 1978). In contrast, the development of emotional experience may not emerge until long after this. Moreover, the link between emotional behavior and emotional experience now becomes an explicit issue, with the obvious possibility that the link changes with development. If there is merit in this line of reasoning, the traditional mode of thinking becomes suspect. For example, we would question the inference that because an infant smiles it likes something and feels happy – the inference that emotional behavior implies subjective emotional experience.

Consider the debate in the literature over the question of when "emotion" (or anger, etc.) first occurs developmentally. In our approach, we would separately ask when physiological activation first occurs (answer: very early), when specific emotional behaviors such as smiling first occur (answer: quite early for many behaviors), and when emotional experience first occurs (answer: probably later). We do not mean to prejudge the empirical issues here, but if, as we suspect, the answers to these different questions are in fact different, then the original question of when "emotion" first occurs becomes ambiguous.

When does the *pattern* that constitutes an emotion first occur? The answer to this question will vary with how closely we demand that the actual pattern and the prototypical pattern match and what units we choose as the components of our pattern. There is no clean division between prototypical and nonprototypical patterns, and there will be no answer to the question that is not arbitrary. We can ask when all three aspects of emotion occur simultaneously (e.g., When does the child become activated, frown, and feel angry simultaneously?), but this sets a criterion for membership in the category of anger that is higher than that set for the everyday use of the term. Thus, the answer given by this criterion will be different from parental report and from the psychologist's own intuitions. The appropriate procedure, then, is to describe the developmental emergence of the pattern rather than worry about when it crosses an arbitrary border.

Should patterns be described in terms of everyday concepts? One difficulty faced by a description of emotion based on everyday folk concepts is *dissociations*. Not all actual states match the prototypical pattern. In fact, the various components that make up the pattern, far from being perfectly correlated, are poorly (and, for some, negatively) correlated. Dissociations can be anticipated on theoretical grounds. Ekman's (1972) concept of display rules implies that expressive behavior will not always correspond to subjective experience and different expressive cues will sometimes be inconsistent. More important, low correlations are a fact. Behavioral, physiological, and verbal measures of, for example, anxiety are often only minimally correlated (Martin, 1961). Individuals who respond to emotionally laden stimuli with more expressive facial patterns tend to show *smaller* psychophysiological responses than do less expressive individuals (Buck, 1976). Rachman (1978) begins his book *Fear and Courage* with a chapter aptly titled "Fear Is Not a Lump." Reviewing the clinical evidence on therapeutic attempts to alter human fears, Rachman found that an interesting result occurred whenever investigators attempted to measure more than one component of fear. Much to everyone's surprise, one component of fear often exists or changes in the absence of others. A patient may claim to experience fear of snakes but be willing to approach and even handle a snake. Another patient may lose his or her behavioral avoidance during the course of therapy but maintain physiological signs of fear. In clinical terminology, the various components of fear are discordant. As Rachman points out, if measures were taken over a broader range of emotional states from extreme calm to extreme fear, positive correlations among the components might be seen. Nevertheless, the potential independence of the components must be recognized. Indeed, Rachman defined courage as occurring when a person feels fear but approaches rather than withdraws from the feared object.

From our point of view, patterns that do not match the folk script are just as real and worthy of study as those that do. The pattern of response in teen-agers that is fear of rejection may differ from the pattern that is a preschooler's fear of strangers or an adult's fear of physical danger. Each pattern should be studied in its own right. Similarly, it matters less whether an individual's pattern of response fits the script of fear than what that pattern is and why it is that way.

Ekman and Freisen (1982) have taken an enlightening step in the description of facial expressions that parallels the approach we are advocating. The English language provides a lexicon for the description of facial actions in such words as *smile, frown, sneer, pout,* and *grimace.* Rather than building on this foundation, Ekman and Friesen (1982) began afresh. They developed an anatomically based system of facial action units (AUs). Each is arbitrarily labeled (e.g., AU 4), and five discernible levels of intensity are defined for each action unit. The system, known as FACS, provides an objective, reliable, and finely grained basis for research on facial behavior. From a developmental perspective, Oster (1978) has made the most significant contribution by adapting FACS to the facial behavior of infants. Research has already shown the value of this approach.

It might be objected that an action unit has no *meaning,* whereas a "smile" does: It is a sign of happiness. Precisely. That is the primary value of FACS. It reminds us that the meaning of a facial expression must be established rather than assumed. And it cannot be established in any simple way. A smile, for example, does not always signify happiness. The polite smile of a greeting, our ability to smile under adversity, and the smile of submission must be weighed along with the evidence that, under some circumstances, amount of smiling correlates with amount of self-reported happiness (Ekman, Friesen, & Ancoli, 1980). From an ethological perspective, Kraut and Johnston (1979) provided arguments and evidence that the primary meaning of a smile is a social statement of friendliness rather than a sign of happiness. Ekman's (1972) concept of display rule provides a different theoretical rationale for the same conclusion: Smile and happiness bear no one-to-one correspondence. And if a smile cannot be equated with happiness, is any other facial expression likely to bear a closer relationship to an inner experience?

To call for setting aside such concepts as emotion, anger, love, hate, and so on invites a number of misunderstandings we would like to avoid. First, we are not denying the *existence* of emotions, anger, love, or the rest. The phenomena are real, of course. The question is how to study these phenomena in the most scientifically useful way. Ekman and Friesen (1982) did not deny the existence of frowns and smiles but provided categories more useful to a scientific description of the phenomena.

Second, our approach is not simply an appeal to study phenomena on a more molecular level. There are patterns among physiological, cognitive, behavioral, and subjective events. The study of those patterns constitutes a molar level of analysis. We do suggest beginning at a more molecular level, but only for practical reasons; we see this as a way of discovering patterns at the molar level.

Third, it might be said that our approach is not new, since that is what psychologists do now anyway. A researcher cannot assess fear but must assess physiological change, behavior, or self-reported experience. This charge we will not deny. Rather, if this is so, it seems a powerful argument for viewing the field as we do. There is now a large gap between the questions researchers ask and the answers research provides. A researcher asks when emotion first occurs, and research provides information on an infant's first smile. Our approach seeks to eliminate this gap by, first, distinguishing those questions that can be empirically answered from those that cannot and, second, suggesting a way in which molar concepts can be created by the sort of research we can actually do.

References

Abelson, R. P. (1981). Psychological status of the script concept. *American Psychologist, 36,* 715–29.

Abelson, R. P., & Sermat, V. (1962). Multidimensional scaling of facial expressions. *Journal of Experimental Psychology, 63,* 546–54.

Andrew, R. I. (1963). Evolution of facial expression. *Science, 142,* 1034–41.

Armstrong, S. L., Gleitman, H., & Gleitman, L. R. (1983). What some concepts might not be. *Cognition, 13,* 263–308.

Borke, H. (1971). Interpersonal perception of young children: Egocentrism or empathy? *Developmental Psychology, 5*(2), 263–9.

Buck, R. (1976). *Human motivation and emotion.* New York: Wiley.

Bullock, M., & Russell, J. A. (1984). Preschool children's interpretation of facial expressions of emotion. *International Journal of Behavioral Development, 7,* 193–214.

Bullock, M., & Russell, J. A. (1985). Further evidence on preschoolers' interpretations of facial expressions of emotion. *International Journal of Behavioral Development, 8,* 15–38.

Caron, R., Caron, A., & Myers, R. (1982). Abstraction of invariant face expressions in infancy. *Child Development, 53,* 1008–15.

Darwin, C. (1872). *The expression of the emotions in man and animals.* London: John Murray (Reprinted by University of Chicago Press, 1965).

Ekman, P. (1972). Universals and cultural differences in facial expressions of emotions. In J. K. Cole (Ed.), *Nebraska Symposium on Motivation 1971* (pp. 207–83). Lincoln: University of Nebraska Press.

Ekman, P. (1976). *Pictures of facial affect.* Palo Alto, CA: Consulting Psychologists Press.

Ekman, P., & Friesen, W. V. (1982). Measuring facial movement with the Facial Action Coding System. In P. Ekman (Ed.), *Emotion in the human face* (2nd ed., pp. 178–211). Cambridge University Press.

Ekman, P., Freisen, W. V., & Ancoli, S. (1980). Facial signs of emotional experience. *Journal of Personality and Social Psychology, 39,* 1125–34.

Fehr, B., & Russell, J. A. (1984). Concept of emotion viewed from a prototype perspective. *Journal of Experimental Psychology: General, 113*(3), 464–86.

Fehr, B., Russell, J. A., & Ward, L. M. (1982). Prototypicality of emotions: A reaction time study. *Bulletin of the Psychonomic Society, 20,* 253–4.

Felleman, E. S., Barden, R. C., Carlson, C. R., Rosenberg, L., & Masters, J. C. (1983). Children's and adult's recognition of spontaneous and posed emotional expressions in young children. *Developmental Psychology, 19*(3), 405–13.

Field, T. M., & Walden, T. A. (1982). Production and discrimination of facial expressions by preschool children. *Child Development, 53,* 1299–1300.

Gates, G. S. (1923). An experimental study of the growth of social perception. *Journal of Educational Psychology, 14,* 449–61.

Gitter, A. G., Mostofsky, D. I., Quincy, A. J., Jr. (1971). Race and sex differences in the child's perception of emotion. *Child Development, 42,* 2071–5.

Gnepp, J., Klayman, J., & Trabasso, T. (1982). A hierarchy of information sources for inferring emotional reactions. *Journal of Experimental Child Psychology, 33*(1), 111–23.

Guthrie, P. T., Smouse, A. D. (1981). Perception of emotions and attribution of acceptance by normal and emotionally disturbed children. *Journal of Nonverbal Behavior, 5*(4), 253–63.

Heider, F. (1958). *The psychology of interpersonal relations.* New York: Wiley.

Hesse, P., & Cichetti, D. (1982). Perspectives on an integrated theory of emotional development. In D. Cichetti & P. Hesse (Eds.), *Emotional development* (pp. 3–48). San Francisco: Jossey-Bass.

Izard, C. (1971). *The face of emotion*. New York: Appleton-Century-Crofts.

Izard, C. E. (1977). *Human emotions*. New York: Plenum.

Izard, C. E. (1982). Measuring emotions in human development. In C. E. Izard (Ed.), *Measuring emotions in infants and children* (pp. 3–18). Cambridge University Press.

James, W. (1929). *The varieties of religious experience: A study in human nature*. New York: Longmans, Green. (Original work published in 1902)

Jones, G. V. (1982). Stacks not fuzzy sets: An ordinal basis for prototype theory of concepts. *Cognition, 12*, 281–90.

Kelly, G. A. (1955). *The psychology of personal constructs*. New York: Norton.

Klinnert, M. D., Campos, J. J., Sorce, J. F., Emde, R. N., & Svejda, M. (1983). Emotions as behavior regulators: Social referencing in infancy. In R. Plutchik & H. Kellerman (Eds.), *Emotion: Theory, research, and experience* (Vol. 2, pp. 57–86). New York: Academic Press.

Kraut, R. E., & Johnston, R. E. (1979). Social and emotional messages of smiling: An ethological approach. *Journal of Personality and Social Psychology, 37*, 1539–53.

La Barbera, J. D., Izard, C. E., Vietze, P., & Parisi, S. (1976). Four- and six-month old infants' visual responses to joy, anger and neutral expressions. *Child Development, 47*, 535–8.

Labov, W. (1973). The boundaries of words and their meanings. In C. J. N. Barley & R. W. Shuy (Eds.), *New ways of analyzing variation in English*. Washington, D.C.: Georgetown University Press.

Lakoff, G. (1973). Hedges: A study in meaning criteria and the logic of fuzzy concepts. *Journal of Philosophical Logic, 2*, 458–508.

Langer, S. K. (1980). *Philosophy in a new key*. Cambridge, MA: Harvard University Press. (Original work published 1942)

Martin, B. (1961). The assessment of anxiety by physiological behavioral measures. *Psychological Bulletin, 58*, 234–55.

Mervis, C. B., & Rosch, E. (1981). Categorization of natural objects. *Annual Review of Psychology, 32*, 89–115.

Odom, R. D., & Lemond, C. M. (1972). Developmental differences in the perception and production of facial expressions. *Child Development, 43*, 359–69.

Osherson, D. N., & Smith, E. E. (1982). Gradedness and conceptual combination. *Cognition, 12*, 299–318.

Oster, H. (1978). Facial expression and affect development. In M. Lewis & L. A. Rosenblum (Eds.), *The development of affect* (pp. 43–75). New York: Plenum.

Rachman, S. (1978). *Fear and Courage*.

Reichenbach, L., & J. C. Masters. (1983). Children's use of expressive and contextual cues in judgements of emotion. *Child Development, 54*, 993–1004.

Rosch, E. (1973). On the internal structure of perceptual and semantic categories. In T. E. Moore (Ed.), *Cognitive development and acquisition of language* (pp. 111–44). New York: Academic Press.

Rosch, E. (1975). Cognitive representations of semantic categories. *Journal of Experimental Psychology: General, 104*, 192–233.

Rosch, E. (1977). Human categorization. In N. Warren (Ed.), *Studies in cross-cultural psychology* (Vol. I, pp. 1–49). London: Academic Press.

Russell, J. A. (1980a). A circumplex model of affect. *Journal of Personality and Social Psychology, 39*, 1161–78.

Russell, J. A. (1980b). *Emotion: Prescriptive and descriptive analyses*. Unpublished manuscript, University of British Columbia, Vancouver.

Russell, J. A. (1983). Pancultural aspects of human conceptual organization of emotions. *Journal of Personality and Social Psychology, 45*, 1281–8.

Russell, J. A., & Bullock, M. (1985). Multidimensional scaling of emotional facial expressions: Similarities from preschoolers to adults. *Journal of Personality and Social Psychology, 48*(5), 1290–8.

Russell, J. A., & Bullock, M. (1986). *On the meaning of preschoolers attribute to facial expressions of emotion. Developmental Psychology, 22,* 97–102.

Russell, J. A., & Bullock, M. (in press). Fuzzy concepts and the perception of emotion in facial expressions. *Social Cognition.*

Russell, J. A., & Ridgeway, D. (1983). Dimensions underlying children's emotion concepts. *Developmental Psychology, 19,* 795–804.

Ryle, G. (1963). *The concept of mind.* Harmondsworth, Middlesex, England: Penguin. (Original work published 1949)

Schlosberg, H. (1952). The description of facial expressions in terms of two dimensions. *Journal of Experimental Psychology, 44,* 229–37.

Schwartz, G. E. (1982). Psychophysiological patterning and emotion revisited: A systems perspective. In C. E. Izard (Ed.), *Measuring emotions in infants and children* (pp. 67–93). Cambridge University Press.

Smith, E. E., & Medin, D. L. (1981). *Categories and concepts.* Cambridge, MA: Harvard University Press.

Tomkins, S. S. (1962–3). *Affect, imagery, consciousness* (2 Vols.). New York: Springer.

Vurpillot, E. (1976). *The visual world of the child.* New York: International Universities Press.

Wittgenstein, L. (1953). *Philosophical investigations.* New York: Macmillan.

Woodworth, R. S. (1938). *Experimental psychology.* New York: Holt.

Zadeh, L. A. (1965). Fuzzy sets. *Information and Control, 8,* 338–53.

9   A conceptual analysis of the meaning of negative emotions: implications for a theory of development

Nancy L. Stein and Janet L. Jewett

When a child says she is angry, what does she mean? What types of events have taken place in order for an emotional reaction to have occurred? Once an emotional reaction occurs, what type of knowledge is used to organize and determine subsequent behavior? These questions grow out of a desire to understand how emotional experiences and knowledge of those experiences affect behavior. The conceptual analysis and empirical study presented in this chapter serve as an initial attempt to answer these questions. Our primary goal is to describe the types of knowledge used to make inferences about the causes and consequences of emotional reactions. By analyzing the causal structure of emotional knowledge, we shall attempt to show how the meaning of different emotions is organized.

Although the study of emotions has been an active concern for nearly a century, the field has been fragmented and wrought with controversy. Problems and disagreements have erupted at both the theoretical and empirical levels. Difficulties at the theoretical level include an absence of a clear definition of emotion, disagreement about the role of cognition in producing emotion, a lack of consensus about the features of a basic emotion, and failure to adopt a consistent set of beliefs about the origins and plasticity of emotional responses (for examples of these controversies see Izard, 1984; Lazarus, 1982, 1984; Scherer & Ekman, 1984; Zajonc, 1980, 1984).

Empirical difficulties stem from the fact that many studies are not grounded in or motivated by a particular theory of emotion. The lack of a consistent theoretical framework often leads to inconsistent data and confusion that could be resolved were a particular theory being tested. For example, in many developmen-

This research was supported in part by a Biomedical Research Support Grant (PHS 2 S07 RR-07029-18) to the University of Chicago and a Spencer Seed Grant to the first author. We thank Lois Bloom, Carroll Izard, Linda Levine, George Mandler, Peter Read, and Tom Trabasso for their helpful comments on an earlier draft.

tal studies, the goal is to describe the changes that occur in children's knowledge of emotional behavior. Often, when younger children perform differently from older children or adults, it is automatically assumed that younger children lack either the prerequisite knowledge or the cognitive operations to perform at a more advanced level (Harris & Olthof, 1983; Harter, 1979; Masters & Carlson, 1984). Upon reconsideration, however, it is often found that younger children's knowledge of emotions is very similar to that of adults (see Harris, 1983; Trabasso, Stein, & Johnson, 1981). Many of these differences stem from the use of inappropriate measurement procedures or from the lack of an adequate theory that would explain how children of different ages might interpret a particular situation. Failure to specify a theoretical rationale also prevents a systematic comparison among studies as well as the systematic accumulation of knowledge.

In order to avoid some of the most common theoretical and methodological difficulties, we proceed here along three dimensions. First, we review some of the literature on children's understanding and use of emotional reactions. This review encompasses studies completed on children's ability to label different facial expressions, as well as studies investigating children's knowledge of the causes and consequences of emotional reactions. Our goal is to link our studies with those of other investigators in the hope of specifying more clearly where areas of ambiguity lie in children's understanding of emotional situations.

We then present a conceptual system that describes the dimensions used to differentiate among three negative emotions. In constructing this analytic system, we have adopted a specific approach to the study of emotion, incorporating many of the assumptions of current cognitive approaches to emotional understanding. Although there is still debate over the role of cognition in arousing emotion (see Izard, 1979; Izard & Malatesta, 1983), there is little doubt that cognitive processes continually interact and influence the motivational system.

Rather than debate about the role of cognition in producing emotion, we have chosen to study those situations in which an event, either externally initiated or internally motivated, precedes an emotional response. In this respect, we attempt to describe some of the events that lead to the arousal of one emotion versus another. Although it can be argued that certain situations do not fit this paradigm, it can also be shown that many situations involving emotional responses occur because of a definite precipitating event that has to be processed and interpreted at some level.

In order to support some of our hypotheses regarding negative emotions, we present data from an empirical study involving 6-year-old children. On the basis of the data, we discuss the implications of our conceptual system with regard to future research in the area of emotional development. It will become increasingly evident, throughout the chapter, that we have begun questioning the results of many previous studies in terms of what children know about emotion and the types of ''qualitative'' changes that supposedly occur in emotional development.

Children's knowledge of emotion: a review

A growing body of information is becoming available about children's knowledge of their own and other people's emotional states. Many investigators have been interested in determining when young children can accurately recognize and label different types of emotional reactions. Chapter 4, by Camras, illustrates this approach. Basically what investigators find is that even very young children can recognize some of the basic emotional expressions if they are asked to pick out the appropriate emotional expression associated with a given label. Perhaps the best example of this ability comes from a study by Smiley and Huttenlocher (1984). These investigators found that many 2- to 3-year-old children can appropriately associate an emotional label with the correct facial expression when required to choose between two expressions. The emotional expressions used in their study were happy, sad, afraid, angry, and surprised. Camras's data show that by the age of 4, children have relatively little difficulty completing a similar task, under even more rigorous conditions. Thus, on the surface, these data suggest that by a very early age children can associate specific words with specific facial expressions.

The data on children's ability to label spontaneously specific emotional expressions are more equivocal. The few studies that exist have shown that even young preschool children have difficulty generating accurate emotion labels for each facial expression. One such study is that of Izard (1971). Upon presenting children with 11 different facial expressions, he found that 2-year-olds could identify only 6% of the pictures accurately, 5-year-olds identified only 49% of the pictures, and 9-year-olds identified only 50% of the expressions correctly. Although he did not report this directly, Izard (personal communication) suggests that certain emotional expressions, like happy, sad, and angry, are identified earlier than other expressions, like fear, surprise, contempt, and disgust.

There could be several reasons for the discrepancy between spontaneous labeling and recognizing emotional expressions. In studies on the recognition of emotional expression (e.g., Smiley & Huttenlocher, 1984) only a small subset of facial expressions was used (e.g., happy, angry, sad, afraid, and surprised). If the same subset of emotions were used in a generation task, the results might correspond more directly to the recognition data. Thus far, no study has compared spontaneous labeling and recognition of the same emotional expression.

Another reason children might experience difficulty in labeling pictures is that some of the features in each facial expression are ambiguous and not unique to one facial expression. Although it is assumed that there are a set of features unique to each type of ''basic'' emotional expression (which adults supposedly can detect), children may have difficulty locating and encoding the unique features of each facial expression, especially when there are 11 different pictures to label. To date, we have no systematic evidence on the similarity of each of the emotional expressions to one another. Nor do we know whether children would categorize certain emotional expressions as highly similar to one another and others as clearly different from one another. That is, we are lacking a basic study on the ability of children to recognize and differentiate, visually, each one of the 11 basic emotions described by Izard (1979).

Finally, young children may experience difficulty in spontaneously labeling emotional expressions because they have not yet acquired a label for some of the facial expressions. Although it is assumed that children as young as 18 months have experienced all of the basic emotions (see Emde, 1983; Izard & Malatesta, 1983; Scherer, 1984), there is little or no evidence to support the notion that children from the ages of 2 to 3 years have acquired the verbal labels to discriminate among the various facial expressions. Although Camras (Chapter 4) reviews many studies on the recognition of emotional expressions, as well as studies that require children to make inferences about emotional states, these studies pertain to children who are 4 years of age and older. We still do not know when and how children from the age of 18 months to 4 years begin to label and understand emotional expressions. Nor do we know when and how children use emotion words in everyday interaction.

A few recent studies (Bretherton & Beeghley, 1983) have reported that children as young as 28 months use the four basic emotion terms of *happy, sad, afraid,* and *angry.* However, there are no data to illustrate the context in which children use these words or how frequently emotion words are used. According to J. Huttenlocher (personal communication), even though children might use emotion words, the frequency of generating these words is very low in comparison with that of generating other internal-state words. Young children between the ages of 2 and 3 are much more likely to generate words for goal states (e.g., want, need) than words for emotion state. This difference has yet to be explained; however, it would seem that the ages of 2 to 3 are ideal for beginning studies on the development of emotional knowledge.

By the time children reach the age of 3, we do have a little more data on their understanding of different emotional states. Borke (1971) was one of the first individuals to complete an investigation on children's ability to recognize correct emotional responses to different situations. Her approach involved selecting specific types of events (e.g., losing a toy or being forced to go to bed) and determining in an a priori fashion which emotional response would be the most appropriate response to a given event. The emotions used in her study were sad, angry, afraid, and happy. Upon presenting a child with each specific event, she asked the child to think about the appropriate emotional response. Then the child had to select a response from one of the four emotions presented.

Borke found that the children had no difficulty picking out the one positive emotion to go with the events she considered to arouse happiness. However, they had more difficulty picking out the appropriate emotions associated with the "negative" events. In particular, they often confused anger with sadness. Borke's conclusions were that young children might have more knowledge about the positive emotions than negative emotions and that knowledge about negative emotions might develop at a later time. She did suggest, however, that a possible reason for the children's confusion may have been that more than one emotional response could be given to each event. It was unclear from her study which of these two hypotheses would best explain her data.

In a subsequent study Trabasso, Stein, and Johnson (1981) investigated 3-year-old children's knowledge of the causes and consequences of both positive and negative emotions. A causal approach to the development of emotional knowledge was used because of the belief that emotional states are a reflection of the success or failure to attain valued goal states and that emotional responses occur most often as part of the problem-solving process. Thus, emotional responses occur as a result of some precipitating event, and once an emotion occurs it in turn influences and organizes subsequent behavior.

Methodologically, the Trabasso et al. study was different from Borke's in the following ways. First, instead of only four emotions, six were used: sad, angry, afraid, happy, excited, and surprised. With six emotions, there was a possibility of obtaining information about more than one positive emotion. Although excitement and surprise could be associated with negative events, these states can also be associated with positive events, and indeed pilot testing with young children showed that to be the case.

Second, instead of predetermining what type of emotional response should be given to each specific event, Trabasso et al. asked children to generate the causes and consequences of each emotional state. For example, children were presented with a picture of a girl (or boy) and told that Jenny (the girl in the picture) was angry. The children were asked one of two questions. Some were asked, "What do you think made Jenny so angry?" Others were asked, "What does Jenny do when she gets angry?" Thus, half the children were asked to generate the causes of an emotional reaction, and half were asked to generate the consequences.

The results of this study showed that 3-year-old children could accurately discriminate both causes from consequences and positive from negative emotional states. Discrimination was measured by the degree to which distribution of the types of answers was correlated for the causes and consequences. The nearly zero correlation indicated little similarity in the kinds of answers given to positive and negative states. For example, almost all reasons given for sadness referred to external states of loss (e.g., she was sad because her mom and dad left her). The reasons given for happiness, however, most often concerned the prevention of a negative state (e.g., he was happy because he didn't go to bed hungry) or referred to an external event in which the child was given a new possession (e.g., a birthday present).

As for the differentiation within each class of emotional responses, the negative emotions were far more differentiated than the positive emotions. That is, children were more likely to give the same causes or consequences to positive emotions than to negative emotions. Happiness, excitement, and surprise were highly correlated, whereas anger, sadness, and fear were less so.

These results are interesting on two counts. First, they show that young children interpret excitement and surprise in a positive light. Second, they indicate that children have little difficulty differentiating among the negative emotions. Fear was the emotion most differentiated from anger and sadness. That is, the events that precipitated fear in these children (usually a monster or an external event that would cause the child harm) did not overlap frequently with the events that caused sadness and anger.

The responses to anger and sadness were more highly correlated, supporting Borke's contention that children give anger and sad responses to the same event. Trabasso et al.'s interpretation of their data, however, is quite different from Borke's. They argue that a single event can arouse either anger or sadness or both and that the co-occurrence of these responses is probably more common than not. As we shall illustrate in our meaning analysis of anger and sadness, when anger is aroused, it is proposed that children have attended to the event that caused an interruption in their ongoing thinking and behavior. When sadness is aroused, it is thought that children have attended to the consequences of an event that has interrupted ongoing behavior.

Similar comments can be made about the overlap among the positive emotions. These emotions might have common features, or two positive emotions could be aroused by the same event. Before concluding that children do not differentiate between certain positive or negative emotions, we must construct a theoretical framework that describes the dimensions children use to discriminate among emotions.

In a dissertation study completed on children from 6 to 12 years of age, Demos (1974) investigated the understanding of emotional states using a procedure similar to that of Trabasso et al. (1981). Demos asked children to generate the causes and consequences of both positive and negative states. Since our study deals with the negative emotions of anger, fear, and sadness, we shall focus on Demos's results for the negative emotions, comparing them with the results from the Trabasso et al. Study.

When asked what types of events made them angry, sad, and afraid, 6-year-old children gave responses that were very similar to those of 3-year-old children. For 6-year-old children, anger was aroused by being attacked by another person or being abused by another. For 3-year-old children, being attacked and having a conflict with a parent were precipitating causes of anger. The primary event mentioned for fear by both 3- and 6-year-old children was the presence of a strange animate being, such as a monster or ghost. Six-year-olds also mentioned the dark as a source of fear. In both groups, sadness was caused by a loss of a valuable possession or rejection by one's parents or peers.

Similarities across the two age groups were also found when the consequences of negative emotional responses were analyzed. Both 3- and 6-year-old children mentioned destructive actions as a consequence of feeling angry. Withdrawal responses were also generated if the cause of anger was a parent. Fear and sadness responses were also similar across the age groups, with the exception that 3-year-old children more frequently than 6-year-olds sought out a parent as a result of fear or sadness. Six-year-olds more frequently tried to change the situation that made them sad or afraid.

Given the similarities between the Demos (1974) and Trabasso et al. (1981) studies, what conclusions can be drawn with respect to children's causal knowledge of emotions? To begin with, certain types of events can be shown to arouse a specific emotion. For example, events that allude to the presence of a monster or the dark almost always arouse fear in children. This type of relationship between event and emotion may be the reason Borke chose to assume that a specific event always arouses a specific emotion.

We have illustrated quite clearly, however, that anger and sadness are quite frequently aroused by the same event. This result was consistent across all three studies we discussed (e.g., Borke, 1971; Demos, 1974; Trabasso et al., 1981). Thus, reliance on the context or situation to arouse a particular negative or positive emotion seems to be an unproductive strategy. More important, the association between an event and an emotion does not tell us why or how children interpret specific situations as causing a particular emotion. As Masters and Carlson (1984) conclude in their review of emotional development:

. . . there remains within the larger categories of positive and negative experiences, ample room for further inquiry to identify the dimensions on which experiences producing emotional reactions may be classified.

Our conceptual analysis attempts to address this issue by describing the dimensions children use to distinguish among anger, fear, and sadness.

A conceptual analysis of anger, fear, and sadness

In undertaking a meaning analysis of emotional-state terms, certain assumptions must be made about the nature of the cognitive system that underlies the interpretation of events and produces physiological arousal. Our belief is that the types and contents of the inferences made upon experiencing or interpreting an event directly influence the type and intensity of an emotional response experienced by a person. For the most part, the processing of event information occurs in a rather automatic fashion, with much of the contents and procedures underlying emotional evaluation unavailable to the participant. On the other hand, emotional arousal is thought to involve some type of discrepancy or violation of expectation, in the cognitive sense, and therefore may require effortful, conscious processing of event information. Because of the somewhat complex nature of emotional knowledge, the methodology one uses must be flexible and sensitive to the verbal as well as nonverbal aspects of emotional information.

Because our study is concerned with the nature and organization of emotional knowledge, a working definition of *emotion* is in order. Because we are interested in the interaction of cognition and emotion, our definition must include a somewhat detailed description of the cognitive processes that occur as a function of experiencing some type of event. The definition offered by Mandler (1975) comes the closest to describing both the physiological and cognitive properties of emotional responses. Also, the specificity of his description allows a fairly straightforward test to be made of the adequacy of some of the dimensions of the definition.

Mandler defines emotional experience in terms of two dimensions: an arousal component and a meaning analysis. The arousal component is produced by either an interruption of ongoing organized mental activity and/or an interruption of ongoing organized action. Arousal is characterized by increased activity of the autonomic nervous system and can be measured in terms of specific events that are independent of and external to the mental system (e.g., increased heart rate and increased GSR [galvanic skin response] activity). Almost any type of interruption can cause arousal, whether the interruption is externally or internally induced.

A critical factor in predicting whether an event will cause an interruption in ongoing plans or actions is the degree of incongruity between what a person expects to happen and what actually occurs. Here, *expectation* is defined in terms of the predictions individuals make about future events. When engaging in overt action or in planning an overt action, people usually have specific expectations about the outcome of that action sequence. If a different outcome occurs, the end state is, by definition, incongruous with what was expected. The degree of incongruity is often an indicator of the intensity of the emotional experience.

Thus, to Mandler, the violation of expectation, the interruption of ongoing activity, and subsequent physiological arousal characterize all emotional experience. These dimensions, however, tell us little about the type of emotional reaction to be experienced. An additional meaning analysis of the interrupting event is necessary. This analysis includes an assessment of the goal states of an individual and the process by which an intervening event has affected the probability of an individual attaining a desired end state.

Mandler (1975, 1982, 1983) is quite specific in considering the importance of goals and values in determining emotional experience. He is less specific, however, in describing the dimensions that are used either to differentiate positive from negative emotions or to differentiate among the negative emotions. A more detailed description is necessary to understand how the knowledge structures are organized for each of the emotions.

The meanings of fear, anger, and sadness were chosen for initial analysis because there is agreement among most researchers (Ekman & Friesen, 1975; Ekman, Friesen, & Ellsworth, 1972; Izard, 1979, 1981, 1982; Plutchik, 1978; Sroufe, 1979) that each of these emotions is distinct in terms of the facial expressions and behavior that accompany it. Also, many investigators believe that Mandler's definition may be more applicable to these emotions than to others (Isen, in press; Sroufe, 1979; Scherer, 1984), even though Mandler (1983) gives ample evidence that the dimensions of incongruity and violation are as central to positive emotions as they are to negative emotions. Our plan is to describe in detail the dimensions of fear, anger, and sadness and then to test the adequacy of Mandler's definition with respect to the dimensions of interruption and violation of expectation.

As we stated previously, an important assumption underlying our meaning analysis is that individuals respond to and interpret events with respect to their own goals and desires. Thus, one of the central dimensions of the meaning analysis is focused on whether an event will lead to the attainment or nonattainment of a desired end state. The determination of successful goal attainment is important because individuals have strong preferences for certain end states and seek to avoid other types of end states. This principle is quite simple and is closely related to Freud's (1915/1948) pleasure–pain principle (which specifies that most of human activity occurs in the service of attaining desirable end states and avoiding unpleasant end states).

In translating this principle into our meaning analysis, we would say that two types of desires exist: those where an individual wants something and those where an individual does not want something (e.g., where the individual seeks to avoid an end state). A second component centers on whether these desired states have been attained. Again two possibilities exist: The desired state is attained or the desired state is not attained. If the two dimensions are paired to generate all possible combinations of want and attainment states, four possibilities exist:

1. A person wants something and does not attain it.
2. A person wants something and attains it.

3. A person does not want something and does not attain it.
4. A person does not want something and attains it.

Roseman (1979) has developed a meaning analysis of both positive and negative emotions that also incorporates these two dimensions. According to Roseman, specific combinations of want and have states are sufficient to differentiate positive from negative emotions. For example, happiness occurs when a person wants something and gets it or when a person does not want something and does not get it. The negative emotions, such as anger, sadness, and fear, occur when a person wants something and does not get it or when a person does not want something and gets it. In our meaning analysis, however, the want and attainment states are *not* symmetrical across the positive emotions or the negative emotions. *Fear* requires a different combination of want and have states than do anger and sadness, primarily because fear concerns the anticipation of state changes whereas anger and sadness are concerned with state changes that have already occurred.

In order to illustrate how fear can be differentiated from anger or sadness, the dimension of *certainty* must be introduced. This dimension refers to the probability that a state change will occur. In situations where a precipitating event has taken place, negative emotional responses can occur for two reasons: Either a person has perceived that the precipitating event *has* caused a change with respect to attaining certain goals, or the person has perceived that a precipitating event *will* cause a change with respect to the attainment of certain goals. When individuals infer a fear response in others or label their own emotion as fear, the precipitating event has set up the possibility that a change of goal state might occur (e.g., the person might fail to attain a particular goal). However, the change in goal state has not yet occurred. When anger and sadness are inferred or evoked, the precipitating event has already caused a change with respect to attaining a particular end state. By combining the dimension of certainty with the dimensions of want and attainment states, we can differentiate the meaning structure of fear from that of anger and sadness.

Fear

The following pattern of inferences should be made about fear as an emotional response. The actor (person experiencing fear) is perceived to be in a particular state and wants to maintain that state. Because a particular precipitating event has occurred, however, the actor perceives that a change in attaining a desired end state could occur. Moreover, the probability of the change occurring is very high. Thus, fear occurs because of the unexpected change in the probability of being able to maintain a desired end state. According to our meaning analysis, we would say that the actor has attained a particular state (e.g., attainment state) and wants to maintain that state (e.g., want state) but that the maintenance of that state is highly uncertain (e.g., the degree of certainty is high that change will occur).

An example of a fear-provoking situation to the child is the following:

One day, upon coming home from school, you come into your house and notice that it is very quiet. You look all around and find that nobody is at home.

In this situation, fear is aroused because the child has been left alone. The state of being alone, however, is not the object of the child's fear. The possible harm that could be inflicted on the child is the dimension that induces the fear. For example, when we ask children why being left alone makes them afraid, a prototypical response is that a robber could break into the house and hurt them badly while their parents were away. Thus, the precipitating event of being alone can put children into a state of uncertainty as to whether their physical well-being will be maintained. A change has not yet occurred in a particular state (e.g., the state of well-being), but the child perceives that there is a high probability that a change will materialize.

In expressions of knowledge about the emotion of fear, most often the emphasis is on the uncertainty of maintaining a positive state (e.g., a state of well-being with respect to physical and psychological dimensions of a person). However, there are times when both children and adults express their fears in terms

Table 9.1. *Dimensions distinguishing fear, anger, and sadness*

Fear	Anger	Sadness
Not want–not attain; want–attain	Want–not attain; not want–attain	Want–not attain; not want–attain
Uncertainty of maintaining end state	End state has already been changed	End state has already been changed
Fear is an "it" emotion focused on the relationship of the self to the external world	Anger is an "it" emotion focused on the relationship of the self to the external world	Sadness is a "me" emotion focused on the fulfillment of self goals
Attention is on the prevention of the anticipated state change	Attention is on the cause of the state change	Attention is on the consequences of the state change
Primary reason for fear is anticipation of physical or psychological harm	Primary reason for anger is a violation of a personal wish or social code	Primary reason for sadness is loss of valued person, object, or event
Primary action of fear is to prevent anticipated state change	Primary action of anger is to get rid of object obstructing goal path	Primary action of sadness is goal abandonment

of a desire to avoid certain states, even though the underlying desire is to maintain a particular end state. For example, upon discovering that a friend is sick with the flu, many children react with fear at the thought of being exposed to the friend. The reason given for their fear would be the desire to *avoid* illness. Thus, in these cases, we can say that fear is caused when there is uncertainty in the ability to avoid certain end states, such as sickness.

We point this out because knowledge of fear responses can be stated either in the positive (e.g., the desire to maintain a particular end state) or in the negative (e.g., the desire to avoid a particular end state). What distinguishes fear from anger and sadness is that, in fear, there has been no overt change in the ability to maintain the desired end state, only in the perception that a change is about to occur. With anger and sadness, the desire to maintain or avoid a particular end state is also present. The difference is that, with anger or sadness, the change in the ability to maintain or avoid a particular end state has already occurred. Table 9.1 lists the dimensions that are used to distinguish the three negative emotions of fear, anger, and sadness.

Anger

The following pattern of inferences should be made when an anger response is identified. Normally, the actor is in a situation where a particular end state is desired (e.g., the want dimension). She engages in some type of action to achieve the desired end state, when a precipitating event occurs to preclude goal attainment (e.g., the attainment dimension). There is no uncertainty about goal attainment as there is with fear. The actor has failed to attain a particular end state. An example of an event that arouses anger in children is the following:

You've been working for a very long time on a picture that you want to put up on the board in your classroom. Just as you finish it, one of your classmates comes over and scribbles big red crayon marks all over your picture.

In this situation, anger is aroused because a desired end state has not been attained. The child's picture has been destroyed and cannot be put up on the board.

As we indicated before, knowledge about the goals and attainment states underlying an emotional reaction can be given in terms of the desire to avoid a particular end state as well as the desire to attain a particular end state. For example, when a 5-year-old boy was asked why he would feel angry if someone scribbled on his picture, he replied:

I'd be real mad 'cause I didn't want him to ruin my picture, and that's just what he did. He ruined it – it's gone. He wouldn't be my friend anymore.

This response is just as valid as one in which the child verbalizes the interruption in terms of wanting to attain a desired end state (e.g., wanting to hang up a picture in front of the class) and failing to do so. Thus, anger can be described in terms of failing to attain a desired end state or failing to avoid an undesired end state.

Sadness versus anger

The dimensions used to infer or generate sadness are similar to those used for anger. In fact, many times a single event can cause both sadness and anger. For example, sadness as well as anger can occur as a function of wanting to hang up a picture in class and having the picture destroyed before it can be hung up. Thus, the want and attainment states are identical in many situations where sadness or anger is inferred. Dimensions other than these must be used to distinguish between the two emotions.

One such dimension concerns the focus of attention once goal failure has occurred. A person can focus on either the cause of goal failure or the consequences of not being able to attain a goal state. Anger involves an orientation to the cause of goal failure, whereas sadness involves an orientation to the consequences of such a failure.

Dahl (1979) has made a similar distinction between anger and sadness and has proposed that anger and sadness can be differentiated in terms of an "it"–"me" distinction. Dahl asserts that anger is essentially an "it" emotion occurring when an actor focuses on external events, people, and objects. An "it" emotion occurs in response to an actor's needs with respect to the external world. For example, fear and anger would both be considered "it" emotions because they arise from an assessment and interaction with the external world.

Although Dahl does not explicitly state the case, "it" emotions occur when an actor focuses on the cause of an interrupted plan or action, which is normally the event that initiated the interruption. For example, when a 5-year-old girl was asked why she was angry when another child scribbled all over her drawing, the child replied:

> Because she ruined the picture, and now I don't have no picture to give to the teacher. She should be punished, because it's her fault. She's not allowed to do that. She shouldn't be allowed to get any treats or anything, and she should never do that again.

According to Dahl, however, sadness is a "me" emotion and has a specific function: to provide feedback about how well things are going (e.g., whether there is success) in terms of the actor being able to achieve her own goals. We would agree with Dahl's speculation and add that a "me" emotion, such as sadness, occurs because the actor has focused on the consequences of an interruption to an ongoing plan or action. The focus on the outcome of an event is evident in this child's sad response when her picture is destroyed by another child:

'Cause now I don't have no picture. I worked real hard on that. It's wrecked and now I won't have anything to give to the teacher. I just couldn't do it over again, so I won't get a chance to have my picture up.

In comparing the anger and sad responses to the same initiating event, one finds both similarities and differences. Both children verbalized the fact that their picture had been destroyed, and both children stated that they would have no picture to give to the teacher. Thus, these children were explicitly aware of the change in state with respect to achieving a particular goal (e.g., stating that their original plan had failed). However, the child who was angry focused on the cause of the interruption (e.g., her classmate) and also indicated that her classmate was responsible for ruining the picture. The child who felt sad also indicated that the picture was ruined but instead focused on the consequences of having a goal blocked (e.g., thinking about drawing the picture again, concluding that she could not do it, and stating the fact that she would have no picture to give to the teacher).

One factor that may influence whether anger or sadness is experienced in interpersonal social situations is whether intentional harm can be attributed to people who cause an interruption in an actor's plans. If the actor perceives that another person intentionally interrupted or blocked the achievement of a goal, when the actor did not expect this to occur, then anger may easily be aroused. If the actor perceives that another person's actions were not intentional or that the other was not responsible for her actions, then sadness may be felt because the actor then focuses on the consequences of the interruption.

The notion of blame may influence whether an anger response will occur, as suggested by Weiner (1982), but anger may also occur in situations where blame or intentional damage cannot be attributed to another person. Many times a person expresses anger at inanimate objects or at people who have not intentionally sought to harm the person. The mere fact that a person or event caused an interruption may be enough to trigger an anger response. In Table 9.1 we indicate that the important dimension in generating anger is the ability to locate the source of interruption. If intentional harm can be attributed to the source, anger will almost always occur. However, if the source of the interruption is unexpected, anger may still be generated as a response in acknowledging the actor's understanding of the causal relationship between the source of interruption and goal failure.

Just as anger, sadness, and fear can be distinguished in terms of the evaluative inferences made upon experiencing an event, these three emotions can also be distinguished by the wishes and plans associated with each of the emotional responses. According to Dahl (1979), the wishes associated with an emotional response can be distinguished along an active–passive dimension. Anger, according to Dahl, is an active emotion and implies a specific consummatory act of getting rid of the object of anger. In our terminology, we would say that anger functions to organize subsequent action directed at removing the source of interruption.

In contrast to anger, Dahl (1979) conceives of sadness as a passive emotion, with no consummatory act associated with its expression. The passivity experienced in sadness stems from the perception that the goal under consideration is not attainable and the probability of reinstating the goal is very low. The only wish appropriate for sadness is either goal abandonment or goal substitution. In many situations, however, formulating a new goal may require too much restructuring and cognitive effort. Thus, the more frequent wish associated with sadness is one of goal abandonment without goal substitution.

Associating passivity with the wishes following sadness is problematic in one respect. Often a person who experiences sadness persists in attempting to attain a particular end state, even though there is an awareness that the end state is unattainable. For example, when children lose a valued object, even though they know the object is gone they may secretly wish that they could have the object again. Much of their thinking may be focused on ways in which they might have prevented the loss, or some of their cognitive effort may be spent in fantasy thinking, in which they can negate the circumstances that caused the loss.

The question arises as to whether the emotional response of sadness organizes these wishful-thinking episodes or whether a change in emotional state enables a person to engage in wishful thinking. It is possible that the first response to sadness is one of goal abandonment, in which no alternative goal is formulated. Because of the distress caused by goal abandonment, however, the person attempts to initiate a state change by engaging in wishful thinking, which involves an attempt to reinstate the goal. The problem is that distress must be differentiated from sadness as an emotional state. Otherwise, we would have to conclude that sadness is an organizer of subsequent action, very much as anger and fear are.

Children's knowledge of negative emotional states: an empirical test

In order to test some of our ideas described in the previous section, we performed a study with 6-year-old children. We chose to study children of this age group because of the well-documented facility with which they can talk about their emotional knowledge (Demos, 1974; Schwartz & Trabasso, 1984). Conversely, the inadequacy of 6-year-olds' knowledge seems to be the primary concern of other investigators (Harris, 1983; Harris & Olthof, 1983; Harter, 1979), who argue that these children lack knowledge about the causes of their emotions or lack the operations necessary to make the appropriate inferences about emotions from a given event. By studying this age group, we could better determine what these children know and do not know about emotional reactions.

Subjects

The participants in the study were 32 first-grade children from a middle-class Catholic school in suburban Chicago. Half of the subjects were boys and half were girls.

Stimuli

Eight mini-episodes were constructed and used to elicit emotional responses from children. All of the episodes contained events that were either generated by children, as causes of negative emotions, or used in previous studies to generate negative emotions. Each of the mini-episodes was constructed so that the participating child could be involved by being referred to with a general *you* term. Each child was asked to imagine that he or she was experiencing the events in the mini-episode. In all episodes, a second person was introduced and performed an action that either interfered with or impinged on the child in some fashion. The eight mini-episodes were as follows:

1. One day, you find out that your family is going to a really good movie. You ask if you can go, but your mother says no and tells you that you have to stay home with a baby sitter.
2. You are playing with your very favorite toy at school and having the best time. Suddenly, the teacher comes over and takes it away from you.
3. One day, when you come home, you find a note that your mom wrote, telling you that she has taken everyone to the ice cream parlor and will be back in ten minutes.
4. You've been working a long time on a picture you want to put up in your classroom. Just when you finish it a boy/girl comes along and scribbles big red crayon marks all over it.
5. One day, you're sick in bed with the flu, and you can't get up and do things with your family.
6. One day, you're playing at school, when the teacher comes over and tells you that you're five minutes late for your reading group and that you are holding the group up.
7. One day, you come in from playing outside when it turns dark outside. You look all over the house and can't find anyone at home.
8. You're working in your classroom when a boy/girl bigger than you comes over and punches you. He/she tells you that if you tell anybody he/she did that, he/she will really hurt you.

In the process of constructing these mini-episodes, it became clear that more than one emotion could easily be inferred during the interpretation process. For example, Miniepisode 8 could elicit anger or fear or both emotions. Thus, the stimulus materials were not designed to elicit a particular emotion. The important question was whether a specific pattern of inferences would lead to the use of a particular emotion-state word.

Design and procedure

The 32 children were randomly assigned to one of two groups, each group containing an equal number of boys and girls. Each group of children was presented with four of the mini-episodes, the first group receiving Episodes 1 to 4 and the second group receiving Episodes 5 to 8. The division of mini-episodes for each group was completed on a random basis, since we had made no a priori hypotheses about which type of emotional response should be elicited for each event.

After the children heard each mini-episode, they were asked six probe questions:

1a. How would you feel if that happened to you? Would you feel: mad, sad, or afraid [forced-choice response]?
   b. Would you feel more than one way? Which way?
2. Why would you feel [child's choice of emotional response]?
3. Do you think the agent [second character mentioned in the miniepisode] wanted to do that?
4. What do you wish you could do, if you could do anything you wanted to when that happened?
5. What would you really do?
6. Why would you do that?

Within each group, the children received the four mini-episodes in random order. Also, when the children were asked how they felt, the three choices of emotional reactions were always presented in a different order, thus preventing the children from forming a response bias in terms of a particular emotional reaction. All of the responses to the interview questions were tape recorded.

Results

The first analysis completed on the data concerned the proportion of times children chose one emotional response versus more than one response when asked the question "How would you feel if that happened to you?" In 89% of the cases, children chose only one emotional response when answering this question. Thus, although more than one emotional response was possible, children displayed a tendency to choose only one emotion.

The types of emotional responses varied as a function of the miniepisodes, as Table 9.2 clearly indicates. Certain episodes were more likely than others to elicit specific emotions. For example, fear was not elicited very frequently by Miniepisodes 1 to 4 but occurred quite frequently in response to Miniepisodes 6

Table 9.2. *Proportion of fear, anger, and sad responses to each of the eight miniepisodes*

Miniepisode	Fear	Anger	Sadness
1	.00	*.53*	*.47*
2	.08	.30	*.62*
3	.07	.40	*.53*
4	.00	*.85*	.15
5	.07	.20	*.73*
6	*.40*	.20	*.40*
7	*.77*	.00	.23
8	*.53*	*.47*	.00

Note: Italicized numbers indicate the statistically significant different proportions when compared with the nonitalicized proportion.

to 8. Anger and sadness were elicited more frequently across all miniepisodes, although there was one (Miniepisode 7) that elicited no anger and one (Miniepisode 8) that elicited no sadness. Over all of the miniepisodes sadness accounted for 40% of the responses, anger for 36%, and fear for 24%.

In terms of the amount of agreement in children's responses to each miniepisode, the data clearly indicated that each miniepisode normally elicited two dominant emotional responses. For example, Miniepisode 1 (which portrayed a child having to stay at home with a baby sitter while the parents went to a movie) elicited sad responses 47% of the time and angry responses 53% of the time. Thus, if we had chosen one response as the appropriate one, similar to Borke's procedures, at least half of the children would have received no credit for their choices.

The next set of analyses pertained to the responses given to the question "Why would you [feel the child's choice of emotion word]?" Our first analysis involved examining the language children used to explain their reasons for choosing a particular emotional response. The reasons were grouped according to the following categories:

1. *Anticipated state.* Response focused on an event that had not yet occurred. The criterion for determining that children were referring to future events was the use of such terms as *might, will, would,* and *could.* Examples are "A burgler could come in and hurt me"; "I might get lost"; "She would really yell at me."

2. *Existing state.* Response focused on an existing state in the environment or an internal state of a person. Examples are "I was all alone"; "It was dark outside"; "I was sick in bed."

3. *Blocked goal.* Response focused on the attainment of a goal and the occurrence of an obstacle blocking the attainment of the goal. Most of these responses

Table 9.3. *Proportions of children's reasons for fear,*
anger, and sadness

Reason	Fear	Anger	Sadness
Anticipated state changes	.92	.02	.07
Existing states	.08	.64	.62
Blocked goals	.00	.34	.31

Table 9.4. *Children's reasons for fear, anger, and*
sadness according to want and attainment dimensions

Dimension	Fear	Anger	Sadness
Want–attain	.00	.00	.00
Want–not attain	.08	.60	.81
Not want–not attain	.89	.00	.02
Not want–attain	.03	.40	.17

contained two components: reference to the goal under consideration and the conditions blocking goal attainment. Examples are "I wanted to go to the movie, but she wouldn't let me"; I wanted to play with the toy, but she took it away."

The reasons for each emotional response were grouped into one of the three categories.

Table 9.3 contains the proportion of responses in each of the three categories as a function of the emotional response given to the miniepisode. The data clearly indicate that the type of reason varies significantly as a function of the emotional response inferred. When children inferred fear as their reaction to an event, 92% of the time their reasons contained an anticipated state change. Anticipated state changes were given less than 4% of the time for both anger and sadness.

Existing states and blocked goals accounted for the majority of reasons for both anger and sadness. Existing states were mentioned twice as frequently as blocked goals. No differences were found in the reasons given for anger and sadness. Both emotional responses led the child to focus on the fact that an action, state, or event had blocked the chance to attain a desired end state.

The second analysis performed on Question 1 pertained to the classification of reasons in terms of the appropriate want and attainment states mentioned in our theoretical analysis. Table 9.4 contains the data broken down by emotion, as a function of the four combinations of want–attainment states.

It is immediately evident from the data that the only combination of want–attainment state that was not generated by the children was a state of wanting something and being able to attain it (e.g., want–attainment). This combination of states would be prototypic for positive emotions such as happiness or joy. Since this study was constructed to elicit negative emotions, one would predict that this combination would not occur frequently, and in fact it was never given by any child.

The failure of children to generate the want–attainment state was interesting in another respect. Theoretically, we proposed that fear could be used to generate two combinations of want–attainment states: one in which the person wanted to maintain a state, and was in fact maintaining it, but perceived that a change was about to occur; and another in which the person did not want a particular end state to occur, and the state had not yet occurred, but the person perceived that a change was about to occur. With the miniepisodes used in this study, the children always talked about fear with respect to *avoiding* a particular end state (e.g., not wanting an end state to occur and not having it occur yet). Almost all of these not want–not attain states occurred with respect to fear, indicating an almost perfect correspondence between the emotional response and the combination of these want–attainment states.

The relationship between a particular combination of want–attainment states and the generation of either anger and/or sadness was more complex. For both sadness and anger, the prototypical response was one of wanting something and not being able to attain it (want–not attain). The combined states of not wanting something and having it were generated for both emotions, but their frequency of occurrence was much lower than that for the want–not attain combination. This was especially true for sadness, where want–not attain states accounted for 83% of all responses. Sadness may be more representative of states of loss than anger, and in fact children may need to express sadness in terms of lack states.

The next set of analyses focused on the answers to Question 3: "Do you think the agent [second character mentioned in the miniepisode] wanted to do that [specific action mentioned to child]?" Two conditional probability analyses were completed on the data, and the results are shown in Table 9.5.

The first relationship to be considered is the judgment of intentional action, given that the subject stated that he or she would feel one of the three emotions. The data indicate that children who express anger are more than twice as likely to infer that an actor's actions were intentional than children who express the other two negative emotions.

The second relationship concerns the type of emotion expressed, given that subjects inferred the action on the part of another to be intentional. Again, subjects were much more likely to express anger than any another emotion, if they made the judgment that another's action was intentional. These data indicate a

Table 9.5. *Relationship between judgment of intent and emotions inferred or anticipated*

A. Proportion of children in each emotion category who said that actor intended action

Emotion	Proportion inferring intentionality
Anger	.50
Fear	.19
Sadness	.22

B. Proportion of children inferring that actor intended action who said that they would feel anger, fear, or sadness

Emotion	Proportion stating emotion would be felt
Anger	.63
Fear	.26
Sadness	.11

fairly strong relationship between intentional action on the part of another and the experience of anger.

Whether anger can occur without the perception of intentional action, however, is still an important question. Not all children who were angry said that another person's actions were intentional in terms of causing an interruption of or an obstacle to goal attainment. Sometimes children expressed anger when one of their expectations had been violated, even when they perceived the actions of another person to be unintentional. It may be that the interruption of plans leading to the attainment of important end states results in anger, whether or not inferences of intentional harm are made. This remains an issue for consideration in future research.

The next group of analyses pertained to the wishes the children generated in response to the events in the miniepisodes. These wishes were grouped into five categories:

1. *Goal reinstatement*. Wish indicating the child's intention to pursue, regain, or attain the goal or end state formulated before the precipitating event occurred. Examples are "I would wish that I could go to the movie"; "I wish that the boy didn't ruin my picture."
2. *Goal substitution*. Wish indicating that the child substituted a new goal or end state to be attained, rather than attempting to achieve the goal formulated before the precipitating event. An example would be "I would want to play with my favorite toy if I couldn't go to the movies."
3. *Goal forfeiture*. Wish indicating that the child abandoned the original goal but did not substitute any new goal. Most often, goal forfeiture was expressed by

Table 9.6. *Proportion of children choosing one of five plans, given the emotion expressed*

Plan	Fear	Anger	Sadness
Goal reinstatement	.07	.21	.38
Goal substitution	.36	.45	.47
Goal forfeiture	.07	.05	.11
Revenge	.14	.27	.02
Preventative action	.36	.02	.02

the mention of passive action such as "I would just sit there with my hands folded"; "I would just sit in my room and do nothing."

4. *Revenge.* Wish indicating that the child had formulated a new goal to destroy or harm the cause of the interruption. Revenge is a type of goal substitution, always directed by and focusing on the source of the interruption. Examples are "I wish I could wrestle him"; "I wish I could punch her for doing that"; "I wish I could get him into big trouble."

5. *Preventative action.* Wish indicating that the child wished to take action to prevent the recurrence of a particular obstacle or to prevent a particular end state from occurring. Examples are "I wish that I could tell the teacher what happened and that he'd never do that again"; "I would go to my friend's house until my mom came home [to prevent anyone from harming the child]."

Table 9.6 lists the types of wishes children generated as a function of the emotional reaction they inferred about the precipitating event. Two findings are apparent. First, the most common wish was one of goal substitution, independent of the type of emotional response generated. Thus, when the children found an obstacle in their path, their most frequent wish was to avoid the obstacle by generating another goal that would not be blocked.

Second, the frequency of generating other types of wishes, however, was governed by the particular emotional response given to the focal event. When a child expressed a fear reaction, the most frequent wish other than goal substitution was one to prevent the anticipated end state from occurring. For example, children who expressed fear about a burglar entering their house and harming them said that they would want to go to a friend's house and wait until their parents came home. In that way, no harm could come to them. The wishes of children who expressed fear about another classmate harming them often involved telling the teacher or parent, with the express purpose of having the parent or teacher

Table 9.7. *Proportion of children choosing one of five means of action, given the emotion expressed*

Action	Fear	Anger	Sadness
Goal reinstatement	.11	.15	.18
Goal substitution	.37	.39	.64
Goal forfeiture	.11	.14	.08
Revenge	.07	.22	.04
Preventive action	.34	.10	.06

prevent harm. Thus, the wishes of a majority of children expressing fearful reactions involved an attempt to prevent an anticipated state change.

For anger, the two wishes most frequently stated were ones involving revenge or goal reinstatement. For sadness, the most common wish involved goal reinstatement. That is, children wished that they could reinstate the goal, even though they had just expressed an accurate awareness that their goal had been blocked and that it would be impossible to attain a particular end state.

The *means* (e.g., plans) by which the children stated they would really solve their problems were similar to their wishes, with one exception (Table 9.7). For sadness, goal substitution was a more frequent strategy than goal reinstatement. Children expressed their awareness that, even though they really wanted to get back what they had lost, it was impossible. Thus, they began to formulate alternative plans involving the attainment of a new goal.

Conclusions and discussion

Several conclusions can be drawn from this investigation. In analyzing the children's reasons for their emotional responses to different events, it is clear that different types of knowledge are elicited to express information about fear as opposed to anger and sadness. Children talk about fear in terms of anticipated state changes rather than state changes that have already occurred. Anger and sadness are most often talked about in terms of blocked goals or existing states that prevent goal attainment. So, again, the data show that fear is clearly differentiated from anger and sadness.

The data from our study also support the notion that different want–attainment states underlie the organization and meaning of emotional reaction words. The children's reasons for fear were most often expressed in terms of not having something happen to them and not wanting something to happen to them but perceiving that there was a high probability that something would happen. Anger and sadness, however, were always talked about in terms of wanting something and not having it or not wanting something and having it. Thus, one of the critical dimensions differentiating fear from anger and sadness is one of possibility. *Fear* connotes a state of anticipation of a possible state change, whereas *anger* and *sadness* signify that the state change has already occurred.

In our description of the want–attainment states that pertain to each of the three emotions, we stated that each emotion could be signified by two of the four combinations of want–attainment states: Fear × Not Want–Not Attain and Want–Attain States, Anger and Sadness × Want–Not Attain and Not Want–Attain States. From the analysis of the children's reasons for choosing specific emotion terms, we found that one combination of want–attainment states was used more frequently than the other combinations. For example, in expressing fear, the children most often said they were afraid of having something happen to them. These children also indicated that nothing had happened yet but that they did not want anything to happen to them, thereby referring to fear in terms of not want–not have states.

Anger and sadness were most frequently talked about in terms of wanting something that was not attainable. There were instances where children did refer to being angry or sad because they were in a state they did not want to be in (e.g., having a picture ruined and not wanting it to be ruined). These references, however, were not nearly as frequent as references to states of wanting something that was lost or unattainable.

What future studies must explore is whether each of the negative emotions can be described as easily by both combinations of want–attainment states, or whether there is a preferred way of talking about emotions. Our study was completed on a limited set of items not varied systematically in terms of the different combinations of want–attainment states that could exist.

More systematic studies would be necessary to determine the type of language most commonly used to describe a particular emotional state. Our hunch is that there may be a preferred way of talking about each emotion. For example, a child may be presented with a situation in which she does not want to get the flu but she gets it. When asked how she feels, her response could easily be one of sadness (e.g., she is in a state of sickness and does not wish to be in the state). When further probed about her reason for feeling sad, however, she might say that she is sad because she wants to play outside and now she cannot do so. In other words, both children and adults may use the word *sadness* to refer mainly to states of loss that arise from being put into undesirable states.

Anger, in contrast, may be used to refer to situations of loss *and* undesirable situations. For example, when children and adults are physically restrained, anger is often expressed. When children are asked the reasons for their anger, they often say that they are angry because someone is holding them down and they do not want to be held. Thus, one difference between anger and sadness may be the degree to which each emotion term is used to express different combinations of want–attainment states.

Another difference between anger and sadness was the degree to which the perception of intentional action was related to the expression of each emotion. The children were more likely to respond to a situation with anger rather than with sadness if they stated that the actor intentionally blocked their goal. This finding indicates that the presence or absence of intentional harm should be investigated in future studies. Our prediction is that the presence of intentional harm will almost always arouse anger, given that the intentional act was unexpected.

Whether anger is aroused without the perception of intentional harm is a more difficult question to answer. It may be that the intentional component is a sufficient condition to arouse anger but not a necessary condition. From anecdotal evidence, we know that people often get quite angry when a physical event or an object is responsible for goal obstruction. The fact that physical events and objects are not animate beings capable of intentional action makes it difficult to suggest that anger always requires the perception of intentional harm. However, children and adults may automatically make inferences about the animate characteristics of physical objects without fully believing that objects and events are capable of intentional behavior. This is an important issue and clearly one for further exploration.

Although our study did not include children in the age range of 2½ to 5 years of age, certain predictions can be made about the development of emotional knowledge from past studies and from current studies in our laboratory. First, it is evident that fear becomes highly differentiated from anger and sadness by the time children reach the age of 3. Children generate different causes and consequences for fear than for anger or sadness, and fear does not co-occur with other emotional responses as frequently as anger or sadness does (Trabasso et al., 1981).

Second, it is evident that children are aware of and can verbalize about their own intentions at a very early age (Hood & Bloom, 1979; Huttenlocher, Smiley, & Charney, 1983). Children as young as 3 also have quite accurate knowledge about whether they or story characters have been able to attain important goals (Stein & Levine, 1984).

The fact that children can accurately identify many of their own needs from the age of 2½ on, especially when asked about them during an ongoing behavioral episode (Stein & Levine, 1984), and the fact that the causes and consequences of anger, sadness, fear, and happiness are well differentiated by the age of 3 (Trabasso et al., 1981) lead us to the conclusion that children would be able to identify the want–attainment states underlying the meaning of anger, sadness, fear, and happiness. In fact, in one of our studies (Stein & Levine, 1984) 89% of all 3-year-old children tested correctly identified the want–have states for anger, sadness, and happiness.

From these data, we would propose that it is the awareness of the combinations of want–have states that enables children to use different emotion words to label their feelings about different precipitating events. The fact that fear is clearly differentiated from anger and sadness also leads us to believe that children should be able to differentiate emotions in terms of whether the emotion is associated with a definite change in the probability of attaining a goal (e.g., anger or sadness) versus the possibility of a change occurring in the ability to attain or maintain a desired end state (e.g., fear).

The child's knowledge of anger and sadness should also be differentiated in ways similar to adults' knowledge. Three-year-old children should be able to differentiate those situations where harm is intentional from those situations where actions are unintentional or accidental (Shultz, 1980). Thus, the presence of intentional obstruction should elicit anger in young children as well as in adults.

If there is any difference in the way adults and young children respond to events that block their goals, we suspect that young children may be more prone to label all types of unexpected obstructions as causes of anger. In contrast, adults may use intentional action in a more systematic fashion to label an emotional response as anger rather than as something else. For example, adults may label a situation frustrating or irritating if physical objects or events obstruct their plans. Also, unintentional acts by others may be labeled differently from those perceived to be intentional. Again, these hypotheses remain to be tested in future studies.

As for the relationship between plans, or wishes and subsequent behavior, our results showed that the specific emotion inferred did predict differential plans and actions to some extent. Revenge was more highly related to anger, goal reinstatement to sadness, and preventative action to fear. The unexpected finding that goal substitution was the most frequent plan and action for all emotions requires an explanation. Several dimensions could account for these results.

Our study was an interview study in which children had the opportunity to reflect on their reasons and actions in situations that could arouse emotions. It may be that, when children are not actually involved in a situation, they can retrieve more information about the likely outcome of their actions. The reason for greater access is that the intensity of the emotional feeling may be absent or quite reduced in hypothetical situations. In real-world situations, the emotion is actually aroused and the plans or wishes may well be an automatic component of the emotion.

However, the fact that children were asked a series of questions about their feelings before deciding on a course of action could have influenced their responses, independent of whether emotional arousal was present or absent. The intervention procedures used in many therapeutic situations are very similar to the ones used in this study. Asking about reasons for anger, as well as evaluating another person's intentions could provide additional information in interview as well as real-life situations. This information could very well change the nature of the planning process.

A third difficulty was that children could very well have inferred the automatic plan or wish that is supposedly associated with each emotion but chose to verbalize a more adaptive plan in response to the questions concerning plans and actions. That is, we had no way of probing the processes children go through before making a response. Often they think of a plan along the way to formulating a more "appropriate" solution. Because we did not tap this process, we have no way of knowing whether the plans generated were the children's first spontaneous thoughts involving their actions.

The data collected, however, do indicate that 6-year-old children know quite a bit about the causes and consequences of emotional reactions. In several recent studies, it has been hypothesized that 6-year-olds do not understand the nature of emotions as well as older children do (Harris, 1983; Harter, 1979). These developmental differences are thought to be related to children's inability to experience two emotions simultaneously, especially when one emotion is positive and the other negative. Harter (1979) proposed that young children have difficulty understanding that they can feel both positive and negative affects toward a person, and Harris (1983) argued that 6-year-olds are much less likely than older children to experience "simultaneous" positive and negative emotional responses to the same event.

In this study we did not systematically investigate whether 6-year-olds can express more than one emotional response to an event. Data from other studies in our laboratory (Stein & Eulau, 1984), however, suggest that even 5-year-olds can express more than one emotion in response to a given event. The expression of two emotions is not "simultaneous" because each emotion is expressed in terms of a different part of the event (much like the expression of sadness and anger to the same event).

We have found that children are quite sensitive to dual emotions, if the questions asked and the methodology used are specific in eliciting this knowledge (Stein & Eulau, 1984). Moreover, the theoretical rationale underlying the elicitation of dual emotions suggests that 4- and five-year-olds should be capable of experiencing and expressing such emotions.

Essentially, the elicitation of positive and negative emotion is evidenced in those situations where the child experiences some type of goal conflict. For example, children can be presented with dilemmas in which a character has to perform some type of action to accomplish a valued goal (positive emotion). In doing so, however, the character has to hurt someone else (negative). When children are asked about their knowledge of such situations, they are aware of both the positive and the negative consequences of such actions (Nezworski, Stein, & Trabasso, 1982; Stein & Trabasso, 1982). This awareness is reflected in answers to probe questions, in moral judgments about the central character, and in the elicitation of positive and negative feelings in our current studies. It would appear that a more rigorous and systematic effort is necessary before it is concluded that young children lack either critical knowledge of emotions or the operations necessary to perform integration of emotional information.

Similar "cognitive deficit" arguments have been made with respect to children's understanding of physical concepts. In their review of the critical literature, however, Gelman and Baillergon (1983) show the errors in such an approach. For most tasks that were once thought to be outside the cognitive capability of young children, studies have shown that these children, especially in the early preschool years, have much more knowledge than originally thought. It is also debatable whether these young children can be said to lack critical operations. Similar arguments can be made in reference to the development and study of social knowledge in young children.

From the review of the literature and from the results of our study, we would predict that much of the change in emotional knowledge has to do with the plans and actions that ensue from a particular emotional response. We would argue that 3-year-olds have a good, fairly stable working knowledge of the conditions and goals that underlie the arousal of the negative emotions, as well as the positive emotion of happiness.

Differences in the knowledge base are more likely to occur in making predictions about what will happen as a result of experiencing an emotion or what will happen as a result of carrying out a particular course of action. Young children have much less knowledge than older children about the obstacles in their path (Goldman, 1982) and much less knowledge about the consequences of their actions (Stein & Trabasso, 1982). Future research will be necessary to explore the developmental implications of our conceptual analysis, both in terms of the causal structure of emotions and in terms of the relationship between emotional knowledge and the experience of emotion.

References

Borke, H. Interpersonal perception of young children: Egocentrism or empathy. *Developmental Psychology*, 1971, *5*, 263–9.

Bretherton, I., & Beeghley, M. Talking about internal states: The acquisition of an explicit theory of mind. *Developmental Psychology*, 1982, *18*, 906–21.

Dahl, H. The appetite hypothesis of emotion: A new psychoanalytic model of motivation. In C. E., Izard (Ed.), *Emotions in personality and psychopathology* (pp. 373–407). New York: Plenum, 1979.

Demos, E. V. *Children's understanding and use of affect terms.* Unpublished doctoral dissertation, Harvard University, 1974.

Emde, R. The pre-representational self and its affective core. In A. J. Solnit, R. S. Eissler, & P. B. Nuebauer (Eds.), *The psychoanalytic study of the child.* New Haven, CT: Yale University Press, 1983.

Ekman, P., & Friesen, W. *Unmasking the face.* Englewood Cliffs, NJ: Prentice-Hall, 1975.

Ekman, P., Friesen, W., & Ellsworth, P. *Emotion in the human face.* New York: Pergamon Press, 1972.

Freud, S. Instincts and their vicissitudes. In *Collected papers* (Vol. 4). London: Hogarth Press and the Institute of Psychoanalysis, 1948. (Original work published 1915)

Gelman, R., & Baillergon, R. A review of some Piagetian concepts. In J. Flavell & E. Markman (Eds.), *Handbook of child psychology: Vol. 3. Cognitive development* (pp. 167–230). New York: Wiley, 1963.

Goldman, S. Semantic knowledge systems for real world goals. *Discourse Processes,* 1982, *5,* 279–303.

Harris, P. L. Children's understanding of the link between situation and emotion. *Journal of Experimental Child Psychology,* 1983, *36,* 490–509.

Harris, P. L. What children know about the situations that provoke emotions. In M. Lewis & C. Saarni (Eds.), *The socialization of affect* (pp. 161–86). New York: Plenum, 1985.

Harris, P. L., & Olthof, T. Children's concept of emotion. In G. Butterworth & P. Light (Eds.), *The individual and the social in cognitive development* (pp. 188–212). London: Harvester Press, 1983.

Harter, S. *Children's understanding of multiple emotions: A cognitive–developmental approach.* Address given at the Ninth Annual Piaget Society Meetings, Philadelphia, May 1979.

Hood, L., & Bloom, L. What, when and how about why: A longitudinal study of early expressions of causality. *Monographs of the Society for Research in Child Development,* 1979, *44*(6), Serial No. 181.

Huttenlocher, J., Smiley, P., & Charney, R. The emergence of action categories in the child. *Psychological Review,* 1983, *90*(1), 72–93.

Isen, A. Affect, cognition, and social behavior. In R. Wyer & Shull (Eds.), *Handbook of social cognition,* in press.

Izard, C. E. *The face of emotion.* New York: Appleton-Century-Crofts, 1971.

Izard, C. E. Emotions as the primary motivators of behavior. In H. E. Howe & R. A. Dienstbier (Eds.), *1978 Nebraska Symposium on Motivation: Human Emotions* (Vol. 26). Lincoln: University of Nebraska Press, 1979.

Izard, C. E. Comments on emotion and cognition: Can there be a working relationship? In M. S. Clarke & S. T. Fiske (Eds.), *Affect and cognition* (pp. 229–42). Hillsdale, NJ: Erlbaum, 1982.

Izard, C. E. The primacy of emotion in emotion–cognition relationships and human development. In C. E. Izard, J. Kagan, & R. Zajonc (Eds.), *Emotions, cognition, and behavior.* Cambridge University Press, 1984, 17–37.

Izard, C. E., & Malatesta, C. Z. *A developmental theory of emotion.* Unpublished manuscript, 1983.

Lazarus, R. S. Thoughts on the relationship between emotion and cognition. *American Psychologist,* 1982, *37,* 1019–24.

Lazarus, R. S., On the primacy of cognition. *American Psychologist,* 1984, *39*(2) 124–9.

Mandler, G. *Mind and emotion.* New York: Wiley, 1975.

Mandler, G. The generation of emotion: A psychological theory. In R. Plutchik & M. Wellerman (Eds.), *Theories of emotion.* New York: Academic Press, 1978.

Mandler, G. The structure of value: Accounting for taste. In M. S. Clark & S. T. Fiske (Eds.), *Affect and cognition* (pp. 3–36). Hillsdale, NJ: Erlbaum, 1982.

Mandler, G. The nature of emotion. In J. Miller (Ed.), *States of mind* (pp. 136–53). New York: Pantheon Books, 1983.

Masters, J. C., & Carlson, C. R. Children's and adults' understanding of the causes and consequences of emotional states. In C. E. Izard, J. Kagan, & R. Zajonc (Eds.), *Emotions, cognition, and behavior* (pp. 438–63). Cambridge University Press, 1984.

Nezworksi, M. T., Stein, N. L., & Trabasso, T. Story structure versus content effects on children's recall of evaluative inferences. *Journal of Verbal Learning and Verbal Behavior, 1982, 21,* 196–206.

Plutchik, R., & Kellerman, M. *Theories of emotion.* New York: Academic Press, 1978.

Roseman, I. *Cognitive aspects of emotion and emotional behavior.* Paper given at American Psychological Association Meetings, New York, August 1979.

Scherer, K. R. On the nature and function of emotion: A component process approach. In K. R. Scherer & P. Ekman (Eds.), *Approaches to emotion* (pp. 193–318). Hillsdale, NJ: Erlbaum, 1984.

Scherer, K. R., & Ekman, P. (Eds.). *Approaches to emotion.* Hillsdale, NJ: Erlbaum, 1984.

Schwartz, R. M., & Trabasso, T. Children's understanding of emotion. In C. E. Izard, J. Kagan, & R. Zajonc (Eds.), *Emotion, cognition, and behavior* (pp. 409–37). Cambridge University Press, 1984.

Shultz, T. Development of the concept of intention. In W. A. Collins (Ed.), *Development of cognition, affect, and social relations: Minnesota Symposium on Child Psychology* (Vol. 13, pp. 131–64). Hillsdale, NJ: Erlbaum, 1980.

Smiley, P., & Huttenlocher, J. *Young children's understanding of facial and situational components of emotion words.* Unpublished manuscript, University of Chicago, 1984.

Stein, N. L., & Eulau, S. S. *Children's thoughts and understanding of emotional experience: A study of shifting emotions.* Unpublished manuscript, University of Chicago, 1984.

Stein, N. L., & Levine, L. *Knowledge structures underlying the meaning of anger, sadness, and happiness.* Unpublished manuscript, University of Chicago, 1984.

Stein, N. L., & Trabasso, T. Children's understanding of stories: A basis for moral judgement and dilemma resolution. In C. J. Brainerd & M. Pressley (Eds.), *Verbal processes in children* (Vol. 2, pp. 161–188). New York: Springer-Verlag, 1982.

Sroufe, A. L. Socioemotional development. In J. Osofsky (Ed.), *The handbook of infant development* (pp. 462–516). New York: Wiley, 1979.

Trabasso, T., Stein, N. L., & Johnson, L. R. Children's knowledge of events: A causal analysis of story structure. In G. Bower (Ed.), *Learning and motivation* (Vol. 15, pp. 237–82). New York: Academic Press, 1981.

Weiner, B. The emotional consequences of causal attributions. In M. S. Clarke & S. T. Fiske (Eds.), *Affect and cognition* (pp. 185–210). Hillsdale, NJ: Erlbaum, 1982.

Zajonc, R. B. Feeling and thinking: Preferences need no inferences. *American Psychologist, 1980, 35,* 151–75.

Zajonc, R. B. On the primacy of affect. *American Psychologist, 1984, 39*(2), 117–23.

Author index

Subject index

274